Y0-AEX-406

Patricia A. L Ehrensal EdD

TEACHING

&

the Law

JACQUI GILLIATT

**KOGAN
PAGE**

Although this book has been carefully prepared, no responsibility for loss occasioned to any person acting, or refraining from action, as a result of any material in this publication can be accepted by the author or publisher.

YOURS TO HAVE AND TO HOLD

BUT NOT TO COPY

First published in 1999

Apart from any fair dealing for the purposes of research or private study, or criticism or review, as permitted under the Copyright, Designs and Patents Act 1988, this publication may only be reproduced, stored or transmitted, in any form or by any means, with the prior permission in writing of the publishers, or in the case of reprographic reproduction in accordance with the terms and licences issued by the CLA. Enquiries concerning reproduction outside these terms should be sent to the publishers at the undermentioned address:

Kogan Page Limited
120 Pentonville Road
London N1 9JN

© Jacqui Gilliatt, 1999

The right of Jacqui Gilliatt to be identified as the author of this work has been asserted by her in accordance with the Copyright, Designs and Patents Act 1988.

British Library Cataloguing in Publication Data

A CIP record for this book is available from the British Library.

ISBN 0 7494 2419 2

Typeset by Kogan Page
Printed and bound by Biddles Ltd, Guildford and King's Lynn

Contents

Contents

Contents

Contents

Contents

Preface

This book has taken me far longer to write than I had hoped. The main reason for that has been the fast, almost overwhelming, pace of legislation that has been passed since I agreed to write it. I am a lawyer and I have found it hard to cope with, so I am only too aware of the difficulties that this will mean for the average teacher. I hope for all our sakes that it is now time for some peace and quiet on the legislative and policy front so that everyone can get on with the difficult business of making it all work. I do not say this in a spirit of opposition to the changes that have been implemented, but feeling sympathy with those who have to take the responsibility for putting the policies into practice and obeying the law when they have barely had enough time to work out what it is!

I started to write this book after my partner decided to become a teacher. Through him I met many trainees and teachers and came to realize that they had a bookful of questions they could not answer. My aim here has been to provide the answers for all those who have been searching in vain, as plainly and as simply as possible.

Acknowledgements

I say thank you to all the teachers I met, both for the questions and their subsequent encouragement in writing the book.

In particular, I would like to thank my partner, Hugh Seckleman, and his colleagues at Kingsmead School, Enfield, especially John Quinlan and Kim Pickering, Leslie Fearney, Mick Young, Chris Christodolou, Maggi Fisher and Giles Bird. I have also been helped by the staff and governors at the school of which I am a governor, White Hart Lane in Haringey, especially Mrs Christina Daubney, Benjamin Smart and Arthur Philips, who have guided me through the practical side of the application of the law.

I also say a very big thank you to all my friends, both new and old, professional and otherwise, who have lent me books, support (of all sorts) and a sympathetic ear, namely Hugh, Louise Rush, Stephen Monkcom, Andrew Thompson, Professor Geoffrey Bennett, Paul and Lynda Humber, Jason and Ila Reece, Paul Green, Tim Eicke, Ann Bevitt, Mark Gay, Karyl Nairn, Peter Tyler and Gwynneth Knowles. Also, thank you to e-mail correspondent Andrew Jones for his useful ideas.

I write this book, too, in grateful remembrance of my own schooldays and so special thanks to Mrs Joy Hancock and her husband Barry and to the other teachers at Brighton and Hove High School who made my time there so happy.

I have done my best to state the law as at 1 September 1998. In any subject area, time never stands still, but at the time of writing, in education, the law is continually spinning, so if you need to be sure of the up-to-date position, you should ask for advice (see Chapter 15 for suggestions on where to get it from).

Table of cases

Table of statutes

Table of statutes

Table of statutory instruments

Table of statutory instruments

Chapter 1

Introduction

Education, education, education

Throughout the first half of the 1990s, legislation concerning education passed through the Houses of Parliament at what many teachers might be forgiven for thinking was an alarming rate. One of the last pieces of legislation passed by Major's Conservative Government was the Education Act 1997. One of the first pieces of legislation – passed by the new Labour Government was the Education (Schools) Act 1997 (which phases out the assisted places scheme, itself only introduced by the Education Act 1996). Education was a focal point of the new Government's election campaign, so the fast pace of change looks set to continue. Indeed, four major pieces of legislation have already been passed.

Political interest in education has gone hand in hand with a high media profile, though which is chicken and which egg may be hard to work out. Unfortunately, whatever the long-term benefits of political intervention and journalistic attention may be, it is not always obvious at the time! News reports have covered the horrific acts of violence against staff and children, such as the murder of the children at Dunblane Primary School, the murder of Headteacher Philip Lawrence, the suffering of children at the hands of bullies or child abusers and the failure of some schools and education authorities to provide an adequate education for pupils. Even apparently good news – such as the continued improvement in A level results – is reported as evidence of a decline in educational standards or of exam rigging.

For much of this bad news, the finger of blame seems to have been pointed at the teaching profession. This could be seen as a compliment and an acknowledgement of the vital importance of the profession (as Harriet Martineau wrote in 1837 in *Society in America,* vol. 3, 'Occupation', 'What office is there which involves more responsibility, which requires more qualifications, and which ought, therefore, to be more honourable, than that of teaching?'), but those in the profession could be forgiven if they see this compliment as being, at best, backhanded.

Such attention is nothing new, as experienced members of the teaching profession know. In 1955, Jacques Barzun wrote in *Newsweek* (5 December), 'Teaching is not a lost art, but the regard for it is a lost tradition'. Every so often, the searchlight comes to rest on teachers, just as at other times it rests on single mothers, society, politicians, social workers and so on.

It has had one apparent consequence, which this book addresses, and it is that, along with physical assaults, politicians' criticisms, journalistic hyperbole and miscellaneous insults, teachers can now expect their actions (or inaction) to come under legal attack. In this they are not unique, but the breadth and complexity of the potential litigation to which teachers find themselves exposed is far wider than that applying to most other occupations.

Teachers may already feel that the ambit of their responsibility is quite wide enough. The job description already includes aspects of the work of social worker, parent, counsellor, administrator and so on. It would be a tall order to expect every teacher to be a legal expert as well. However, just as a car driver needs to have a rudimentary understanding of the law affecting their use of the public highways, so any professional teacher needs to understand the legal framework in which their role sits.

The intention of this book is to provide teachers with an introduction to that legal framework, at least as far as it affects education in primary and secondary schools in England and Wales.

Of course, many car drivers break the law on an almost daily basis, and it can be argued that if they did not do so traffic in most major cities would come to a grinding halt. How many drivers can honestly say that they have never (even inadvertently) driven above the speed limit or parked their car illegally? I do not wish to suggest for a moment that teachers should break the law deliberately, particularly not the criminal law, but, to quote George Bernard Shaw, 'Whenever you wish to do anything against the law, Cicely, always consult a good solicitor first' (Sir Howard, in *Captain Brassbound's Conversion,* Act 1). It is important to be aware of the consequences that may flow from the different types of law-breaking that go on across the country all the time and to give some thought to how to avoid both the law-breaking itself and its sometimes unpleasant consequences.

Whenever litigation in a new area is discussed, there is an almost inevitable comparison with practices and habits in the United States. Lord Denning once said, 'As a moth is drawn to the light, so is a litigant drawn to the United States. If he can only get his case into their courts, he stands to win a fortune'. Stories abound of cases in America where apparently unworthy litigants use the legal system to obtain compensation and large amounts of it in circumstances where it might be thought that they had only themselves to blame. There is some truth in this. There really was a case in which a teenager who fell through a skylight in a roof while trying to steal a floodlight, recovered damages. I do not wish to join in the general trend of bashing the American legal system – often a closer reading of all of the facts of a case will explain everything. It should also be remembered that there are many advantages to the different approach taken in the US, particularly if you look at the way in which groups of ordinary and impecunious individuals have clubbed together and successfully taken on large companies, which have acted in ways that put lives in danger.

The main point is that it is a quite different legal system (or, more accurately, several different legal systems). There are a number of ways in which, in England and Wales, Parliament and the courts step in and offer protection to public officials carrying out their duties, as will be seen later in this book. Judges may not always seem to be the most streetwise of individuals, but in their judgments they demonstrate that they are aware that life is a risky business and it is both impractical and undesirable to eliminate all risk.

An example is found in one of the most often cited education cases – *Hudson* v *the Governors of Rotherham Grammar School and Selby Johnson* (1937). Mr Justice Hilberg said:

> If boys were kept in cotton wool, some of them would choke themselves with it. They would manage to have accidents: we always did ... we did not always have action at law afterwards. You have to consider whether or not you would expect a headmaster to exercise such a degree of care that boys could never get into mischief. Has any reasonable parent yet succeeded in such care as to prevent a boy getting into mischief and, if he did, what sort of boys would we produce?

The legal system does not just offer a shield to teachers, it can be used as a sword as well, particularly in the fields of employment and human rights law. In other words, the law may be an ass, but it is an ass that can sometimes be ridden.

How to use this book

I hope that with the help of this book you will understand a little more both about how to work within the legal system and how to make it work for you. With at least 11 major statutes (and no doubt more to come) directly affecting the field of primary and secondary education, and countless other statutes relevant to the work of teachers, such as the Children Act 1989 and numerous acts relating to employment matters, I can, of course, offer no more than a summary of the main provisions. In most circumstances, this will be all that a working teacher needs to know. When more than that is required, I hope this book will serve to show you where to look it up, where and how to seek legal advice and how to make the best use of that advice.

Being a lawyer myself, I have to confess that I find the law quite fascinating. Apparently there are some people who do not feel the same way. I therefore cannot promise that this book will be a cracking good read, one you want to take on holiday with you. It is a reference book and so I do not suggest or expect – unless you have a similar fascination with the law – that you read it from cover to cover in one go. Rather, it is intended that you read the chapters or sections on issues you need to know about and return to the book to find out more about other matters over time. Also, you should be aware that the details given can only be a completely accurate statement of the law at the time of publication. First, as I said in the Preface, the law is constantly developing and regulations come and go in the blink of an eye. Second, each case depends on its facts and it is impossible for a general book to be able to indicate exactly what a court or tribunal would do faced with your particular problem. Third, I am only human and, although I have done my utmost to avoid them, it is not impossible that there are some inaccuracies .

There are some topics that I have not included in any detail in this book, such as target setting. This is because developments, regulations or detailed guidelines are expected to be published in 1999, so there seems little point going into great detail when the law is not yet fully formed. You ought to be told about them as the developments occur (in fact, a DfEE circular on *Target Setting* has already been issued – DfEE Circular 11/98). In some cases, I have not talked about certain topics or details because, although schools are involved in particular processes, they are regulated by policy considerations or are purely the responsibility of the LEA and of little interest to the teacher or else they are of much more interest to another party than to teachers, such as a parent (for example, details of the procedural aspects of appeals to a special educational needs tribunal).

This is what the book does contain. Chapter 2 tells you where the law comes from and a little bit about the court system. Chapter 3 tells you about the legal basis for the various bodies involved in providing education and where their powers and duties come from. After that, there are chapters that deal with particular issues I believe are important to teachers. Chapters 4 to 6 deal with issues of employment law. Further topics covered are copyright, lesson contents, equal opportunities, information and records, children and parents, discipline, assault, negligence and, finally, a chapter on legal remedies, which includes advice about going to court as a witness and instructing lawyers.

You will find some useful background information at the back of the book in the appendices, including a summary of the main relevant acts and a list of abbreviations, plus useful addresses (and Internet addresses) and further reading sections.

While I have referred to particular sections of some Acts, I have tried to keep legal details to a minimum. If you do want to look directly at the law, you can probably work out which section you need by looking at the index or contents list of the act itself.

Sources of help

Throughout the course of this book, I mention a number of organizations and publications that can help schools and teachers to help themselves to comply with the law. As far as possible, I have listed these in the Useful addresses and Further reading sections at the back of the book. I cannot stress enough the contribution that the unions and staff associations have to make in supporting union representatives and individual teachers, assisting schools to manage to meet their legal obligations and defending themselves if they are accused of failing to do so. The NUT, for example, has worked with SIMS Educational Services to produce a package called *Law Management Software*. Indeed, there is much more on offer than that which I refer to in the appendices as there simply is not room to mention it all. Also, do not leave it until you are in trouble to join a union. They are there to help you *avoid* getting into difficulties in the first place, too.

Chapter 2

Beginning at the beginning

Where and what is the law?

The first step in understanding the legal framework of education law is to understand how something acquires the status of law in the first place.

Primary and secondary legislation

Primary legislation

The most authoritative source of law is an act of Parliament (also known as a statute). This is what is meant by 'primary legislation'. A draft bill is put before the House of Commons for consideration. It may be discussed by the whole of Parliament in an open debate or referred to a standing or select committee for detailed analysis. Amendments will be proposed and finally the House of Commons will vote to approve the bill. It then passes to the House of Lords and goes through a similar procedure there. Finally, the bill must be given royal assent (which, in practice, is a formality). The process can also happen in reverse, that is to say with a bill starting in the House of Lords and then passing to the House of Commons, as was the case with the Teaching and Higher Education Bill.

Some acts introduce a complete change in the law, while others are mainly 'consolidating' acts, which means that they bring together and update a number of previous acts, but do not necessarily make great changes to the law. The Education Act 1996 is a good example of this type of act. However, even consolidating acts will usually give effect to any developments in the courts. In theory, the courts and judges do not create law, they merely interpret and apply it, but, in practice, it can be difficult to see the distinction. In some circumstances, for example, the courts have to fill gaps in the law to cover situations that had not been foreseen before the act was passed.

A word of warning. Just because an act has been passed by Parliament does not necessarily mean that all or any of it is then actually in force. Some parts of the act may come into force immediately, whereas others will be phased in. Sometimes the date on which an act comes into force ('the commencement date') will be stated in the text of the act itself. Sometimes the commencement date will be found in separate, secondary legislation (see below). One act may also be amended by subsequent acts and/or parts of it may be repealed (deleted).

There are three ways of referring to an act of Parliament:

- by its short title;
- by its official reference;
- by its full title.

For example, the Education Act 1997 is the short title. The official reference is the Education Act 1997, Chapter 44 (this means that it was the 44th act to be passed in 1997). The full title of the Act is:

Education Act 1997
1997 Chapter 44

An Act to amend the law relating to education in schools and further education in England and Wales; to make provision for the supervision of the awarding of external academic and vocational qualifications in England, Wales and Northern Ireland; and for connected purposes.

In this book, references will be made to the short title of an act, for obvious reasons!

At the beginning of each act, you will find a list of contents. Somewhere in the act there is usually a section that defines the meanings of certain words used throughout the act. This is often placed near the beginning or end of the act. A long act will usually be divided into several parts, each dealing with a particular aspect of law. For example, Part 1 of the Education Act 1997 deals with the assisted places scheme, Part II with school discipline and so on. Each part may be further subdivided into chapters. Each main clause is separately numbered and clauses are referred to as sections. For example, Section 4 of the Education Act 1997 sets out the circumstances in which it will be lawful for a teacher to restrain a pupil. At the end of the act there will be a number of miscellaneous provisions, such as those that do not conveniently fit anywhere else or saying when the act will come into force and so on. Finally, there may be schedules to the act, which will usually include one setting out the way other acts have been amended.

If you want to look up an act of Parliament, there are several ways of doing so. Statutes are contained in a number of publications, including Halsbury's *Statutes* and *Current Law Statutes*. These will often be found in main public libraries. Another word of warning. You need to be careful to check the additional volumes of each series to see whether or not there have been any amendments to the law. Copies of individual acts can be purchased from the Stationery Office Limited. Acts passed after the beginning of 1996 are available on the Internet (at the HMSO's web site – see the Useful addresses section for the address) and can be downloaded free. However, this can take a long time and be quite a fiddly process if you want a copy of the whole thing. Again, you will need to look elsewhere to see if the act has been amended. Halsbury also publishes a separate volume entitled *Is It In Force?* in which you can check whether or not an act or a part of it has come into force or been repealed.

There are other useful publications, such as the looseleaf *Butterworth's Education Law* (Kenneth Poole, John Coleman and Peter Liell, Butterworth, 1997). These can be found in law libraries (which may be difficult to get into–you will usually need special permission). Otherwise, some schools may have copies of these publications or they may be held by your local education authority. The legal departments of the trade unions may also have copies.

Appendix I contains a list of the main legislation in the education field. For further information on relevant publications, see the Further reading section. The Useful addresses section includes addresses from which the publications may be obtained.

Secondary legislation

It is rare these days for any act of Parliament to be the last word on the subject and so Parliament delegates power to someone else –

usually the relevant secretary of State – to deal with the detail, such as to allow the phasing in of certain functions, or for annual amendments to pay scales and the like. For example, Section 467 (1) of the Education Act 1996 provides that 'Regulations may make provision for requiring the proprietor of a registered or provisionally registered school to provide the Registrar of Independent Schools from time to time with such particulars relating to the school as may be prescribed'. There is usually a cross-reference to any regulations that have been made in the footnote to the section giving power to make them.

There are various procedures for exercising these delegated powers. The main method you will see reference to in this book is by 'statutory instrument' (SI). Usually the SI must be laid before Parliament and will not become law until a certain time has elapsed, during which MPs can bring them up for discussion. In addition, they will be considered by a committee, which will also put them to Parliament for discussion in certain circumstances. In practice, relatively few SIs are scrutinized in a public debate. Delegated legislation is sometimes referred to as 'subordinate' or 'secondary legislation'. SIs are often referred to as 'regulations', and you may also see reference to 'orders', which are similar to SIs.

One vital difference between primary and secondary legislation is that an act of Parliament cannot be questioned in the courts, although its meaning may be debated. That is to say, no matter how much a court might disapprove of the legislation or its effect in a particular case, it must apply the law set down by Parliament. There is greater scope to argue about secondary legislation if it can be said that the Secretary of State has acted outside the powers given to them in the act (*ultra vires*) in making the regulations or the regulations are unreasonable or there is a conflict with European Union law (see Chapter 15).

Each statutory instrument is allocated a number. The SI's number includes the year in which it was passed, followed by another number. For example, 'The Education (Particulars of Independent Schools) Regulations 1997' (made under Section 467(1) of the Education Act 1996 referred to above) are known by the reference SI 1997/2918.

Copies of SIs can be obtained from the Stationery Office. Alternatively, SIs made since 1997 are published on the Internet. They may also be found in public libraries and in the publications I have already referred to.

As with statutes, care needs to be taken that the regulations have not been amended or, indeed, entirely superseded. This is what lawyers get paid for!

Case law

When judges make a decision in a particular case, the decision may become part of the body of the law (also known as precedent law). This will only happen if the decision concerns some point of principle that can be applied to other cases and is not just unique to the facts of the particular case. For example, sometimes the court has to decide what a word used in an act of Parliament means in a particular context. This commonly occurs with the word 'reasonable' and has given rise to all sorts of legal arguments. Sometimes the courts have to decide when a particular body is liable to an individual for any acts of wrongdoing. For example, whether or not a school is responsible when a pupil runs into the road outside the school and is run over.

Not all judicial decisions are equal – there is a hierarchy of courts. The lower courts are bound to follow the decisions of the higher courts, but not the other way around. The decision of a magistrate or County court judge will not be binding on any other court (although it may still have some influence as 'persuasive' authority). The decision of a High Court judge must be followed and applied by the lower courts, but another High Court judge can ignore it and make a different decision in similar circumstances. In the Court of Appeal, judges sit in groups of two or three and their decisions must be followed by the courts below it, but not by other benches of the Court of Appeal. It has been known for it to take years before a conflict of decisions is resolved because a case is taken as far as the House of Lords, the highest-level court that binds everyone else. Even the House of Lords can go back on its own decisions, although it rarely does so.

Court structure

Figure 2.1 shows the basic structure of the courts and summarizes the work of each.

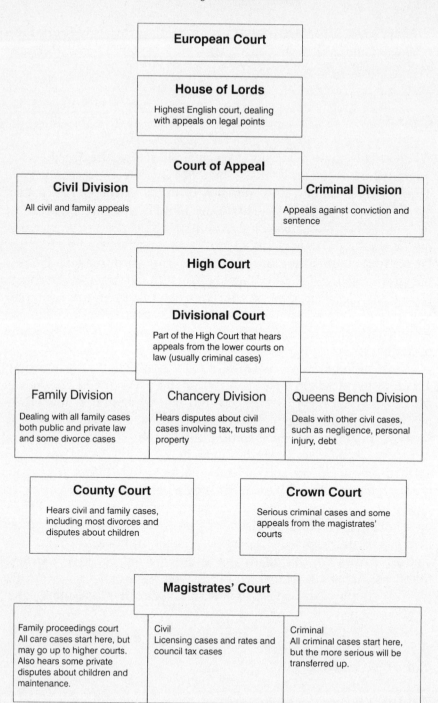

Figure 2.1 The hierarchy of the courts

Law reports

There are literally hundreds of publications in which case law can be found, either the full text of a judgment or in summary form. One series, the *Weekly Law Reports*, also records the arguments submitted to the courts by the advocates before the decisions were made. Some series are available in public libraries and some in law libraries. In relation to education law, some decisions are published in the *Family Law Reports* and the *Education Law Reports*. Summaries may be found in numerous journals, including *Education and the Law* (Geoffrey Bennett and Paul Meredith, eds, Carfax). At the moment, there is very little case law published on the Internet, except by subscription services, but the House of Lords has published its decisions since 14 November 1996.

When reference is made to a particular case, it will usually be by the names of the parties involved in the case, followed by the year of the decision, the series of the report (in abbreviated form) and the page number. A list of common abbreviations may be found in Appendix II. Some education and family cases may only refer to a party by an initial, which is usually because that party is a child whose identity must be kept confidential.

European law

So far, the role of European law with regard to education has been very indirect, but it is there and it is growing. It has had a more direct influence on employment rights. European human rights laws have also had a significant impact and this looks set to increase with the domestic legislation currently being debated (though it is not likely to become law until the year 2000). A detailed consideration of European law will not be tackled in this book, but reference will be made to it where relevant.

Interpreting the law

In addition to legislation, regulations and case law, there are several other documents that do not have the full force of law, but act as guidance and aids to interpretation of what the law itself says or means. These include circulars issued by the Department for

Education, local education authorities, guidance from the Health and Safety Executive and so on, as well as codes of practice, such as the Code of Practice on Special Educational Needs.

Although general readers, lawyers and courts may find these publications helpful, they are really just one department's view of what the law says or ought to say. Having said this, if you follow the guidance issued, unless it is fairly obvious that it is wrong, you will probably get through life without being sued.

Sometimes the law requires that a body must take these documents into account before making a decision (as is the case with the SEN Code). Circulars may also be important because they tell the courts the date from which a person or organization ought to have known about something. For example, if the Health and Safety Executive issues a leaflet about the safe handling of chemical X, from that moment on you will be expected to be aware that chemical X is probably dangerous and the recommended procedures ought to be followed.

So, tempting as it may be, don't throw such leaflets in the bin without reading them first. These documents will be referred to throughout the rest of this book and in the Further reading section. They may be obtained from a number of different sources depending on the publisher. See the Useful addresses section for details of either publishers or other sources of material.

The court system

Reference has already been made to the fact that there is a hierarchy of courts (see Figure 2.1). There is also a table in Chapter 15 (Table 15.1) that sets out the courts you are most likely to encounter in the teaching profession, and another with information on how to address the judge or members of the tribunal (see Table 15.2).

Criminal courts

Criminal cases are always begun in the magistrates' courts. Cases will be dealt with in the magistrates' courts if the offence is not itself particularly serious (such as many road traffic offences) or a not very serious example of a particular offence (such as a minor assault not resulting in serious injury). Magistrates have limited sentencing powers. Most offences committed by minors will be tried in the youth court, a specialist court within the magistrates' court.

There are some professional magistrates who are qualified lawyers. They usually hear cases sitting on their own and are called 'stipendiary' magistrates. The vast majority of magistrates are volunteers from the local community and will sit in groups of two or three. They are assisted by an official called a 'clerk' who may be legally qualified and who can advise them about the law and procedures.

More serious criminal offences are tried in the Crown Court, which also hears appeals by way of rehearing from the magistrates' court. In the Crown Court, the case will be decided by a jury if the defendant is pleading not guilty. The judge will give guidance to the jury about the meaning of the law. They will also decide on sentencing once a verdict of guilty has been given. If the case is an appeal from the magistrates, it will be heard by a judge sitting with two magistrates who will hear the case from scratch, rehearing all the evidence.

Appeals from the Crown Court and the magistrates' courts on points of law go to a section of the High Court called the Divisional Court. Appeals from the Crown Court against a verdict and/or sentence go to the criminal division of the Court of Appeal and from the Court of Appeal to the House of Lords. When hearing these sorts of appeal, the courts do not usually hear any live evidence.

Civil courts

The magistrates' courts deal with some civil cases, such as applications for licenses to sell alcohol. They also hear many disputes about children and almost all care cases start in the magistrates' courts.

The majority of civil cases start in a County Court. These include personal injury actions, actions to recover debts and so on.

More complicated civil cases and those where the level of damages claimed is over £25,000 (£50,000 in personal injury cases) generally start in the High Court. This is also the court that hears applications for judicial review, which often feature in the context of education (see Chapter 15). There are various subdivisions of the High Court that deal with different types of cases.

Appeals from a County Court or the High Court are dealt with by the civil division of the Court of Appeal, and after that by the House of Lords.

Tribunals

Governments have not always felt that the court system proper is the best way in which to resolve disputes. A court hearing can be costly and it can take a long time for a decision to be made. The atmosphere of a court is formal and the judge may not know very much about the factual background to a dispute. In an attempt to overcome these perceived drawbacks to the court system, several tribunals have been established to hear specialized disputes. The special educational needs and employment tribunals are well-known examples. Often a tribunal is chaired by a lawyer sitting together with two lay members with some specialist knowledge relevant to the subject matter of the dispute.

Whether or not tribunals do provide all the advantages claimed for them may be debatable.

Depending on the tribunal, there may be a right of appeal to a court. For example, an appeal against a decision of an industrial tribunal will be dealt with by the Employment Appeal Tribunal (EAT). This is a three-person court, chaired by a High Court judge. The two lay members are usually national officers of employers' organizations and trade unions. An appeal against a decision of the EAT can be made to the Court of Appeal (and then to the House of Lords).

All tribunals are overseen by the Council on Tribunals and this includes bodies such as the panels constituted by the local education authorities to hear admissions appeals and exclusion appeals (there is talk of the Special Educational Needs Tribunal taking over exclusion appeal hearings).

Chapter 3

Who's who in education

What follows is a brief summary of the main bodies and people involved in the provision of education and the main legislation from which they derive their powers and responsibilities or in which they are defined.

The Secretary of State for the Department for Education and Employment

David Blunkett currently holds this position and has various powers and duties bestowed on him by numerous acts, in respect of England. Similar powers and duties have been given to the Secretary of State for Wales, Alun Michael. They are assisted by a number of Ministers, principally Estelle Morris, the Minister of State for School Standards, and Charles Clarke, Junior Education Minister. Baroness Blackstone is the current Minister for Education and Employment in the Lords.

David Blunkett has established a number of task forces (such as the Standards Task Force) to advise him on particular aspects of education, but their role is advisory only and they have no legal standing. In exercising some of his powers, he is obliged by statute to consult with particular people before forming a conclusion.

The Secretary's primary duty is found in Section 10 of the Education Act 1996, which is to promote the education of the people of England and Wales. He is also ultimately responsible for all the bodies that receive public funds to provide education and ensure that they improve standards, encourage diversity and increase opportunities for choice (Section 11, Education Act 1996). These general duties cannot be directly enforced through the courts. Rather, the Secretary is the ultimate arbiter if a dispute arises between a funding authority and an LEA (see below, although funding agencies are to be abolished) or between a governing body and the LEA or between LEAs (Section 495, Education Act 1996).

Other responsibilities include the publication of school performance tables, decisions on school closures, appointment of school inspectors, decisions about barring teachers from future employment, the registration of independent schools, and the establishment of education associations to run failing schools. Under the School Standards and Framework Act 1988, the Secretary now has additional powers, including the power to intervene in the running of an LEA and the power to set up education action zones (see below).

Local education authorities (LEAs)

These are defined in Section 12 of the Education Act 1996 as London borough councils, county councils, unitary authorities and metropolitan councils, and there are currently about 128 of these. The main functions of the LEAs are set out in Section 13 ff, which are, essentially, to secure efficient education at primary, secondary and higher level. Under the School Standards and Framework Act 1998, the LEA has an additional duty to promote high standards in education.

Education services must be tailored to suit particular local needs and the abilities and aptitudes of children in the LEA's catchment area (Section 14(3)) and must include education for children with special educational needs (SEN; Section 14(6)). An LEA has no duty to provide education for children under 5 (Section 14(4)), but may do so (Section 17). The School Standards and Framework Act 1998 imposes a duty on LEAs to prepare education development plans and set up education committees, including parent representatives, and gives them power to intervene in schools causing concern.

The Funding Agency for Schools (England) and the Schools Funding Council for Wales

Section 20 of the Education Act 1996ff deals with the functions of these quangos, which, is in essence, overseeing grant-maintained schools and the funding for them. In fact, the Welsh Council was never established and both agencies have been abolished by the School Standards and Framework Act 1998 with effect from 1999.

Schools

Section 4 of the Education Act 1996 (as amended by Section 51 of the Education Act 1997) defines a school as follows:

> an educational institution which is outside the further education sector and the higher education sector and is an institution for providing:
>
> (a) primary education,
> (b) secondary education, or
> (c) both primary and secondary education,
>
> whether or not the institution also provides part-time education suitable to the requirements of junior pupils or further education.

Education

This term is not defined in any statute. However, it has been defined in one case by a judge as 'the development of mental powers and character and the acquisition of knowledge through the imparting of skills and learning by systematic instruction'. He added that it should prepare children for life in a modern civilized society and enable them to achieve their full potential (*Harrison and Harrison* v *Stevenson*, Worcester Crown Court 1981).

Primary education

This term is defined by Section 2(1) of the Education Act 1996 as full-time education suitable for the requirements of junior pupils (under 12 years' old) below the age of 10 years 6 months (and those older children whom it is expedient to educate in the same school). There are about 20,000 maintained primary schools (including grant-maintained schools).

Secondary education

This term is defined by Section 2 (2) of the Education Act 1996 as full-time education suitable to the requirements of pupils of compulsory school age who are senior pupils (aged 12 to 19), such junior pupils as it is expedient to educate in the same school, pupils who are over compulsory school age but under 19 and educated together at the same school as those below compulsory school age (that is, not a sixth form college). There are about 4000 secondary schools (including grant-maintained schools).

Types of school

Under the School Standards and Framework Act 1998, from September 1999, schools have to be redefined into different types as follows:

- community;
- foundation;
- voluntary (including voluntary aided and voluntary controlled);
- community special;
- foundation special.

Foundation schools will essentially replace grant-maintained schools. Most schools will be deemed either community (county schools) or voluntary, but they may be able to move to foundation status in the future. Foundation, voluntary and foundation special schools will have charitable status, but will be exempt from the Charities Act 1993. Each LEA will have to establish a school organization committee and prepare a school organization plan showing how it intends to fulfil its duties to secure the provision of education in its area. Both old and new terminology are used below.

There are approximately 28,000 primary and secondary schools in England and Wales.

Community school/county school

Defined in Section 31(1), Education Act 1996, and Section 20, School Standards and Framework Act 1998 as a primary or secondary school that was established by or is maintained by an LEA. A subcategory of county special schools will now be known as community special schools.

Maintained school

Sections 34, Education Act 1996, and 20, School Standards and Framework Act 1998 define a maintained school as one funded by an LEA. The majority of maintained schools now have delegated budgets with which comes a great deal of autonomy in respect of finances and staffing. There are a very few schools without delegated budgets or the delegated budget of which has been suspended so this will not be dealt with in much detail in this book. In January 1998, 92 per cent of all pupils were being taught in the maintained sector.

Foundation school/grant-maintained school

The definition in Sections 183, Education Act 1996, and 20, School Standards and Framework Act 1998 is that this is a primary or secondary school that has acquired grant-maintained status by following the procedure set out in the Education Act 1996. This requires a secret postal ballot of parents as to whether or not they wish a school to acquire grant-maintained status and for the approval of the Secretary of State. If a school acquires grant-maintained status, a new governing body is set up and the LEA stops funding the school. Instead, funds are provided by the Funding Agency. There are about 650 grant-maintained secondary schools and about 450 grant-maintained primary schools.

Voluntary school

Section 31(2), Education Act 1996, and Section 20, School Standards and Framework Act 1998, state that a voluntary school is a primary or secondary school that was not established by an LEA and has not been maintained by one. Many such schools are Church schools or are run by a charitable foundation. There are three subcategories of voluntary schools: controlled, aided and special agreement (see below).

Voluntary controlled/controlled school
Section 32 (2) of the Education Act 1996 defines a voluntary school as one that is not an aided or special agreement school. In practice, these are voluntary schools that enjoy some autonomy but require some State funding to meet their maintenance expenses. There are more than 3000 voluntary controlled schools.

Voluntary aided/aided school
In Section 32 (3) of the Education Act 1996, a voluntary school is designated as such by an order made under Sections 48, 51, 54 or 58 of the 1996 Act, Section 15 of the Education Act 1944, Section 2 of the Education Act 1946 or Section 54 of the Education (no. 2) Act 1986. These schools are almost completely controlled by their governing bodies, but must make a 15 per cent contribution to maintenance costs. There are about 5000 voluntary aided schools.

Voluntary aided/special agreement school
Section 32 (4) of the Education Act 1996 says that a voluntary school is designated as such by an order made under Section 15 of the Education Act 1944. No new special agreement schools can be established, and those that do exist will be included in the voluntary aided category. There are only about 100 special agreement schools. The LEA has to pay a contribution of 50 to 75 per cent of building or enlarging the school premises, but other arrangements for the payment of maintenance costs and so on are as for voluntary aided schools.

City technology college (or city college for the technology of the arts)

Under Section 482 of the Education Act 1996, these are schools authorized by the Secretary of State to provide education with a special emphasis on science and technology or the performing or creative arts that are located in urban areas. There are about 15 city technology colleges.

Independent schools

These, according to Section 463 of the Education Act 1996, are schools with more than 5 pupils providing full-time education for pupils of compulsory school age that are neither maintained by the LEA, nor are special schools (maintained or otherwise) or grant-maintained. Independent schools must be registered with the Registrar of Independent Schools (appointed by the Secretary of State). Of all pupils 7 per cent were being taught in independent schools in January 1998.

Special schools

Section 337 of the Education Act 1996 defines such a school as being one that is organized to make special educational provision for pupils with special educational needs and approved as such under Section 342. Special schools may be maintained, grant-maintained or independent. There are about 1350 such schools and 1 per cent of pupils were attending either special schools or pupil referral units in January 1998.

Grouped schools

Section 89, Education Act 1996, covers these. An LEA may organize schools in groups that will be run by a single governing body. They may be county, aided, special agreement, controlled or maintained special schools.

Education action zones

The powers to set up education action zones are contained in the School Standards and Framework Act 1998. It is expected that there will be about 25 of these zones set up initially, with about 5 of them up and running by September 1998. Each zone will contain 2 or 3 secondary schools, with a cluster of up to 20 primary schools.

The National Curriculum will be suspended in the zones, which are expected to run for five years, overseen by an education action forum made up of a representative governor from each of the member schools, parents, community groups, businesses and the LEA. Employment conditions in the zones may also be different from those in non-zone schools if they have been exempted by the Secretary of State.

Governing bodies

The Education Act 1996 contained a number of sections dealing with the constitution and functions of a school's governing body in different types of school. In general terms, the governing body is responsible for the overall management and direction of a school. Sections of The School Standards and Framework Act and the Schedules of that Act (Schedules 9 to 13) replaced these provisions, but the broad framework will remain the same. The governing body is deemed to be a body corporate.

Instruments of government

Section 76 of the Education Act 1996 requires every county, voluntary and maintained school to draw up an instrument of government setting out the governing body's constitution. Section 218 contains equivalent provisions for grant-maintained schools.

Articles

According to Sections 127 (for community, voluntary and maintained schools) and 218 (for grant-maintained schools), all schools are required to draw up articles of government to show how the school is to be run.

Governors

Section 36 of the School Standards and Framework Act 1998 and Schedule 9 define the different categories of governors and the number of each type depending on the size of school. In some circumstances, the Secretary of State may also appoint governors and both the Secretary of State and the LEA will have additional powers to appoint governors in 'failing' schools.

Governors must be over 18. They must not be bankrupt or have been sentenced to more than three months in prison in the previous five years. Other provisions about governors and governing bodies are contained in Schedules 10 to 13 of the School Standards and Framework Act 1998.

Types of governor

Foundation governors
Foundation governors are members of the governing body of voluntary schools appointed to represent the interests of the organization (often a church) that supports the school.

Partnership governors
The equivalent of foundation governors in foundation schools that do not have a foundation.

Parent governors
Parent governors are elected by the parents of all the pupils currently at the school, but they can remain as governors after their children have left until the end of their term of office. If no one volunteers for election, the other governors may appoint a parent to the governing body.

Teacher governors
Teachers at the school have the right to elect representatives on to the governing body, but teacher governors can only stay in office as long as they work at the school.

Representative governors
The LEA has the right to appoint members to the governing body and can also remove them from office so long as it is reasonable to do so.

Co-opted governors
The governing body can co-opt members on to the body by a two-thirds majority vote. Once appointed, they cannot be removed from office. The governing body must take into account the need for its membership to be balanced and should consider ensuring that the local business community has some representation.

Charitable trusts

Some independent schools are run as charities and must act in accordance with the laws relating to charities (mainly in the Charities Act 1993), as well as complying with any relevant education requirements, such as the requirement to register the school with the Registrar of Independent Schools. Foundation schools, voluntary schools and foundation special schools are charities, but specifically exempt from the provisions of the Charities Act.

Headteachers

There is no statutory definition of the term 'headteacher' as such, but there are many different acts that spell out their role. The Education Act 1996 makes it compulsory for every headteacher to be allowed to be a governor and contains numerous other provisions about the powers of headteachers (for example, to exclude pupils) and their obligations (such as publishing information). The responsibilities and employment conditions of headteachers are also set out in the annual School Pay and Conditions Order (see Chapter 6). The Teaching and Higher Education Act 1998 (when fully in force) enables the General Teaching Council to require all headteachers to have a professional headship qualification.

Teachers

Again, there is no statutory definition of the term 'teacher', though there are definitions of certain types of teachers. As with headteachers the employment conditions and so on for teachers in the public sector are set out in the annual School Pay and Conditions Order. There were about 458,000 full-time teachers in 1997, of whom 13,800 were employed in maintained special schools, 1800 in pupil referral units (see below), 1100 in non-maintained special schools and 54,800 in independent schools.

Reserved teachers

This term is used in Sections 54(6) and 58 of the School Standards and Framework Act 1998. It does not mean the shy and retiring type, but a teacher who is specifically appointed for their competence to teach religious education in a voluntary controlled school (where the numbers of reserved teachers must not exceed one fifth of the total number of teachers). The headteacher cannot be a reserved teacher.

The foundation governors on the governing body can require the

LEA to dismiss the teacher if they are not satisfied with their performance in delivering religious education. A teacher in an aided school who is employed to teach religious education but fails to do so suitably and efficiently may also be dismissed by the governing body.

Education Association

As set out in Section 31, Schools Inspection Act 1996, this is a body appointed by the Secretary of State to run a school that requires special measures because it is failing or likely to fail (Section 13(9) or to implement an action plan if the Secretary does not believe that the action plan will be effectively carried out by the school or LEA or the Secretary does not approve the action plan itself or as the action plan is put into practice it becomes obvious that it is not working.

Pupil referral units (PRU)

In Section 19, Education Act 1996, and Schedule 1, as amended by Section 47, Education Act 1997, a PRU is a unit (which may be a school or part of a school, but not a county or special school) for the education of pupils of compulsory school age who would not otherwise receive an education because of illness, exclusion from school or other reason. PRUs are run by management committees rather than governing bodies (Section 48, Education Act 1997).In January 1998, 1 per cent of pupils were being educated in special schools or PRUs.

OFSTED and other school inspections

OFSTED is shorthand for the Office for Standards in Education and is a quango led by the Chief Inspector for Schools for England. Similar provision is made for Wales.

The current framework for the work of OFSTED in inspecting schools is set out in the School Inspections Act 1996. The Education Act 1997 amendments add provisions giving OFSTED the power to inspect local education authorities as well as schools. Most OFSTED inspections occur on a periodical basis, but the Act also allows *ad hoc* inspections, inspections by LEAs and inspections of religious education, carried out by people chosen by governors. OFSTED has also been invited to advise the Secretary of State on other areas, including literacy and numeracy strategies, access and equal opportunities, curriculum and assessment, pupil behaviour and attendance, failing schools, special educational needs, drugs education, schools' partnership with parents, initial teacher training, induction of newly qualified teachers and training for headship.

Assisted places scheme

Section 479 of the Education Act 1996 created this scheme, but it has already been abolished by the Education (Schools) Act 1997. However, transitional provisions have been made to allow children already in the scheme to continue at the same schools until they leave or finish their primary education.

School Curriculum and Assessment Authority

A victim of the Education Act 1997, this has been replaced by the Qualifications and Curriculum Authority and the Qualifications and Curriculum Authority for Wales.

Qualifications and Curriculum Authority and QCA for Wales

These bodies were set up by the Education Act 1997 (Sections 21 and 27) and replace the School Curriculum and Assessment Authorities and the National Council for Vocational Qualifications. Members are appointed by the Secretary of State for Education.

The main purpose of these Authorities is to advise the Secretary of State on matters relating to the curriculum and in respect of examinations.

Advisory Councils on Religious Education

Section 390 of the Education Act 1996 instructed all LEAs to establish these councils to advise them on matters connected with religious worship and religious education.

Independent Schools Tribunal

This body's existence is now governed by Section 476 of the Education Act 1996 and related regulations. It deals with disputes about objections to a school's continuation by the Secretary of State and disqualifications of staff employed in independent schools.

General Teaching Council (GTC)

This is a new body created by the Teaching and Higher Education Act 1998 to oversee the registration and training of teachers. It has been given disciplinary powers ranging from reprimand to de-registration of a teacher. The GTC is not expected to be set up until some time in 1999.

Council on Tribunals

The Council on Tribunals is responsible for supporting the administration of all tribunals and for guidance and support of a number of quasi-judicial bodies, such as the local authority panels that hear exclusion appeals and admissions appeals.

Commission for Local Administration/local government ombudsman

The local government ombudsmen (there are three) investigate complaints of injustice arising from maladministration by local authorities and certain other bodies. They can investigate complaints about educational matters, but not if the complaints relate to the internal affairs of an individual school. See Chapter 15 for further details.

Chapter 4

Subject to contract – the employment relationship

Who is the employer?

The vast majority of teachers are employed by the LEA in the sense that this is the body with whom the contract of service is made. Table 4.1 shows the identity of the employer in this sense for each different type of school.

Table 4.1 Who is your employer?

Type of school	Employer
Community/county	LEA
Voluntary aided (including former special agreement schools)	Governing body
Voluntary controlled	LEA
Foundation/grant-maintained	Governing body
Independent	Proprietor or Board of trustees or governing body
Community special	LEA
Grouped	Governing body of group
Pupil referral unit	LEA
City technology college	Governing body

Change of employer

See the Frequently asked questions section at the end of this chapter for information about the situation when the employer changes. This can happen, for example, when a school changes from maintained to grant-maintained (foundation) status.

Dismissal and appointment of staff

Maintained schools

Appointing staff
The roles of the governors and the LEA are set out in Schedule 16 of the School Standards and Framework Act 1998. Table 4.2 shows what the division of labour between them is.

Governors now have additional powers under the School Standards and Framework Act 1998 to appoint any teacher (including a headteacher) in an emergency if they think that a vacant post will not otherwise be filled. They can only appoint a teacher who has all the necessary qualifications and, if they use this power, the person concerned will not become an employee of the LEA.

Under the School Standards and Framework Act, the Secretary of State has the power to make regulations to govern the employment of non-teaching staff who will be LEA employees.

Maintained schools with suspended budgets

Under Section 54(2) of the School Standards and Framework Act 1998, the LEA takes over all matters relating to the appointment, suspension and dismissal of all staff. They may consult the governing body and headteacher if they think fit.

Dismissal of staff

The governing body can recommend to the LEA that any person employed at a school or the clerk to the governing body should be dismissed. Before doing so, they must allow the person an opportunity to make representations and take those representations into account before reaching their final decision. They must also allow

Table 4.2 The roles of the governors and LEA in appointing staff

Task	Governors	LEA
Appointment of headteacher	Governors must notify the LEA of vacancy. Governors must advertise vacancy. Governors must appoint selection panel of at least 3 governors. Governors recommend candidate to LEA.	The LEA must appoint recommended candidate unless staff qualification requirements are not met.
Appointment of deputy headteacher.	Governors must advertise vacancy. Governors must appoint selection panel of at least 3 governors. Governors recommend candidate to the LEA.	The LEA must appoint recommended candidate unless staff qualification requirements are not met.
Appointment of head and deputy headteachers.	Governors must consider advice before making decision.	Chief executive officer must be allowed to offer advice as to appointment of head and deputy headteachers.
Appointment of other teachers.	Governors must draw up job specification and send copy to the LEA. Governors decide whether or not to accept LEA nominee. Governors may recommend existing teacher in school. Governors may advertise (and may interview LEA nominee if they think fit, and must advertise if they reject the LEA recommendation). Governors recommend candidate to the LEA. Governors may delegate above functions to selected governor(s) and/or the head-teacher. The headteacher must be allowed to attend all interviews (except interview for the headteacher post itself).	The LEA may nominate a candidate for consideration who is an existing LEA employee (in aided schools, governors must consent to this). The LEA must appoint recommended candidate unless staff qualification requirements are not met. The CEO may offer advice on the appointment if requested to do so by the governing body.
All appointments.		The CEO (or nominee) must be allowed to attend all interviews.
Appointment of non-teaching staff.	Governors may recommend candidate to the LEA, including recommendations about terms of service. Governors must consult headteacher. If new post is for more than 16 hours, governors must consult the LEA.	The LEA must appoint the recommended candidate unless staff qualification requirements are not met.
Clerk to governing body.	Governing body selects candidate after consulting the LEA.	The LEA must appoint recommended candidate.

opportunities for an appeal. Both the headteacher (unless it is the headteacher whose neck is on the block) and the CEO are entitled to attend any meetings or hearings dealing with potential dismissal and may give advice that must be taken into account. Ultimately, the LEA must follow the governors' recommendation. The LEA must also meet the costs of any dismissal (Section 137, Education Act 1996) that the governors decide should be paid unless there is a good reason for the costs to be met from the school's budget.

The only circumstance in which the LEA can itself institute dismissal proceedings is if dismissal is required under Section 218(6) of the Education Reform Act 1988 (due to be replaced by provisions in the Teaching and Higher Education Act 1998). Regulations have been made under this Section (The Education (Teachers) Regulations 1993 SI 1993/543) that a person must not be appointed or continue in employment if they do not meet prescribed health and physical capacity standards or if they have been barred by the Secretary of State from employment in a school on medical, educational or misconduct grounds.

The School Standards and Framework Act (Schedule 16) gives an LEA a right and a duty to make a report to a governing body when it has concerns about the performance of a headteacher. It also imposes a duty on governors to consider an LEA's report and tell the LEA what action they propose to take.

Independent schools

In independent schools, the situation is much clearer as to the hiring and firing of staff because there is no sharing of responsibilities. Either the proprietor of the school is the employer or the governing body or the Board of Trustees and whichever it is will be responsible in law for all the consequences of decisions about staff.

General Teaching Council (GTC)

The Teaching and Higher Education Act 1998 sets up a General Teaching Council (GTC) to be responsible for the registration of teachers and for disciplinary matters. All teachers will have to be registered before they can be employed in schools. Under Schedule 2 of the Act, the GTC (when established) will be able to exercise a disciplinary jurisdiction when it is alleged that a teacher is:

- guilty of unacceptable professional conduct;
- guilty of serious professional incompetence;
- has been convicted at any time of a relevant offence.

If satisfied after hearing evidence and representations from the teacher that the allegations are proved, the GTC will have the power to impose one of a range of penalties:

- a reprimand;
- a conditional registration order – under which the teacher remains registered provided they comply with certain conditions;
- a suspension order – suspending the teacher from registration for a period of up to two years;
- a prohibition order – suspending the teacher from registration indefinitely (the teacher can apply for reinstatement, but not for at least two years after the date the order takes effect).

Teachers will be able to appeal against any disciplinary order imposed by the GTC to the High Court, but no further.

Voluntary aided schools

Appointment and dismissal of staff is a matter for the governing body (Section 137 of the Education Act 1996 and Schedule 17 of the School Standards and Framework Act 1998).

The procedures to be followed are extremely similar to those applying to community schools. The governors must notify the LEA if they dismiss a member of staff and explain their reasons for doing so in writing. The CEO has advisory rights (Section 138) if the governors agree or if the Secretary of State requires it, and, if the CEO has those rights, they must then be allowed to attend all meetings and hearings.

These schools have a free hand in employing non-teaching staff unless they agree otherwise with the LEA.

In Roman Catholic voluntary aided schools, the major superior of the order is the person to be notified of vacancies. He will recommend candidates to the governing body and they must appoint one of his recommendations unless that person is not qualified or there is some other good reason (not defined) for non-appointment.

Reserved teachers

Reserved teachers (who are appointed to teach religious education) are now appointed under Section 58 of the School Standards and Framework Act 1998. In voluntary aided schools with a religious character, the procedures for appointment are as for other teachers, but one fifth of all teachers may be selected because of their fitness or competence to teach religious education. The foundation governors must be satisfied of this competence before appointment and may require dismissal of the teacher or teachers if they cease to be fit and competent.

Proposed changes

It is not yet clear what the procedures will be in the education action zones if the Secretary of State grants them exemption from the nationally agreed contractual provisions or what the impact of this will be on appointments and dismissals.

The employment contract

Every employee has a contract of employment made up of a number of terms that are said to be agreed between the employer and the employee. These may be express, implied or statutory:

- 'express' terms are those that are agreed between the employer and the worker, sometimes in writing and sometimes orally;
- 'implied' terms may be implied by law into every contract – for example, the duty of good faith (see below) – or implied into the particular contract because it has been the custom and practice of a particular area of employment;
- 'statutory' terms are those that become part of the contract because of an Act of Parliament.

What is unusual about the employment situation of teachers in the public sector is that, although the contract of employment will almost always be with the LEA, it is the governing body of the school that will make all the major decisions.

Along with all other employees, teachers must be given a written statement containing information about their employment. This is dealt with in the Employment Rights Act 1996, a consolidating act in which the main provisions on employment protection are now found. The written statement can be provided in several parts over a two-month period from the date of starting work. It must include the following information:

- the name of the employer and the employee;
- the date the employment began;
- the date on which continuous employment began – this may be the start date of previous employment;
- salary details;
- details of working hours;
- holiday entitlement;
- terms relating to illness;
- pension details;
- notice period;
- job title and brief job description;
- length of employment, if fixed term;
- place of work and address of employer;
- information about relevant collective agreements;
- disciplinary rules, grievance and appeals procedures, except health and safety matters.

The written statement can contain cross-references to other documents that contain further details, so long as these are reasonably accessible to the employee. Every employee should be given details of any amendments to the above information in writing within a month of the change (this does not mean that the employer can simply impose changes to the contract unilaterally). In addition, an employee is entitled to an itemized pay statement with or before every payment that shows gross and net amounts and any deductions.

School teachers' pay and conditions document

The main documents to which cross-reference will usually be made are to the annual school teachers' pay and conditions document. This not only deals with the all-important annual pay changes, but also sets out some of the duties of teachers. There follows a summary of those duties.

The pay and conditions document applies to teachers employed by:

- LEA;
- education associations;
- a joint committee;
- the governing body of a voluntary, grant-maintained or grant-maintained special school (foundation schools);
- the governing body of a group of grant-maintained or grant-maintained special schools (foundation) (unless they have obtained a special exemption).

It does not apply to an establishment maintained by a local authority in the exercise of a social services function. The right of grant-maintained (foundation) schools to opt out of the Pay and Conditions Orders is to be repealed. Having said that, there has been recent press coverage indicating that, in addition to suspending the order in the education action zones, the Government is considering moving away from a nationally negotiated contract in the longer term.

Union agreements

The majority of LEAs have agreed to follow the Conditions of Service for Schoolteachers in England and Wales ('the Burgundy Book'). The Conditions deal in detail with a number of aspects of the employment of teachers and are often incorporated into their contracts. In many grant-maintained (foundation) schools, a similar 'Blue Book' has been adopted. There is no similar document in respect of City Technology Colleges.

Independent schools

Independent school teachers should have a written contract and the Employment Rights Act 1996 and other general employment legislation will apply to teachers employed in independent schools. However, the annual pay and conditions document will not apply and, generally speaking, neither will the collective union agreements. The terms and conditions of service under which teachers work in independent schools are entirely a matter for the school, although they will still be subject to some statutory regulation, such as the general disciplinary matters referred to above under General Teaching Council and in the next chapter under List 99.

The role of governors

One of the terms in a teacher's employment contract is that they must follow the reasonable instructions of headteachers and so on. Other aspects of the teacher's employment may be affected by decisions of the governing body, the duties of which include:

- appointing, suspending and dismissing staff;
- deciding on staff numbers;
- deciding on pay where they have some discretion (such as to responsibility points);
- setting disciplinary rules and procedures and hearing grievances;
- deciding on the timing of school sessions (in consultation with the LEA, head and parents).

In grant-maintained (foundation) schools, governors are also responsible for appraisal arrangements. All governors can take part in making the above decisions – there is no embargo on any particular type of governor taking part in general decisions about pay, for example, and this includes teacher governors. However, a governor must withdraw from any discussion or decision about a matter where their own interests might conflict with those of the school if they have a personal interest in the outcome of a decision (say about pay or discipline in the case of a teacher governor or about exclusion in the case of a parent governor whose child was being discussed).

The duties of headteachers

Headteachers must carry out their duties in accordance with any relevant statutory and regulatory provisions, such as the Education Act 1996, and must follow any rules, regulations or policies laid down by the governing body as well as those of the employer.

Headteachers are deemed to be responsible for the 'internal organization, management and control of their schools' in consultation with governors, the LEA, parents and staff, as appropriate. More specific duties include:

- formulating the aims and objectives of the school and implementation policies;
- participating in the appointment of staff;
- managing all staff and allocating duties;
- delegation of duties to deputy headteachers;
- arranging for cover for absent teachers;
- disseminating information to teachers;
- liaising with unions and other staff representatives;
- overseeing the school curriculum;
- ensuring attendance at daily collective worship;
- evaluating standards;
- supervising and participating in teacher appraisal;
- making arrangements for staff training and the support of newly qualified teachers;
- ensuring pupils' progress is recorded and monitored;
- devising and implementing a policy for the pastoral care of pupils;
- maintaining discipline and promoting self-discipline, a proper regard for authority and good behaviour on the part of pupils;
- keeping parents informed about the school and pupils' progress;
- advising, assisting and reporting to the governing body;
- allocating, controlling and accounting for resources;
- making arrangements for the security and effective supervision of the school buildings and grounds;
- participating, as appropriate, in teaching duties, including providing cover.

The headteacher is entitled to a break of reasonable length in the course of the school day, but there is no entitlement to a break at a particular time.

The duties of deputy headteachers

A deputy headteacher must generally carry out any of the duties that the headteacher delegates to them and is expected to play a major role in the management of the school. A deputy is entitled to a break of reasonable length as near to the middle of the day as is practicable.

The duties of teachers

A teacher must carry out their duties as *reasonably* directed by the headteacher and the LEA. Those duties are defined as including:

- planning and preparing lessons;
- teaching, setting homework and school work and marking it;
- assessing and reporting on pupil progress;
- promoting the well-being of pupils;
- guiding and advising pupils;
- recording and reporting on the personal and social needs of pupils;
- communicating and consulting with parents and others;
- attending meetings for the above purposes;
- participating in the appraisal of the performance of teachers, including themselves;
- participating in further training;
- advising the headteacher and other teachers on course preparation, teaching programmes and pastoral arrangements;
- maintaining discipline and safeguarding pupils, both in school and out;
- providing cover for teachers who are absent for fewer than three days;
- participating in arrangements for examinations;
- participating in appointments, training and appraisal of other members of staff and related management functions;
- attending assemblies and registering pupil attendance.

The document also deals with the teachers' hours of work. Full-time teachers must be available for 195 days in a school year, on 190 of which they may be required to teach. They must perform their duties at times and places specified by the head, up to a maximum of 1265 hours a year (the so-called 'directed' time). The time allocation must be reasonably spread amongst the days on which a teacher is required to teach. The time limit does not include any travelling time. A teacher is not required to supervise at lunchtime and is entitled to a reasonable break between 12 noon and 2 pm. In addition to directed time, a teacher is expected to work such additional hours as may be necessary to carry out all the duties listed above, in particular, lesson preparation, marking and report writing.

Part-time and supply teachers

The Pay and Conditions Document says that teachers in part-time service or employed on a casual basis shall be entitled to be paid in proportion with the hours they work. The other conditions referred to above apply to all teachers, including part-time teachers, except in respect of directed time, which does not apply to them.

The Employment Rights Act 1996 also deals with part-time workers. There is no longer any restriction on the right to apply to an industrial tribunal in respect of unfair dismissal and so on the minimum number of contracted hours. Part-time workers are in the same position as full-time workers and claim relief when they can after they have been in service continuously for two years.

At the moment, part-time and supply teachers do not have the same pension entitlements as their full-time colleagues. On 5 February 1998, the House of Lords referred a number of important questions about the rights of part-time workers (one of whom is a teacher) to the European Court of Justice. Their decision when it comes may force a change in UK law to bring part-time teachers into line with full-time teachers in terms of pension rights.

Some supply teachers are employed by the LEA as part of a pool, but many are now employed by agencies and their employment contracts are likely to be different from those of their local authority counterparts. It is not possible to generalize about these contracts as they will vary from agency to agency. See also the DfEE circular on the *Use of Supply Teachers* (7/96).

Rights under the Employment Rights Act 1996

The working life of teachers, along with other employees, is further regulated by the Employment Rights Act 1996. This includes the following entitlements:

- not to have unauthorized deductions made from your pay;
- not to suffer detriment at the hands of the employer for acts done in the capacity of staff representative (including in relation to health and safety matters), complaining about risks to health and safety, refusing to work in dangerous conditions or protecting oneself or others from risk of harm;

- the right to take a reasonable amount of paid time off to carry out public duties, including serving as a councillor, tribunal adjudicator, police authority, board of prison visitors and so on;
- the right to take paid time off for antenatal care;
- the right to take a reasonable amount of paid time off to work as a trade union representative or stand for election;
- the right to be paid if suspended for a period of less than 26 weeks on medical grounds;
- a right to maternity leave and to return to work at the end of it;
- the right not to be unfairly dismissed.

The Government has announced new arrangements that, it claims, will speed up dismissal procedures in respect of incompetent teachers. These are based on recommendations from a joint body, including employers and the teaching unions. These will apply to all teachers, including head and deputy headteachers.

The procedures enable incompetent teachers to be dismissed within six months or, in extreme cases, four weeks. The School Standards and Framework Act 1998 provides that, while it is generally for the governing body to devise its own disciplinary rules and procedures, it must take into account any guidance issued by the Secretary of State as to assessing the capabilities of staff and allow the Secretary to impose rules and procedures on the governing body. In fact, the Secretary of State does not currently intend to use these powers to impose the dismissal procedures nationally. The procedures will still be subject to the unfair dismissal protection offered by the Employment Rights Act and must also be in line with the ACAS code of practice providing for complaints in writing, rights of representations at hearings, appeals and timescales for each stage. Furthermore, there is an expectation that the employer will have to consider a period of support and training for any teacher felt to be below the required standard. The whole purpose of a disciplinary procedure is to cure problems, not just legitimate dismissals. It therefore seems highly unlikely that the vast majority of teachers will feel any effect from the 'new' procedures. Some employers are already operating similar or even more stringent procedures.

Frequently asked questions

Can my employer make me work for a probationary period and then not renew my contract?

For most LEA employees, the question of a probationary period should not normally arise. However, there is nothing intrinsically unlawful about a period of probation, and, indeed, it used to be compulsory for newly qualified teachers. The Teaching and Higher Education Act 1998 requires newly qualified teachers to undergo an induction year before they can be accredited with registered teacher status, which looks like a probationary year to me. In addition, newly qualified teachers and other teachers are increasingly being offered fixed-term or temporary contracts that may have exactly the same result. About one in ten teachers in LEA schools work under such contracts.

It should be noted that many employment rights cannot be asserted in an employment tribunal until there has been continuous service for a period of two years (although there are constant challenges to this in the courts and in the European courts). In other words, it is quite lawful not to renew a fixed-term contract or to dismiss an employee once that fixed term has expired (except where the dismissal is for reasons connected with maternity, sex or race discrimination or trade union activity where there are no continuous service requirements). However, successive fixed-term contracts in the teaching context have been held to count as continuous service. It was even held that flexible pool working counts as continuous service in some circumstances. In one case the court has also held that the expiry of a fixed-term contract does not count as a termination of employment so a teacher cannot claim any entitlement to early retirement benefits (for example, *Teacher's Pension Agency* v *Rosemary Hill* (1998) *The Times*, 20 July 1998 – leave to appeal has been granted in this case). As with all matters relating to your employment position, it would be wise to speak to your union, which can make representations on your behalf.

There is a case on its way to the European court at the time of writing that challenges the two-year rule on the basis that it discriminates against women. The thinking is that the time limit may be reduced to one year. In the meantime, all cases involving this point in the UK are on hold.

Can I take early retirement?

Early retirement has been much in the news in the last few years, surrounded by a great deal of uncertainty about the future. First, teachers were encouraged to take early retirement, then the government realized the cost implications and attempted to place the responsibility for paying back with the LEAs. The statutory superannuation scheme allows a teacher who has served a minimum qualifying period to leave work at any time with their pension being frozen until the time when it would normally have fallen due for payment. If a teacher is asked to retire early and aged between 50 and 59, they may be entitled to a pension and a lump sum. If you are considering early retirement, you should seek advice from your union and from the Teachers' Pension Agency (TPA). Current thinking is that an application should be made to the TPA about six months in advance of the desired retirement date. The pension scheme is complicated and constantly changing. For example, changes were made to regulations during the course of 1997 that have made it harder to qualify for ill health benefits and it is now necessary to prove permanent incapacity to work.

Any teacher granted ill-health benefits will not be able to return to work at all, whether on a part-time basis or, in some other capacity, such as librarian.

I am a teacher at a school that has changed from maintained to grant maintained / foundation. Does this have any effect on my employment rights?

There are numerous ways in which a teacher is specifically protected in this sort of situation, even though the employer has changed. When a school becomes grant-maintained, Section 202 of the Education Act 1996 provides that a teacher's contract is treated as if it were originally made between the teacher and the new employer (that is, the governing body and that all the former employer's rights, powers, duties and liabilities (including for past action) are transferred to the new employer. This has the effect of preserving continuity of employment for unfair dismissal purposes and so on. In other words, the teacher is treated as having been employed by the new employer from the date that they were originally employed by the old employer. Similar provisions have been incorporated into the School Standards and Framework Act 1998.

The employee is therefore entitled to exactly the same contractual conditions as they would have been before the transfer. This does not mean the contract cannot be varied, but it does mean that any variation has to be agreed to by the employee or they may be able to claim constructive dismissal. This echoes similar provision in the Employment Rights Act 1996 (Section 218) under which when any act has the effect of substituting one employer for another – it will not break the continuity of employment. The same section says that an employee of a local education authority who is then taken into the employment of governors of a maintained school and *vice versa* will have their first period of employment aggregated with their second. Thus, not only is continuity of employment rights preserved but the right to redundancy pay for the whole period of both employments.

Chapter 5

You won't get me, I'm part of the union – the employer's rights and duties

The employer's duties

The obligations under the contract of employment go both ways. As with the duties of the employee, an employer's duties towards an employee come from a variety of sources, including statutory duties and duties that have been imposed as a result of judicial decisions (common law duties), which are more than usually important in this area.

Common law duties

Safety and the work environment
The case law says that an employer must take reasonable care for the safety of employees by providing:

- competent fellow employees;
- a reasonably safe system of work;
- reasonably safe equipment.

This duty is personal to the employer, who will be responsible to an employee both for the wrongdoing of another employee acting in the course of employment and the wrongdoings of any third party who creates a risk in the workplace.

The following sections deal with some aspects of common law liability, which are of particular relevance in the teaching environment, namely stress, the behaviour of other people and bullying.

Stress

According to a 1997 survey sponsored by the *TES* and carried out by Brunel University, 38 per cent of teachers quit due to ill health (compared with say 9 per cent of nurses) and one stress expert has described teaching as now being one of Britain's most stressful occupations. An HSE survey in 1995 suggested that 37,000 of teachers or former teachers suffered from stress, anxiety or depression. A further 26,000 suffered from some physical illness that they believed to be due to stress at work. This amounts to 4 per cent of current and recently working teachers who feel themselves to be under stress. Teachers may have a particular interest, therefore, in knowing whether or not they have any comeback against their employer if their health suffers as a result of stress.

An employer has a duty to take reasonable care of an employee's physical and mental health. The duty to maintain a reasonably safe system of work includes a duty to ensure that intolerable stress is not put on an employee. In practice, it is not easy to pin liability on an employer for the effects of stress because it may be difficult to show that they were aware of the problem. This may get the employer off the hook the first time, but it will not work more than once. In *Walker* v *Northumberland County Council* (1995] IRLR 35, a social worker was given leave to sue a local authority when he suffered one breakdown owing to the pressure of work, was sent back to work in the same conditions and then had a second breakdown. The judge said:

> He had been trapped in a situation where on the one hand he was unable to control the increasing volume of stressful work and where on the other he was unable to persuade superior management to increase staff or give management guidance as to work distribution or prioritization.

The social worker recovered damages of £175,000 as a result of an out-of-court settlement, but the court had accepted that the employer was liable in the circumstances.

The Health and Safety Executive has published updated guidance aimed at both teachers and school managers on how to avoid and reduce the health risks associated with work-related stress.

The booklet is entitled *Managing Work-related Stress: A guide for managers and teachers in schools.*

Risks arising out of the behaviour of others
The employer's duty to provide a reasonably safe system of work includes ensuring that employees are not exposed to obvious risks arising out of the behaviour of other people. This includes pupils. There are several duties imposed on headteachers to impose discipline and maintain order. In practice, it may be difficult to prove that the employer is to blame for the effects of stress as, with the best will in the world, it is not always possible to control the behaviour of someone who is really determined to cause trouble or who flares up unexpectedly. However, once bitten, twice shy. A teacher recovered damages from Coventry City Council of £82,500 when she was assaulted by a violent 10-year-old pupil. The employer was well aware of the pupil's disruptive behaviour, but had failed to transfer him to a special school despite repeated requests to do so.

Bullying
Bullying in the workplace is not a new problem and I cannot comment on whether or not it was more prevalent in the past in the teaching environment than in other workplaces. It certainly seems to be a significant problem in some schools now and one cannot help but speculate as to whether or not the pressure to achieve good results in the form of league tables, OFSTED inspections, so-called fast-track dismissal procedures and increased parental criticism have made things worse. The National Workplace Bullying Advice Line has found that 20 per cent (of 3000) of callers are teachers or other employees in the education field. Its web site on the Internet (see Useful addresses) contains much useful information and a specific section written by REDRESS (the bullied teachers' network).

In a case in 1998 that, at face value at least, bears a remarkable similarity to the Walker case mentioned under Stress, a teacher was awarded £100,000 in damages (in an out-of-court settlement). He alleged that he had been the victim of a campaign of harassment and bullying at the primary school in which he worked. He also alleged that he was sent back to work in the same school despite his complaints and having had one nervous breakdown and so then suffered a second breakdown.

The legal principles involved in such a case are very similar to those arising in questions of stress management and sexual harassment.

The difference is that it is not quite so obvious what sort of systems an employer can put in place to prevent it from happening. The most important procedural implication from the point of view of avoiding litigation is to have a clear grievance policy for dealing with complaints about bullying and take appropriate action when it is reported, both in terms of supporting the victim and dealing with the bully. Training can certainly help to improve employee awareness and provide them with confidence and techniques for dealing with the problem. Equally, it may help the budding bully to realize the impact of their behaviour on others.

The obvious source of support for teachers facing bullying at work is their union. The National Association of Schoolmasters/Union of Women Teachers (NASUWT) has even produced two relevant booklets – *No Place to Hide: Confronting workplace bullies* and *Stop Personal Harassment*.

Statutory duties

In addition to an employer's common law duties, there are a number of statutes that may affect them (which are also relevant to potential liability to pupils who are injured on school premises – see Chapter 14), as discussed below.

Occupiers' Liability Acts 1957 and 1984

Any occupier of premises – that is, the person or persons in control of the premises (which is likely to be the governing body and/or the LEA in the majority of schools) – has a 'duty to take such care as in all the circumstances of the case is reasonable to see that the visitor will be reasonably safe in using the premises for which he is invited or permitted by the occupier to be there'.

One complication in the case of schools relates to the division of responsibility between the LEA and the governing body for repairs to the premises. The LEA owns the building and is responsible for major items of repair, but day-to-day maintenance is down to the governing body. In order to figure out their respective liabilities, it may be necessary to have a look at which of them is responsible for an individual item of repair and the DfEE circular 2/94: *Local Management of Schools* is relevant here.

If an occupier hires an independent contractor to do work on the premises and someone is injured as a result of something the contractor does or does not do, the contractor – not the employer – will be liable. However, an employer is always liable towards an employee, even though the person at fault is the contractor. There is a very old case that suggests that a local authority carrying out its statutory duties will be liable even though the real fault lies at the door of the contractor. This might apply in circumstances where the LEA is carrying out its duties to repair school premises, but this argument has not been used recently and is wildly out of synch with most modern authorities. An employer will not generally be liable to the contractor unless some special danger exists that could not have been obvious to the contractor (or part of their job to deal with) but was known to the employer.

There is a helpful Health and Safety Executive briefing aimed at schools on the use of contractors entitled *Contractors in Schools*.

The Health and Safety Act 1974 and related regulations
This legislation exists primarily for the protection of employees, but also for those who are not at work but may be at risk from the activities of those who are. This includes, for example, pupils on work experience, teachers and others inspecting the premises and so on. The general duty is to 'ensure, so far as is reasonably practicable, the health and safety and welfare at work of all his employees'. The courts have held that it is reasonable for an employer to take into account the cost of repairs or procedures (in terms of money, time and disruption) to ensure health and safety and balance them against the likely benefit.

All organizations with more than five employees must have a policy statement dealing with health and safety issues. Among other things, this should spell out who is responsible for identifying hazards, assessing risks and keeping them under control. In LEA schools, this policy will usually be drawn up by the LEA as employer, but governing bodies are encouraged to adapt the standard policy to their own needs and add to it as appropriate.

The devil, as they say, is in the detail and it is the regulations that are made under the Act that set out what must be done and to what standard. These include:

- The Health and Safety (First Aid) Regulations 1981 (SI 1981/917);
- The Workplace (Health, Safety and Welfare) Regulations 1992 and Code of Practice (SI 1992/3004);
- The Management of Health and Safety at Work Regulations 1992 (SI 1992/2051) and Code of Practice;

- Control of Substances Hazardous to Health Regulations 1994 (SI 1994/3246);
- The Reporting of Injuries, Diseases and Dangerous Occurrences Regulations 1985 (SI 1985/2023);
- The Personal Protective Equipment at Work Regulations 1992 (SI 1992/2966).

The Health and Safety Executive publishes numerous guides on the effect of regulations and the duties they impose, including *Workplace (Health, Safety and Welfare) Regulations 1992: Guidance for the education sector, The responsibilities of school governors for health and* safety and *Managing health and safety in schools*.

The Management of Health and Safety at Work Regulations 1992 make it compulsory for an employer to:

- carry out a risk assessment, the results of which should be recorded in writing;
- appoint competent people to assist them in the measures needed to comply with health and safety law (this may include an LEA safety officer or an outside consultant.

When health and safety tasks are entrusted to employees, the employer must take into account the capabilities of the employee as regards health and safety. Any system of risk prevention and control must be monitored (usually by school managers as part of their normal management duties). The risk assessment must include a consideration of the risk of stress in the workplace (Regulation 3).

The Workplace (Health, Safety and Welfare) Regulations 1992 (which took full effect with regard to existing workplaces in January 1996) make it compulsory for an employer to:

- maintain the workplace and equipment in an efficient state;
- ensure that there is safe access to the premises and within the school premises;
- ensure that all windows and other glazing meets certain safety standards;
- provide drinking water;
- provide rest rooms and secure storage for the outdoor clothing of employees – rest areas must incorporate suitable arrangements to protect non-smokers from tobacco smoke and suitable

facilities must be available for pregnant women (for example, somewhere to lie down).

Reporting accidents

Certain types of accident that may occur in schools or during educational activities elsewhere must be reported to the Health and Safety Executive. The HSE has produced an information sheet on the duties placed on schools – *Reporting School Accidents*. The two main types of accident that must be reported are those resulting in a death or major injury and any accident that prevents the injured person from working for more than three days. The term 'accident' now includes any act of non-consensual violence to staff. The term 'major injury' includes:

- any fracture other than to fingers, thumbs or toes;
- dislocation of the shoulder, hip, knee or spine;
- loss of sight, whether permanent or temporary;
- any chemical or hot metal burn to the eye or any penetrating injury to the eye;
- any injury resulting from electric shock or burn leading to unconsciousness or requiring resuscitation or admission to hospital for more than 24 hours;
- any other injury leading to hypothermia, unconsciousness, requiring resuscitation or admission to hospital for more than 24 hours;
- loss of consciousness or other illness caused by asphyxia or exposure to a harmful substance or biological agent, toxin or infected material.

Accidents to pupils and other visitors to school premises need not be reported unless the person involved is killed or taken to hospital and the accident arises out of, or in connection with, work. This means an accident that occurs because of the way the work is organized (such as the supervision of a field trip), the plant or substances (say, lifts, machinery, experiments and so on) or the condition of the premises. The HSE guidance specifically notes that playground accidents due to collisions, slips and falls are not reportable unless they happen because of the state of the playground or the level of supervision. Notification must be made without delay by telephone, followed by a written report within ten days.

The Education (School Premises) Regulations 1996 (SI 1996/360)
These Regulations are made under the Education Act 1996 and replace complicated, detailed provisions that existed before. They set standards for the structure of the buildings and fire safety precautions and it is the responsibility of the LEA in the case of maintained schools or the governing body in the case of grant-maintained (foundation) schools to ensure that those standards are met. There is DfEE guidance on these regulations in *The 1996 School Premises Regulations* (Circular 10/96).

Environmental Protection Act 1990
In a really serious case, the state of the premises may give rise to a criminal prosecution for causing a statutory nuisance under this Act. The first prosecution of this kind was brought by pupils in a Liverpool school in October 1997 – and they were successful. The circumstances that were alleged to amount to a statutory nuisance included constant water flooding down the blackboards from leaking roofs, rotten window frames, loose tiles, blocked gutters and potholes. The pupils asked the court to make an order requiring the repairs to be carried out and the court granted it. Of particular concern to the court was the proximity of water to electricity.

Such prosecutions are normally brought by local authorities, but may be brought by any person 'aggrieved' by the nuisance, even against the local authority itself. Lack of finance to carry out the repairs is not a good defence. It is not yet clear whether or not this lead will be followed up, but it is certainly one way of short-circuiting the system. In theory, it seems to me that the school itself could take the LEA to court just as the pupils did. Whether or not they would want to is another matter!

Insurance
In keeping with all employers, employers of teachers must carry insurance in respect of liability for injury to employees arising out of their employment (Employers' Liability (Compulsory Insurance) Act 1969). In maintained schools, insurance is usually arranged by the LEA, but it is important for the governing body of every school to have an awareness of exactly what is and what is not covered by the policy by checking with the insurer if necessary. If members of staff are asked to do something that is outside their usual terms of employment, they may not be covered, particularly if the insurer has not been notified. For example, excursions out of school to

church services, school trips and so on may not be covered. The same applies for insurance cover in respect of pupils at the school. See, for example, the section on 'Work Experience' in Chapter 12.

Equipment

An employer may be liable in respect of any faulty equipment (this includes plant, machinery and clothing) that causes injury (Employers' Liability (Defective Equipment) Act 1969) either because the defect was down to the employers' negligence (for example, in not replacing it) or because the defect was caused by a third party, such as the supplier (even though the employer had no direct hand in causing the fault in the first place). In theory, this saves the employee from having to identify the supplier or manufacturer, but, in fact, it is necessary to show that the third party has been negligent, which may not always be easy without knowing who they are! Often the negligence will be obvious, however. If a relatively new piece of equipment, which has been properly looked after and is being used for its proper purpose, breaks, that may in itself be enough to establish negligence.

Teachers

It should not be forgotten that teachers also have a duty to protect themselves and their colleagues, follow good practice in health and safety matters and cooperate with the employer and anyone else with health and safety responsibilities so far as is necessary to ensure that legal duties are complied with. This includes warning an employer about any unsafe conditions or practices. You and your employer may be liable for negligence if you do not draw these to their attention. Having said that, you are not expected to be a health and safety expert.

Equal treatment

An employer must treat all employees equally and not discriminate against them on the grounds of gender, race or disability. For further details, see Chapters 5 and 9.

Pay

It may seem obvious, but an employer must actually pay for work done by the employees. They must also provide a written pay statement and not make unauthorized deductions from the payslip. Incidentally, if an employee is overpaid, in most circumstances the employer will be entitled to repayment of the excess unless the employee can show that they are not in a position to restore the payments and accepting them was a genuine mistake. If you notice an overpayment and you keep quiet about it, you may be committing a criminal offence under the Theft Act.

Treatment of staff

The courts consider that a relationship of trust and confidence is expected between employer and employee and neither are to do anything to undermine that relationship. An employer must not, for example, do anything calculated to humiliate an employee or single them out unfairly for adverse treatment or fail to support someone who has been the victim of sexual harassment. If this were to happen, the employee might be entitled to claim constructive dismissal (see Chapter 6).

In addition, the courts have said that an employer is under a duty to provide some way for employees to air their grievances. Depending on the nature of the job and the size of the staff, this procedure may be more or less elaborate. Most schools should have a well-documented grievance procedure (although tracking down a copy may be a different matter).

References

There is no legal entitlement for an employee to be provided with a reference, although I am not aware of this ever having been a particular problem in the teaching context. If a reference is provided, however, it must not be malicious or defamatory or inaccurate.

The employer's rights

There are several general duties owed by all employees to their employer, which are to:

- obey reasonable and lawful orders;
- exercise reasonable care and skill in carrying out their job;

- attend for work;
- take reasonable care of the employer's property;
- not conduct themselves in a manner that is calculated or likely to destroy or seriously damage the relationship of trust and confidence between employer and employee.

More will be said about these expectations in the following chapter.

Perhaps one of the most controversial areas for teachers is the obligation to obey the reasonable and lawful instruction of an employer, particularly as to the use of their time. For, although directed time is limited in terms of the number of hours and the majority of those hours are taken up by the school day, there are so many calls on the surplus time that there is still plenty of scope for argument as to what may be a reasonable direction on the part of an employer. It should also be noted that there is no provision in the school pay and conditions document for holiday time as such. However, holiday entitlement is usually dealt with in other documents that form part of the contractual entitlement and, by implication, a teacher's time outside that which is directed and needed for the preparation of coursework and so on is their own.

In addition, from 1 October 1998, the Working Time Regulations 1998 (SI 1998/1833) implement an EU Directive giving workers rights to a certain amount of rest during the normal working week and to annual paid holiday. A cap of 48 hours is imposed on the working week, unless the worker agrees in writing to waive this requirement. An adult worker will be entitled to a rest period of not less than 11 consecutive hours in every 24-hour period and a minimum of uninterrupted rest of not less than 24 hours in every 14-day period (and more if it is agreed by the employer and forms part of the employment contract). Rest breaks during any working day of more than six hours are also provided for, if they are contained in a workplace or collective agreement. Finally, for the first time in UK law, there is a right to annual leave of about 3 weeks (after the first 13 weeks of employment). Certain types of employment are exempted from the Regulations, but teaching is not one of these exempted categories.

It remains to be seen what practical impact, if any, the Regulations might have on the working arrangements for teaching staff. It should be noted that there is a let-out clause that might apply to teachers. The Regulations do not apply in relation to a worker when, on account of the specific characteristics of the activity in which they are engaged, the working time is not measured or predetermined or else it is up to the worker how to determine their working time. Examples given in the Regulations of such instances include managers, executives or other people with autonomous decision-making powers. There is a further let-out to cover exceptional circumstances and emergencies or where there is a risk of an accident if the time limits are not suspended.

Frequently asked questions

Can I recover damages if I am injured slipping on the corridor floor?

This is now a very big question and one whole book has been written about the law on slipping and tripping. It will depend whether or not the employer has a reasonable system for regular inspection of the school and it was being followed. It may depend on the type of flooring that is being used and whether or not it is suitable for the pounding it is likely to receive in schools, particularly if it is near a doorway and likely to get wet (see the cases referred to in Chapter 14). It will depend on the nature of any spillage, how obvious it was and so on. If you slip because the floor is uneven, it is easier to prove liability than for a spillage, especially if the unevenness has existed for some time or it has been reported.

If you are injured in this way, then all these matters will need to be investigated and enquiries made about previous accidents and previous complaints. Speak to your union representative as soon as possible. Of course, any accidents should be reported and recorded in an accident book. Make a note of what happened as soon as you possibly can because you will soon forget the details and personal injury actions can take a long time to come to court. Similarly, keep a running total of all your expenses, such as hospital trips (both for you and visiting relatives), prescription charges, damaged clothing and so on.

I forgot to lock a door to the chemistry lab. A pupil wandered in and was injured by some broken glass that had not yet been cleared up. Will I be liable for damages?

Potentially, yes. Again, it will depend on all the surrounding facts.

How old the pupil was. Whether or not they should have known not to go into the lab unattended. Whether or not the door was marked 'No Entry'. Whether or not anyone else was responsible for making sure the door was locked. Whether or not anyone else was responsible for clearing up the glass.

In theory, if you are to blame, the pupil could sue you personally. In practice, cases are brought against both the teacher and the employer, and it is the employer who pays (or, more usually, the employer's insurance company).

Could the school be held responsible for illnesses that result from too much exposure to the sun?

A topical question arising out of a 1998 Health Education Authority report concluding that 40 per cent of children are sunburnt every year, and one that leads us into a legal minefield. I think the answer at the moment is 'probably not'. First, there is little agreement about how long you have to be exposed to the sun for this to result in serious damage or what is the best type of protection (a school has recently banned children from bringing suntan lotions into school because of concerns about allergic reactions). Second, it is probably the responsibility of the parents to decide what protection their child should have. It would be a different matter if the individual pupil had some particular problem that meant they needed special protection from exposure to certain dangers.

Chapter 6

Working to rule – the teacher as employee

The duties of teachers

The last chapter discussed some of the general duties of teachers with regard to their employers. Further specific duties are usually set out in the contractual documentation that generally includes the job description. In addition a teacher is under an obligation to obey the reasonable and lawful instructions of their employer. If a teacher does not fulfil the terms of their employment contract, they may be disciplined by their employer and, in serious cases, their behaviour may lead to dismissal.

In law, it has long been recognized that certain types of behaviour on the part of an employee may justify an employer in dismissing them. The type of conduct considered unacceptable may be clear from the contractual documentation. However, it is rare that an exhaustive list will be given and it is certainly not always clear what level of disciplinary penalty may be imposed for any particular 'offence'.

List 99

One source of guidance for teachers is DfEE circular 11/95 – *Misconduct of Teachers and Workers with Children and Young Persons*. As well as the contractual rights of an employer to discipline or dismiss a teacher for misconduct, the Education Reform Act 1988 gives the Secretary of State power to bar a person from future employment as a teacher or restrict their employment by imposing conditions. Certain procedures have to be followed before these powers can be exercised and these are set out in the Education (Teachers) Regulations 1993 (SI 1993/543), which provides extensive rights to the teacher to make representations and to appeal. The court can also be asked to review the action of the Secretary of State. Once the Secretary of State has made a final decision to ban someone from teaching, their name is entered on the so-called 'List 99', which should be checked whenever a teaching appointment is being made

If a teacher or worker with children or young persons at any school, including an independent school, is dismissed for misconduct or resigns after being accused of misconduct before enquiries into the misconduct have been completed, their employer has a duty to notify the Secretary of State.

If a teacher commits one of a list of criminal offences they will automatically be added to List 99. The listed offences include not only sexual offences against children and young persons, but buggery, gross indecency between men, indecent assault on a man or woman and any offence involving the taking or distributing of indecent photographs.

The guidance also states that barring is likely to result from the following examples of behaviour:

- violent behaviour towards children or young people;
- a sexual or otherwise inappropriate relationship with a pupil (whether or not they are over 16);
- a sexual offence against someone over the age of 16;
- any offence of serious violence;
- any drug-related offence;
- theft of school property or money;
- any deception in the obtaining of employment as a teacher or at a school, for example, misrepresentations about qualifications;
- any other conviction that results in a sentence of more than one year;
- repeated convictions for less serious matters.

Although not specifically referred to in the guidance, the commission of other offences involving child pornography, such as publishing pictures on the Internet, would also lead to a teacher being barred. While the circular itself acknowledges that it is not the last word on the law relating to misconduct, the types of behaviour listed above are, in many circumstances, viewed by the courts and tribunals as the sorts of conduct that will justify dismissal.

At least one local education authority seems to be maintaining a second list that they have dubbed 'List 98'. On it they record the names of teachers they do not wish to employ but who do not fit the criteria for inclusion on List 99. It seems highly likely that this practice is unlawful and it may be challenged in the courts.

From a procedural point of view, the above will change when the provisions of the Teaching and Higher Education Act 1998 are implemented, setting up the General Teaching Council as a disciplinary body to oversee the registration, discipline and deregistration of teachers.

Disciplinary offences

The above examples of misconduct that will result in a teacher's name being added to List 99 are also those that are likely to be seen by an industrial tribunal as the sorts of behaviour that might justify dismissal, depending on the circumstances. Others include:

- other examples of serious dishonesty, even if these are not directly work-related;
- persistent lateness or unauthorized absenteeism;
- failure to carry out reasonable and lawful instructions;
- use or abuse of drugs and alcohol;
- bringing the school into disrepute;
- disclosure of confidential information.

These specific areas of misconduct will be discussed in more detail below.

Unfair dismissal

An employer is not allowed to dismiss an employee unfairly. If they do so, the employee can take action through an industrial tribunal and claim compensation or reinstatement (provided they have been continuously employed for a period of two years, whether part-time or full-time). A dismissal on the grounds of misconduct, however, will not be unfair so long as:

- the employer has formed a genuine and reasonable belief in the guilt of the employee and has carried out an appropriate investigation into the circumstances;
- the misconduct is sufficiently serious that dismissal is within the band of reasonable responses of an employer to the behaviour.

Industrial tribunals will take account of a number of factors when deciding whether or not the above criteria apply. Here are some examples of these.

- If an employer's belief that misconduct has occurred is based purely on rumour, this will not be considered reasonable. The employee should be told the nature of the suspected misconduct and given a chance to explain what has happened.
- Where disciplinary procedures are laid out (as will be the case for most teachers), they must be followed or not doing so may, in itself, amount to unfair dismissal.
- The principles of natural justice will apply to any investigation. For example, the accuser should not take part in the investigation or decision-making process.
- Even in the most extreme cases, an employer should consider, however momentarily, whether or not other penalties short of dismissal (such as redeployment) should be considered.
- An employer must also be even-handed in treatment of all employees and ensure that use of sanctions for misconduct is consistent.
- A dismissal may be a fair response even if some employers would not dismiss on the same facts. Even in a borderline case, dismissal may be justified so long as it falls within the reasonable band of responses to the misconduct.
- The ACAS Code on Disciplinary Rules and Procedures stipulates that conduct outside of work should lead to dismissal only if it affects the person's suitability for their job. The difficulty for teachers is that they are in a position of at least great potential to influence young people, such that particularly high standards are usually expected of them and, therefore, industrial tribunals may be more sympathetic to a teacher's employer for dismissing because of misconduct away from work than would be the case for those in other occupations.

See also the comments on capability dismissals in Chapter 4 (so-called 'fast-track dismissals').

Automatically unfair dismissal

Some reasons for dismissal will automatically be considered unfair. In most of these cases, there is no requirement for there to have been any particular length of service before a complaint can be made to an industrial tribunal and in the case of maternity-related dismissals, no ceiling on the compensation that may be awarded. For example:

- any dismissal due to pregnancy or maternity or connected reason (such as pregnancy-related illness, taking maternity leave);
- dismissal for asserting a statutory right or for bringing proceedings to enforce such a right – the relevant statutory rights include the right to a minimum notice period, an itemized pay statement, not to have unlawful deductions made from pay, have time off for trade union activities and so on;
- dismissal for taking any reasonable step to protect themselves or others if in serious or imminent danger;
- dismissal for membership of a trade union;
- dismissal for taking industrial action if the employee is singled out for adverse treatment – that is, the employer has to sack all concerned or none of them.

Conduct dismissals

Violent behaviour
See also Chapter 13.

Such behaviour will be viewed very seriously in the teaching context and will often give rise to dismissal. However, an employer should investigate all the circumstances of such behaviour. The use of force may be justified, for example, if it is with the intention of preventing a criminal act or breaking up a fight between pupils. Even if the behaviour is unacceptable or unprofessional, it may be that an employer should consider a lesser remedy than dismissal. When the other party to the dispute was behaving in an outrageously provocative manner or the force used was out of proportion to that required, but was such because of a lack of good judgement rather than any intention to cause serious harm or because the teacher concerned was under severe stress would be examples of when dismissal would be too harsh a measure.

Abusive behaviour in the workplace may be a disciplinary offence in itself or it may go to undermine a relationship of trust and confidence, and this goes both ways. In one tribunal case in 1976, an employee was able to claim unfair dismissal when an employer called her a 'bitch'. In a later case, a tribunal said that it should be careful not to attach too great an importance to words used in the heat of the moment or in anger, but there will come a time when neither an employee nor an employer should have to tolerate bad language.

In the teaching environment, a great deal will depend on the circumstances in which bad or abusive language was used and to whom it was directed. If pupils are involved, then it is more likely to result in disciplinary action. If a parent is abused by a teacher, this is likely to be a disciplinary offence no matter how extreme the provocation, though not necessarily a dismissible offence. If abusive language is used between colleagues, a great deal may depend on the context. For example, did it occur at a meeting where others were present? Did the abuse go both ways? Was the recipient really offended by the behaviour?

Sexual misconduct

If it is proved that there has been a sexual relationship between a pupil under 16 and a teacher, dismissal will inevitably be justified. In 1975 (*Vogler* v *Hertfordshire County Council*), a male teacher was dismissed by a local authority for having a sexual relationship with a 16-year-old female pupil at the school where he was employed. He tried to argue that there was nothing in his contract to prevent this. It was held that there was an implied term not to behave in such a way that was unbefitting of someone in his position.

It is hard to imagine a situation in which a sexual relationship between a teacher and a pupil over the age of 16 would not also justify dismissal and I am not aware of any recent tribunal ruling to the contrary. In another case reported in the newspapers in 1998, a teacher resigned in the face of a likely dismissal and the city council took the view that the teacher's name should be put on List 99.

In another case in 1998 that reached a tribunal, a teacher in a Roman Catholic school (herself an atheist) was dismissed when it came to light that not only had she had an affair with another member of staff, but had three children by different fathers, one of whom was a former pupil whom she had met in a nightclub. He was 16 and had left the school to do his A levels at a sixth-form college. The senior managers at the school did their utmost to get rid of her and she claimed they made her life extremely difficult. Her claim for unfair dismissal was rejected. Her argument that she had been discriminated against was also rejected on the basis that a man would have been treated in the same way and there was no evidence to suggest that the behaviour expected of her was any different because of her gender.

A case in 1991 gave rise to the same decision. An unmarried mother in a private school was dismissed when she became pregnant. She did not intend to marry. The tribunal found that she had not been discriminated against and that the dismissal was justified – it was because she was not married that she had been dismissed, not just for being pregnant.

In *Wiseman* v *Salford City Council* (1981), a drama teacher was twice charged with gross indecency involving adult males in a public lavatory. His dismissal was upheld as fair. It had been argued that there was no risk to the young people in the teacher's charge, but an employment appeal tribunal felt that the subject was a controversial one and the employer's response in dismissing him fell within the band of reasonable responses. In other words, another employer might not have dismissed him in the same circumstances, but it was not unreasonable for that particular employer to do so.

Less extreme behaviour may not justify dismissal but may, none the less, attract some sort of disciplinary penalty. In 1998, a teacher was suspended and disciplined when she accepted a kiss from a sixth-former at a school party. She was not dismissed.

Sexual relationships between members of staff are not usually considered to be the business of an employer and special care needs to be taken to guard against inaccurate rumours – it really is possible for people to be just good friends! However, if the behaviour has an impact in the workplace, it may then become the business of an employer. For example, if the parties concerned are behaving 'inappropriately' towards one another in the school environment (kissing and cuddling behind the bicycle sheds, for instance) or the relationship begins to affect their job performance or relationships with other colleagues. It would also be a problem if one of the parties was the other's manager or superior.

Even if there is a problem, it does not mean that an employer's reaction should be to dismiss either of the people involved (and it is amazing how often in these cases it has been the woman who has been dismissed or badly treated). If the problem is behaviour, the employee concerned should be given an opportunity to put that right. If the problem relates to their management function or there is ill feeling in the school, then relocation ought to be considered.

Dishonesty

Dishonesty in the workplace often justifies dismissal and almost certainly disciplinary action. This includes not just obvious and criminal dishonest behaviour, such as theft, but also all forms of deceitful behaviour if they concern work matters or have an adverse effect on the relationship of trust and confidence. Examples of such behaviour would be deliberately misrecording assessment results or exam results or giving pupils advance notice of examination questions.

Dishonesty about personal matters is much less likely to be the business of an employer. If a person lies about their personal circumstances, it may not be relevant to their employment and there may be a fine line between excusable self-delusion and deliberately misleading somebody! However, it may be different if a person is asked a particular question about their health or background in an interview, say, and they give an untruthful or misleading answer. The more directly the question is related to the person's capacity to carry out their job to a satisfactory standard, the more likely it is that this dishonesty will breach the employment relationship. Of course, the question itself must be a proper one and not discriminatory in any way. It would be discriminatory to ask only female employees about their intentions to have a family, for example.

In most employment situations, by virtue of the Rehabilitation of Offenders Act 1974, an employee does not have to reveal the fact that they have been convicted of a criminal offence once a certain period of time has elapsed after the conviction (when the conviction is said to be 'spent'). Teachers, however, cannot rely on the Rehabilitation of Offenders Act and, if asked, must disclose any criminal convictions, otherwise considered spent or not. In fact, a teachers' record is checked before employment is offered.

At the time of writing, no such obligation is imposed on those embarking on a teacher training course. However, anyone with a criminal conviction should seek advice before starting a course as to the view likely to be taken of their offending behaviour when they would come to apply for a teaching job.

Lateness and absenteeism

Absence arising from illness or accident will not usually justify dismissal or disciplinary action until it has been a problem for a considerable period of time.

Time off for certain activities is a legal right, as we saw in the previous chapter). Incidentally, one such not mentioned there is jury service. Allowing employees time off for this reason is an obligation for any employer. Having said this, if there is a particular reason why the timing of the period of jury service presents a problem for the employer, the courts will usually be sympathetic to a request to postpone, at least on the first or second occasion. The difficulty is that jury service cannot be scheduled for a more convenient time as jurors must be selected randomly.

The Burgundy Book also contains some references to permitted absences for personal reasons, such as compassionate leave. In addition, there may be a local agreement that a certain level of absence or reason for absence is acceptable. For example, some schools allow teachers to take a specified period – say, two days off a year during term time – for particular reasons, such as family functions – weddings and so on – or sitting exams. Many LEAs also have policies about going to funerals, even to the extent of listing which relatives' funerals it will normally be acceptable to attend. There is often an agreement that teachers be allowed a day off for moving house. Incidentally, even if time off is allowed, it may have to be taken as unpaid rather than paid leave.

Time off for antenatal care is specifically covered by the Employment Rights Act 1996 (Section 55ff). If an employee is advised by her medical practitioners that she should attend an appointment for the purposes of antenatal care, she is entitled to do so and be paid for the time she is absent. The employer can insist that documents be provided as confirmation.

Persistent lateness or absenteeism may ultimately justify dismissal, but not usually before other procedures, such as warnings, have been followed. Teachers should bear in mind that while an employer may be expected to tolerate temporary or unexpected difficulties (for example, the sudden loss of a carer for children) it is a teacher's responsibility to make arrangements to remedy these difficulties during directed time. In a school context, a teacher's primary duty is to the children at the school.

Absence because of illness may justify dismissal (or medical retirement) after a reasonable period of time. A tribunal will look at the contractual provisions for sick pay and will not normally consider dismissal to have been justified if those arrangements have not yet been exhausted. Eventually, it may be argued that long-term illness 'frustrates' the employment contract and that, therefore, the contract is at an end.

Recurrent illness is much more problematical for both employee and employer. A tribunal will uphold a dismissal if there is recurrent absence over a long period of time. This is a complicated area and is not helped by the change in regulations under the superannuation scheme.

Failure to carry out reasonable and lawful instructions
This is a particularly problematical area for teachers in light of the concept of directed time. There is a great deal of uncertainty about what it is reasonable for a headteacher to expect from a teacher, particularly with regard to meetings outside normal school hours and cover for extracurricular activities. A PE teacher, for example, may be less able than other teachers of other disciplines to argue that they should not supervise extracurricular activities as they have for so long been expected to do so. Negotiations are ongoing about some of these points between the government and the unions with a view to reducing the bureaucratic burden on teachers.

There is a general expectation in industrial tribunals that an employee will cooperate with an employer in responding to changes in the workplace – for example, with the introduction of new technology or reorganization. However, there is also an expectation that an employer will introduce such changes reasonably by providing training and proper guidance and giving reasonable advance notice. An employee will only be able to resist these sorts of changes for a relatively short time unless there are good reasons to object, such as the health and safety of staff or pupils will be affected.

Use or abuse of drugs and alcohol
As with other misconduct, the question for an employer in this regard is whether or not the behaviour is criminal or adversely affects the performance of the teacher concerned.

If the behaviour is criminal, even if it has not resulted in criminal proceedings, dismissal is more than likely to be justified in a school context because of the poor example it sets to pupils. However, in *Norfolk County Council* v *Bernard* (1979) IRLR 220, a drama teacher was sacked after being convicted of possession of cannabis. The tribunal held that the dismissal was unfair because the LEA did not take into account the fact that other members of staff and parents supported the continued employment of the teacher, and the teacher had an otherwise exemplary record. On the other hand, another tribunal has upheld a dismissal in connection with a conviction for possession of cannabis when the offence took place away from the employer's premises (a dental laboratory), during the employee's own time, after five years of trouble-free service (*Mathewson* v *R B Dental Laboratory* [1988] IRLR 512, EAT). These cases show how difficult it can be to make predictions about how behaviour will be viewed and why it is important for employers to exercise discretion rather than automatically apply a particular sanction.

If the drug or alcohol use affects a teacher's performance, their employer's reaction must depend on how it does. Counselling and support may be appropriate responses at first, with dismissal being reserved for situations in which the abuse continues to be a problem despite support. A teacher who is drunk or under the influence of alcohol during the course of working hours will be on a very sticky wicket, particularly if their duties include responsibility for dangerous equipment.

Bringing the school into disrepute
A much more controversial topic than the last as there is plenty of scope for disagreement about what might bring the school into disrepute – so much is subjective.

An example occurred in 1998 when a teacher returned to work after beginning the process of changing sex. The teacher concerned taught science in a Church of England school. The case law indicates that dismissal on grounds of gender change will rarely be justified unless it is genuinely necessary for the job to be carried out by a person of a particular gender. It has been suggested that this might apply to PE teachers and those working in boarding schools. With regard to the former, I doubt very much that this is a sustainable argument as there is generally no embargo on PE teachers being in charge of pupils of a different gender from them, although difference in gender may dictate that certain behavioural boundaries should be observed.

Public criticisms of a school are almost bound to bring it into disrepute. In 1998, a pupil who publicized her criticisms of her school in the local paper was suspended. Ultimately, she was reinstated and it was considered that she had behaved perfectly properly. However, as a pupil she was under no contractual obligation to the school and she was 'vindicated' by the school's OFSTED report. A teacher is clearly in a different position.

As well as turning to the teaching unions for advice, there are two other organizations that support employees who are under pressure not to speak out in public about matters of concern in their workplace or who have done so and are being victimized. These are Public Concern At Work and Freedom to Care (see Useful addresses section for the addresses). It is impossible to give detailed guidance here about when this will be appropriate and when it might be deemed to be a breach of the employment contract as each case will depend very much on its own facts. Bear in mind, though, that it is always a serious and risky step to go public and so should not be entered into lightly.

It may well be that this sort of behaviour will be addressed in school policies and so on. A teacher would then be under a duty to comply with the policy if instructed to do so, so long as that instruction was reasonable. This really only brings us back to the beginning in considering what will or will not amount to misconduct requiring some kind of disciplinary action.

What can be said is that, if at all possible, a teacher should ensure that any reasonable complaints are made, first, informally, then through the grievance procedure and, if possible, raised at a governors' meeting, perhaps via a teacher governor. In the unlikely event that this does not result in a satisfactory response, then the teacher may be justified in speaking out if the problem is a really serious one, but advice should be taken from unions before doing so.

The Employment Rights Act 1996 gives employees specific protection in cases where they either bring proceedings against an employer to enforce a statutory right or allege that such a statutory right has been infringed (whether or not it has been), so long as the allegation is made in good faith. The special protection afforded to union representatives and health and safety representatives (or other staff members where it is not practical to refer the matter to health and safety representatives) might also cover them if they speak out about health and safety matters so long as it is reasonable to do so. For example, if an emergency occurred in a school and a teacher had to bring it to the attention of people at the school and outsiders, they could not be dismissed for doing so, provided they believed that danger was serious or imminent and the steps taken were appropriate ones in all the circumstances.

Disclosure of confidential information
In considering whether or not this sort of behaviour should attract a disciplinary penalty, much will depend on the circumstances. For

example, was the disclosure deliberate? It may not have been obvious that the information was confidential or should not have been disclosed to the particular third party. For example, a great deal of confusion has arisen over disclosure of information about children to parents. The right to information flows from having parental responsibility. Parents who have been married will have parental responsibility. Those who have not been married may acquire parental responsibility by agreement or court order. It may not be obvious to the teacher who has the right to information, particularly if the separation of the parents is recent. If a mistake is made in these circumstances, it may be more important to review procedures than to reprimand the teacher concerned.

If there is no doubt that the information was confidential, then an employer must consider the effect of the disclosure, the reason for wanting to keep the material confidential in the first place and the reason for breaking the confidence.

Frequently asked questions

Can I refuse to obey the instructions of the headteacher to cover for PE/science lessons?

Not necessarily. You do not have to provide cover if a colleague is absent for more than three days, so long as your own commitments amount to 75 per cent of the normal teaching day. Before that, however, the headteacher must satisfy themselves that it is safe for all concerned for the particular person to supervise the lesson by considering your experience, the nature of the lesson you are expected to teach, the number of pupils involved, your familiarity with them (and their individual education plans) and the nature of the particular classroom environment. You should not normally be expected to teach a lesson that involves the use of equipment or materials with which you are unfamiliar and, in my view, the Employment Rights Act 1996 protection might well justify your refusal to teach. Cover lessons should be devised to avoid this wherever possible.

If dangerous, or potentially dangerous, equipment is in the classroom, even if you are not actually expected to supervise its use, the headteacher must be satisfied that you are able to control the particular pupils. If some pupils in a particular year 8 group, say, are known troublemakers, you might be justified in refusing, even if all they are supposed to be doing is private study. If you do not feel confident about the situation, you are not likely to be able to assert control and it is best to say so and see whether you can get some back-up.

Can school management tell me what I have to wear to school?

Provided that nothing about any dress code is discriminatory (even female barristers can now wear trouser suits!) and it is reasonable, in theory, the answer is yes. I doubt it would be considered unreasonable to expect a teacher not to wear jeans in the classroom in most schools. Stipulations about dress will more obviously be reasonable in certain situations, such as a gym or science lab. Nor is it likely to be unreasonable to expect a teacher broadly to comply with those requirements imposed on pupils, up to a point. Whether or not an employer could require a teacher to dress in a uniform is highly questionable and has not yet been tested.

Whatever the dress code, what it costs to comply with it should be in proportion with the average teacher's salary.

The subject of dress codes has attracted a great deal of press attention, but not much case law exists. In a somewhat surprising case in Germany in 1998, a female newly qualified teacher who was a Muslim was refused a job because she wanted to wear her headdress in the classroom. It is widely expected that this decision will be overturned. I would very much hope the same attitude would not be supported in the UK. A major problem in this case is that there was no employment contract that was breached. If it did happen here, it would be difficult to see what remedy would be accepted as it would not count as sexual discrimination.

Can I have a second, part-time job?

Provided it does not affect your ability to perform your main contractual duties or bring the school into disrepute, there is no reason, in theory, for not having a second job. A difficulty that might arise, however, is that you may quite lawfully be directed to attend after-hours meetings and you must be sure that you can meet those requirements if reasonable. There is no legal reason for you to necessarily consult senior management before accepting other work, but, in practice, it may make sense to do so. You may, as usual, be able to get some indication of an employer's likely reaction by consulting a union representative.

Do I have to declare my criminal convictions?

Yes. A teacher cannot claim the protection of the Rehabilitation of Offenders Act 1974. See above.

Can my employer make me work in a different school?

Yes, in theory, provided the request is a reasonable one and you are given proper advance notice. If it were to cause you great disruption because of transport difficulties or childcare arrangements, it might not be reasonable. Similarly, if there were some particular reason you did not want to teach in that particular school, such as harassment or bullying there previously, this would not be reasonable.

Do I have to supervise lunchbreaks?

As a result of a working party report in 1968, the power of LEAs to require teachers to supervise lunchbreaks was withdrawn. The report recommended that if teachers were to supervise during a midday break (including clubs, coaching and so on as well as lunch itself), they should be entitled to a free school dinner (how could they resist?!) It is now contained in conditions of employment that teachers (other than headteachers and their deputies) 'shall not be required under his contract as a teacher to undertake midday supervision and shall be allowed a break of reasonable length between school sessions or between the hours of 12 noon and 2.00pm'. Deputy headteachers shall 'be entitled to a break of reasonable length as near to the middle of each school day as is reasonably practicable'. For headteachers, more flexibility is expected: 'A headteacher shall be entitled to a break of reasonable length in the course of each school day, and shall arrange for a suitable person to assume responsibility for the discharge of his functions as headteacher during that break'.

Do I have to attend meetings after hours and for training on INSET days?

You are required to obey the headteacher's reasonable instructions regarding directed time, which would extend to non-contact time for meetings and INSET training. Some schools hold sessions during the daytime on a day when the pupils are not at school. Some prefer to hold training sessions in the evening to preserve the integrity of the holiday period. This can cause problems for those with childcare responsibilities. This is all a matter for local negotiation, with the assistance of union representatives and teacher governors as appropriate. It may, of course, be possible to vary the times of INSET training sessions, particularly for non-subject-specific training. You are undoubtedly entitled to reasonable notice of anti-social hours work requirements.

Chapter 7

Reproduction – copyright law

What is copyright?

The main legislation dealing with copyright is the Copyright, Designs and Patents Act 1988 referred to as 'the Act' in the rest of this chapter). It is a long and complicated piece of legislation that has resulted in some extremely expensive litigation. Unless you are a teacher who happens also to be a best-selling author, however, the Act should hold little fear in its practical application in the classroom. For these reasons, I shall not include many references to the specific sections of the Act.

Copyright is a 'property right' subsisting in:

(a) original literary, dramatic, musical or artistic works;
(b) sound recordings, films, broadcasts or cable programmes; and
(c) the typographical arrangements of published editions.

All these expressions are further defined in the Act.

A 'literary work' is any work that is not dramatic or musical but is written, spoken or sung. This includes a computer program. Artistic merit is not relevant when considering whether or not a work is literary and the courts have tended to take a fairly wide view, including most written or printed material as being literary works.

A 'dramatic work' includes a work of dance or mime.

Further areas defined in the Act include:

- 'artistic work' – graphic works, photographs, sculptures or collages, architectural works, including both buildings and models of buildings and works of artistic craftsmanship;

- 'sound recordings' – includes recordings of poetry recitals and other non-musical recordings;
- 'films' – a recording on any medium from which a moving image may be produced;
- broadcasts;
- cable programmes;
- published editions.

There cannot be any claim to copyright unless the work is committed into writing or recorded. There is no copyright protection for 'ideas, procedures, processes, systems, methods of operation, concepts, principles and discoveries'. It is only when an idea has been expressed in a particular way that one can talk of there being any property rights in it. A speech may attract copyright protection if, for example, it is recorded or transcribed.

Ownership of copyright

The first owner of copyright is the author or creator of the work (but see below for a more detailed consideration of work that is produced in the course of employment). If there are joint authors, they will share the copyright. An author can choose to either keep the copyright rights or sell them on to a third party.

A distinction is drawn between copyright in a literary work, for example, and copyright in the published edition. An author may either transfer their copyright ownership to a publisher or simply grant the publisher rights to reproduce the text. That publisher will have their own copyright in respect of the published copy of the work. The situation is similar for film makers. A film may be considered a different work from written screenplay, for example, and there will be separate copyright vested in the author and the film maker.

Employer's copyright

Where a literary, dramatic, musical or artistic work is made by an employee in the course of their employment, the copyright will normally be owned by the employer, unless there is some agreement to the contrary. That is, it is customary within that area of employment that copyright remains with the employee or there is something in the contract of employment that specifically says that the employee will have the copyright.

It will mainly be obvious when a work has been created in the course of employment. It is slightly more difficult in the case of teachers as there is not a particularly clear distinction between working hours and non-working hours – as many teachers are all too uncomfortably aware!

Some guidance can be given. If a teacher devises, say, a scheme of work that is actually used by them in the teaching of pupils at the school in which they work, the copyright will probably be owned by the employer (unless the contract provides otherwise). Equally, if a teacher is specifically directed by an employer to produce certain written materials, the copyright will belong to the employer.

If you are in the fortunate position of having a publisher who wants to publish your materials, you will need to check with your employer what their attitude is likely to be. Some LEAs have a policy of not asserting copyright. Their real concern is likely to be to ensure that you are devoting adequate amounts of your professional energies to your pupils. If, however, you were asked to contribute to a book about your experiences as a teacher or on educational theory, this would be much less likely to be subject to any copyright claim by your employer. In one case (*Stephenson Jordan* v *Harrison Ltd* v *Macdonald* [1952] RPC 10), an accountant gave a course of lectures. These were published in book form. The work in preparing the lectures had been done in his own time, but some of the typing had been done by his secretary in the office. The court took the view that, despite this, the copyright belonged to the accountant. The purpose of his employment was to advise clients, not to give lectures. There was only one section of the book in which the court found the copyright vested in his employer and that was based on a report the account had written for one of his employer's clients.

Author's moral right

In order to give an author some say in what happens to their work even when they no longer own the copyright, the Act also recognizes what is known as the 'moral right 'of the author. This involves, first, the right to be identified whenever the work is performed or published (sometimes called the 'paternity right') and, second, the right to object to the 'derogatory' treatment of the work by others (the 'integrity right'). This last does not mean that the work cannot be criticized, but that it cannot be treated in a way that amounts to a distortion or mutilation of the work.

There are many exceptional circumstances in which moral right protection cannot be asserted. For example, no moral right protection is extended to computer programs, sound recordings or broadcasts. Nor is there protection for work written for, and published in, newspapers and magazines, encyclopaedias, dictionaries and other similar reference works (if written for the particular publication in which it appears). The moral right only applies to commercial publication or public performance.

There are two particular exceptions that are significant in the context of the teaching profession. The first is that where the first owner of the copyright in the work is the author's employer, then the right does not apply in respect of acts done by, or with, the authority of the copyright owner. In other words, not only does your scheme of work not belong to you, you do not have to be named as the author and so on either.

The second relates to examination questions. The author does not have to be identified as such when an extract from their work appears on an examination paper. However, in practice, the author is usually named, unless of course, it would defeat the whole purpose of asking the question in the first place.

It does not count as derogatory treatment of a work to edit it to take out passages that would, if published, amount to a criminal offence or, in the case of the BBC, would offend against good taste or decency, encourage crime and so on.

An author also has the right not to be falsely accused of creating a particular work.

All the above rights can be waived by an author, as can the assertion of copyright by the owner, but only if there is a signed document stating that the author has waived their rights.

How long does copyright last?

The claim to copyright has a shelf-life.

- For literary, dramatic, musical or artistic works, the copyright expires 70 years after the end of the calendar year in which the author died.

- For computer-generated work, the copyright expires 50 years from the end of the calendar year in which it was created.
- For Crown copyright, the copyright expires 50 years from the date on which the work was first published commercially (if published commercially within 75 years of first publication) or 125 years if it is not commercially published. Note that, at the time of writing, Crown copyright generally is under review and the law may change following public consultation.
- For sound and film recordings, copyright expires 50 years from the end of the year in which it was first made.
- For typographical arrangement, copyright expires after 25 years.

A well-known exception is J M Barrie's *Peter Pan*, the copyright in which has been granted permanently to Great Ormond Street Hospital for Sick Children.

Moral rights generally last for the same length of time as ownership rights (except the right not to be falsely accused of creating a work, which lasts for only 20 years after death). As with property rights, moral rights can be asserted by whomever acquires the rights on death as a result of probate law.

Copyright protection

The owner of the copyright is the only person who is entitled to take and distribute copies of their work or to perform it publicly or to broadcast it and so on. Anyone else must usually ask the owner for permission to do any of these things, or at least if they are going to use a substantial part of the work, and the owner will be entitled to make a charge for giving their permission. In general terms, if this rule is broken (and the copyright is thereby 'infringed'), the copyright owner may pursue a number of legal remedies, including seeking an injunction to prevent repetition or claiming damages. It can even be a criminal offence to arrange for a public performance of a work in breach of copyright.

The law does allow the copying of work without permission to be carried out in some circumstances, but the strict provisions are specifically relaxed in the case of educational use.

Defences in cases of copyright infringement

There are several defences that the Act makes available, some of which are general and some of which apply exclusively to schools, colleges and libraries. Copyright will not be infringed if:

- the person doing the copying, reproducing or performing of a literary, dramatic, musical or artistic work is doing so for the purpose of giving or receiving instruction in a manner that does not involve the use of a photocopier or similar equipment – that is, it can be copied down from the blackboard into a notebook or read out in class from a published edition;
- a copy of a film or film soundtrack is made for the purposes of instruction in the making of films or film soundtracks by the person giving or receiving instruction;
- it involves copying for the purposes of holding an examination (except in the case of photocopies of musical works that are to be performed as part of the examination, when permission must be obtained);
- not more than 1 per cent of a work is reproduced in any quarter, unless there is a licence in force, in which case the terms of the licence dictate what can be reproduced, but there may also be a defence even if copies of more than 1 per cent of the original are made as it can be argued that this is not a substantial amount, (but the courts have not yet decided this clearly);
- copying is done under the terms of a licence from the Copyright Licensing Agency;
- a literary, dramatic or musical work is performed by pupils, teachers and others for the purpose of instruction, although if there are other people present at the performance, such as doting mums and dads, then this will not fall within the exemption – it must be to people directly connected with the activities of the educational establishment (however, the performers do not have to be pupils or teachers, so long as the performance takes place at the school, and, conversely, if the performance only involves teachers and pupils, it can take place outside school premises);
- the copying is done in a library, involves the taking of no more than one copy of an article in a periodical, say, or a reasonable proportion of a text, and the copying is done for an individual pupil who pays the librarian a photocopying charge (the librarian should obtain a signed certificate from the pupil to the effect that

no previous copies of the same material have been taken and that the material is required for private study);

- the copying of a literary, dramatic, musical or published work is done by an individual for the purpose of their own private study (this defence will not be available in every circumstance: it will depend on how much of a text, say, is copied and so on, and note that private study is not the same as private use – taping a friend's CD and listening to it at home would infringe copyright);
- extracts of reasonable length and in proportion to the length of the work in which they are quoted are quoted for the purpose of criticizing or reviewing the work;
- a copyright work is included in an anthology that mainly contains non-copyright work intended for use in educational establishments and does not contain more than two extracts from the author's work published by the same publisher over any five-year period;
- a computer program is copied as a back-up copy (Copyright (Computer Programs) Regulations 1992 (SI 1992/1427);
- an extract from a published literary or dramatic work of reasonable length is read out in public and the author is acknowledged (that is, you can read out poems in assembly!);
- a sound recording is played in public for charitable, religious, educational or social welfare purposes;
- a recording of a television or cable programme is shown to an audience of teachers, pupils and other people directly connected with the educational establishment or is shown in public by an organization the objective of which are charitable or educational, but no charge is made.

Privacy

In general terms, the 'right to privacy' is not yet a right that is recognized in English law. However, there is a limited protection offered by the Copyright, Designs and Patents Act 1988. Under Section 85, if a photograph or film has been commissioned for private and/or domestic purposes, it cannot be issued to the public, shown in public or broadcast on television without the permission of the person who commissioned it (if there is more than one 'commissioner' all of them have to give permission).

Frequently asked questions

Can I use my own worksheets to write a book?

See the section earlier in the chapter headed 'Employers' copyright'. There will be many circumstances where, for a teacher, the answer is no or not without permission from the employer. Arguably, if you wrote a worksheet or lesson plan entirely in your own time and did not ever use it yourself, you would own the copyright. Of course, you would have no way of knowing if it was effective as an educational tool, which might be a bit of a drawback to any prospective publisher. One bright spark has suggested that you could write something and then get a colleague to try it out. However, I think that would probably fall under the heading of 'in the course of employment'. If, however, you wrote and used a work scheme exclusively in the capacity of your self-employment as a home tutor, say, then the copyright would belong to you. In practical terms, the best thing to do is to speak to your employer and see what their attitude might be.

Can I photocopy a short story or poem to hand out to pupils?

You should remember that you may be infringing more than one copyright owner's rights here. If the story is published in a collection and constitutes more than one per cent of the whole book, then you will be breaching the publisher's rights. You may also be breaching the author's rights. However, if there is a licensing scheme in force, as there often will be, it will depend on the terms of the scheme. If you have not been provided with guidance on this, the best person to ask in the first instance is probably a librarian.

Does a pupil have any say over what you do with their essay in the summer holidays?

Yes, just the same as any other author. Strictly speaking, you should get the pupil's permission if you want to copy it for the benefit of the rest of the class or include it in a school magazine.

Chapter 8

Object lessons – lesson contents

Lesson contents

EDUCATION – At Mr Wackford Squeer's Academy, Dotheboys Hall, at the delightful village of Dotheboys, near Greta Bridge, in Yorkshire, Youth are boarded, clothed, booked, furnished with pocket-money, provided with all necessaries, instructed in all languages living and dead, mathematics, orthography, geometry, astronomy, trigonometry, the use of the globes, algebra, single stick (if required), writing, arithmetic, fortification, and every other branch of classical literature. Terms, twenty guineas per annum. No extras, no vacations, and diet unparalleled.

Charles Dickens, *Nicholas Nickelby*, 1839

In between all the other onerous tasks imposed on teachers, they must also endeavour to teach their charges something, which may sometimes seem an incidental burden. As with every other aspect of school life, the curriculum is heavily regulated.

The National Curriculum

Regulation of the National Curriculum, which must be followed in all schools except independent and special schools, is now found in Section 350ff of the Education Act 1996 (referred to in this chapter as 'the Act'). Since September 1997, all schools should have been delivering the National Curriculum in full.

The Act requires that a school's curriculum must:

- be balanced;
- promote the spiritual, moral, cultural, mental and physical development of pupils and of society;
- prepare pupils for the opportunities, responsibilities and experiences of adult life.

Secular education

The secular education that must be delivered comprises:

- all the core subjects – that is, mathematics, English, science (and Welsh in Welsh-speaking schools in Wales;
- foundation subjects – that is, technology (design and information) and PE (at all ages in secondary school), history, geography, art, music (not compulsory after year 3), a modern foreign language (from year 10).

The technology requirement was applied with effect from September 1996 for pupils who reach Key Stage 4.

Foreign languages

If only one foreign language is offered at a school, it must be one of the following:

- Danish;
- Dutch;
- French;
- German;
- Modern Greek;
- Italian;
- Portuguese;
- Spanish.

Provided that pupils are also offered the opportunity to study one of the above languages, they may also be offered the opportunity to study one of the following:

- Arabic;
- Bengali;

- Chinese (Cantonese or Mandarin);
- Gujerati;
- Modern Hebrew;
- Hindi;
- Japanese;
- Punjabi;
- Russian;
- Turkish;
- Urdu.

More specific detail on the recommended study programmes for the National Curriculum has also been published. Special arrangements have been applied to primary schools for a period of two years from September 1998. The Secretary of State has relaxed the requirements for primary schools to allow them to concentrate on literacy and numeracy. However, primary schools must still deliver the National Curriculum in English, mathematics, science and IT (and religious education, see below). The foundation subjects will still have to be taught, but the detailed study programmes will not have to be followed. The Government has promised that there will be no further alterations to the National Curriculum arrangements until the year 2000.

Key stages

The Act divides pupils into four key stages, which roughly correspond to year groups as follows:

- Key Stage 1 – years 1–2, ages 5–7;
- Key Stage 2 – years 3–6, ages 7–11; Key Stage 3 – years 7–9, ages 11–14;
- Key Stage 4 – years 10–11, ages 14–16.

It is also a requirement of the Act that, at each of Key Stages 1 to 3, all pupils are tested in English and mathematics at the ages of 7, 11 and 14. At 11 and 14, they will also be tested in science. Achievement targets have been laid down by the Secretary of State. At the age of 7, pupils should have attained at least Level 2, at 11 Level 4 and at 14 Levels 5 and 6. The highest level is 8. In music and art, there are descriptive attainment targets rather than target levels.

In the case of Key Stage 1, pupils are assessed by being asked to perform standard tasks and by means of teacher assessment of classroom work. At Key Stages 2 and 3, assessment is by externally administered test (standard assessment tests – SATs) and by teacher assessment.

There are now new requirements to set targets for pupils that are set out in the School Standards and Framework Act 1998, and the DfEE has issued a circular to schools on the subject (Circular 11/98).

In addition to the numerous powers of the Secretary of State to monitor and evaluate the delivery of the National Curriculum, there is also power to:

- suspend the requirement to teach the National Curriculum in any given school for the purposes of research (the LEA and governing body have to consent to this);
- make regulations to suspend the requirement to teach the National Curriculum or to modify it;
- suspend the National Curriculum in the case of a pupil whose statement of special educational needs recommends that it be suspended or varied;
- enable the headteacher of a maintained school to direct that the National Curriculum shall not apply in the case of a particular pupil for a maximum period of six months;
- suspend the National Curriculum for an individual pupil in order to facilitate work experience (see Chapter 12).

Religious education

Religious education is not actually part of the National Curriculum, but, under Section 352 of the Education Act 1996, it must be taught to all children in maintained schools as part of the 'basic curriculum', as must sex education (see below).

Agreed syllabus

The School Standards and Framework Act 1998 requires every LEA to have an agreed syllabus for the teaching of religious education. This syllabus must 'reflect the fact that the religious traditions in Great Britain are in the main Christian whilst taking account of the teaching and practices of the other principal religions represented in Great Britain'.

Standing Advisory Council for Religious Education (SACRE)

Each LEA must establish a SACRE, on which sit representatives from a number of religious groups, teachers' associations and LEA representatives. This body is an advisory one, but it can formally require an LEA to review the agreed syllabus. On an *ad hoc* basis, LEAs are required to establish an agreed syllabus conference to make recommendations about the agreed syllabus. This conference must be convened at least once in every five-year period. Schedule 31 to the Education Act 1996 sets out who is to be invited to attend the conference (essentially as for SACRE).

Nature of education to be provided

Most schools must follow the agreed syllabus, but some schools, particularly aided and special agreement schools (and grant-maintained schools that used to be aided or special agreement) may follow the trust deed if it makes provision for religious education or carry on providing religious education in accordance with their former practice. Parents are entitled to request that religious education be provided as set out in the agreed syllabus or the trust deed provision or previous practice (whichever is not being provided) if they would prefer that and the governing body or LEA must make appropriate arrangements unless it is not reasonable to do so. Parents can also make arrangements for their children to receive denominational religious instruction or ask an LEA or governing body to make appropriate arrangements. Maintained boarding schools must also allow pupils the opportunity to take part in acts of worship and religious education outside normal school hours. In many cases, however, an LEA or governing body will not be under any obligation to incur costs in making alternative arrangements.

Collective worship

Schools are also obliged to provide a period of collective worship of a broadly Christian nature (but not distinctively of any particular denomination) on a daily basis, which may be either for the whole school or in groups (this is stated in the School Standards and Framework Act 1998). There is some flexibility in that not every act of daily worship must be Christian so long as the majority of them are and the balance can be more or less depending on the ability to provide collective worship in groups rather than on a whole-school basis and on the family backgrounds of pupils at the school. In addition, a SACRE can disapply the need for broadly Christian worship in a particular school or for particular groups of pupils.

The right of parents to withdraw pupils

In provisions given in the School Standards and Framework Act 1998, a parent can withdraw their child from both religious education and collective worship, and, subject to certain caveats, may also take a child out of school to receive religious education elsewhere. A child can be withdrawn from all or part of the education concerned. In other words, a parent can specify that their child should only be involved in teaching about a particular religion.

DfEE guidance

Guidance on religious education and collective worship has been issued by the DfEE in Circular 1/94 – *Religious Education & Collective Worship*. This circular suggests that where a parent wishes to withdraw their child from religious education or worship, it might be helpful for the headteacher to discuss the implications with that parent. However, it should be remembered that it is an absolute right of a parent to withdraw their child and schools should not be obstructive or critical about the parent's decision. Neither can they lawfully insist that the parent take part in any discussion. On the other hand, schools are encouraged to meet a parent's reasonable request for alternative religious education or worship.

Special schools

Special schools are not under quite the same obligations as other schools to provide religious education, but the Education (Special Schools) Regulations 1994 SI 1994/652 state that arrangements for religious education and daily collective worship should be made, as far as practicable, unless the parent withdraws their child.

Complaints about RE

LEAs must establish a complaints procedure with regard to the provision of the National Curriculum, including complaints about religious worship, as must grant-maintained and grant-maintained special schools. The procedures need to be approved by the Secretary of State. Only after the procedures have been exhausted can a case be taken to court.

An unsuccessful attempt was made to require a wholly Christian approach to the act of collective worship in the case of *R* v *Secretary of State for Education ex-parte Ruscoe and Dando* [1994] ELR 495. Parents of children at a school in Manchester argued that multifaith worship could not amount to collective worship of a broadly Christian nature as required by the law. The judgment concentrated on the use of words such as 'most' and 'mainly' and 'broadly' in the legislation and held that multifaith worship was not precluded. In terms of the detail, however, it is still not particularly clear whether or not there is a line that, if crossed, would pitch an act of collective worship on to the wrong side of the law.

Disagreement between parents

If parents do not agree as to the nature of the religious education to which their children should be exposed, they can invite the court to make a decision under the Children Act 1989. Thus, it should not simply be left to schools to arbitrate in such a difficult situation.

Sex education

In secondary schools, sex education must be provided as part of the basic curriculum. DfEE circular 5/94 –*The Education Act 1993: Sex Education in Schools* – contains guidance on how this should be done.

In primary schools and independent schools, a governing body can decide whether or not sex education should be provided.

Written policies

Section 404 of the Education Act 1996 says that a governing body of any maintained school must have a separate written statement of their policy about sex education and this must be made available for parents to inspect or take a copy. A governing body should consider whether or not to adopt its LEA's curriculum statement or vary it in the particular context of their school.

In primary schools, a governing body should consider whether or not sex education should be provided at all and, if so, what it should consist of. The headteacher must be consulted and any representations from members of the local community, including the chief police officer, should also be taken into account.

Voluntary aided and special agreement primary schools need not comply with the detailed procedures set out in the Act, but are encouraged by the guidance to consider whether or not to provide sex education at some stage.

The content of sex education

'Sex education' in this context includes education about HIV/AIDS and other sexually transmitted diseases, but not the biological aspects of reproduction that are separately covered in science lessons.

Section 403 of the Act requires that, in the provision of sex education, an LEA, governing body and headteacher must ensure that, so far as practicable, it is given 'in such a manner to encourage those pupils to have due regard to moral considerations and the value of family life'.

Homosexuality

Under Section 28 of the Local Government Act 1988, 'A local authority shall not intentionally promote homosexuality or publish material with the intention to promote the teaching in any maintained school of the acceptability of homosexuality as a pretended family relationship.'

The law also states that this is not to be taken to mean that a local authority is prohibited from doing anything for the purpose of preventing the spread of disease.

Without wishing in any way to imply approval of the above law, it is clear that, in practice, it has not needed to have much impact on the way homosexuality is discussed in the classroom, although teachers have been understandably confused by the mixture of complicated guidance they have been given on the subject.

The embargo in Section 28 is on LEAs, not teachers. An LEA

might just be in difficulties if it failed to prevent a teacher who was promoting homosexuality. Having said that, I do not think that the expression of personal opinion by one teacher – particularly if set in a context where it was made clear that the view is a personal one with which others might disagree – would constitute the promotion of homosexuality. The Section does not, in my view, have the effect of prohibiting all discussion about homosexuality, which, in any case, would not sit easily with the requirement to provide education about HIV and AIDS.

The Department of the Environment said as much in its Circular, issued when Section 28 was enacted:

> Section 28 does not affect the activities of school governors, nor of teachers. It will not prevent the objective discussion of homosexuality in the classroom, nor the counselling of pupils concerned about their sexuality.

In DES guidance in 1987 (Circular 11/87 – *Sex Education At School*), it was stated that teaching advocating homosexual behaviour, presenting it as the norm, or encouraging pupils to experiment with homosexuality had no place in schools.

The current DfEE guidance (Circular 5/94 – *Education Act 1993: Sex Education in Schools*), which supercedes the 1987 guidance, states:

> ... The purpose of sex education should be to provide knowledge about loving relationships, the nature of sexuality and the processes of human reproduction. At the same time it should lead to the acquisition of understanding and attitudes which prepare pupils to view their relationships in a responsible and healthy manner. It must not be value-free; it should also be tailored not only to the age but also to the understanding of pupils. The Secretary of State believes that schools' programmes of sex education should therefore aim to present facts in an objective, balanced and sensitive manner, set within a clear framework of values and an awareness of the law on sexual behaviour. Pupils should accordingly be encouraged to appreciate the value of stable family life, marriage and the responsibilities of parenthood. They should be helped to consider the importance of self-restraint, dignity, respect for themselves and others, acceptance of responsibility, sensitivity towards the needs and views of others, loyalty and fidelity and they should be enabled to recognize the physical, emotional and moral implications, and risks, of certain types of behaviour, and to accept that both sexes must behave responsibly in sexual matters. Teachers need to acknowledge that many children come from backgrounds that do not reflect such values or experiences. Sensi-

tivity is therefore needed to avoid causing hurt and offence to them and their families; and to allow such children to feel a sense of worth. But teachers should also help pupils, whatever their circumstances, to raise their sights.

There is no specific mention of homosexuality, except in a passing reference to the existence of Section 28 and to the age of consent for gay males. The guidance does suggest that teachers should inform the headteacher if they have reason to believe that a pupil is likely to do anything unlawful and this would include a homosexual relationship under the age of 18. This is guidance only and so the appropriate action should be considered in the context of general considerations about confidentiality.

It is not possible to come to a categorical conclusion as to what might or might not be acceptable teaching about homosexuality in terms of the current state of the law as it has never been tested in the courts. As mentioned earlier, I do not think the expression of a personal opinion in a certain context would be likely to be held to be unlawful. No doubt most teachers would probably want to avoid a situation in which sex education became too personal in any event. I cannot see either that there would be anything wrong with giving pupils information on sources of further information about sexuality issues.

Contraception

Similar controversy apparently surrounds the question of contraceptive advice, not so much in the context of whole-class teaching but in connection with requests from individual pupils.

The DfEE guidance (*Education Act 1993: Sex education in schools*, DfEE Circular 5/94) states:

> Particular care must be exercised in relation to contraceptive advice to pupils under 16, for whom sexual intercourse is unlawful. The general rule must be that giving an individual pupil advice on such matters without parental knowledge or consent would be an inappropriate exercise of a teacher's professional responsibilities. Teachers are not health professionals, and the legal position of a teacher giving advice in such circumstances has never been tested in the courts.

Quite! The legal position has never been tested. I do not agree that it would necessarily be unlawful for a teacher to give such advice, although saying nothing certainly keeps things simple. Of course, if a teacher were to purport to give advice about medical aspects of forms of contraception that would clearly be dangerous as they are not really qualified to do so. However, to tell a pupil where to go to get that sort of advice is quite a different matter. Indeed, later in the guidance, there is a reference to advising pupils about seeking advice in appropriate circumstances from a health professional (but no clues are given as to when this would be appropriate).

What has been tested in the courts is the position of healthcare professionals in providing contraceptive advice and treatment. In the case of *Gillick* v *West Norfolk and Wisbech Area Health Authority* [1986] 1 AC 112, the House of Lords decided that a doctor who gave contraceptive advice and treatment to a girl under 16 without the consent of her parents did not commit a criminal offence. It was obvious that in doing so the doctor would be facilitating the commission of a criminal offence – that is, unlawful sexual intercourse with a girl under 16. The court held, however, that so long as the advice and treatment was given with the intention of avoiding an unwanted pregnancy and not with the intention of promoting the commission of a criminal offence, in circumstances where the doctor considered that the minor was of sufficient understanding to consent to treatment, then the doctor would escape criminal liability.

There have been many criticisms of this judgment, the gist of which is that the House of Lords has twisted the criminal law relating to intentionality in order to achieve the outcome it desired. There may be something in this, but the end result is the same and I cannot see any logical reason for a teacher (or, for that matter, a parent) to be treated any differently. Thus, in my personal opinion, if a teacher honestly believes that it is in a pupil's interests to receive advice and is concerned to avoid the consequences of unwanted pregnancy or disease, then the teacher could not be said to be committing a criminal offence any more than a doctor could. It would, of course, be sensible and in keeping with the other statutory requirements and guidance about sex education to ensure that the pupil is aware that sexual intercourse below the age of 16 constitutes a criminal offence and encourage them to discuss the matter with their parents or other trusted adult before doing something they might well regret.

Confidentiality

It is also suggested in the current guidance that if a teacher becomes aware that a pupil is involved, or likely to be involved, in behaviour that puts them in 'moral or physical danger or in breach of the law', the following should happen.

- the teacher should advise the pupil about the risks of such behaviour;
- the teacher should urge the pupil to seek advice from parents and, if appropriate, healthcare professionals;
- if the pupil is under 16, the teacher should inform the headteacher;
- the headteacher should make sure that the pupil's parents are told, preferably by the pupil;
- the headteacher should arrange for counselling, if appropriate;
- the headteacher should consider whether or not to involve other services, such as health professions or the LEA.

Again, this is guidance only. It is hard to imagine that any teacher in the difficult position of having been told about, say, sexual behaviour by a pupil under 16, would face legal criticism for breaching that child's confidentiality if it was done with the intention of protecting that pupil's best interests, even if the decision to disclose turned out not to be the right one. In some circumstances, it will be perfectly obvious from a child protection standpoint that the confidence cannot be kept – for example, where a pupil reveals that they are being sexually abused by a relative.

However, in my opinion, this does not mean that in every such circumstance a teacher is under a positive obligation to disclose the facts to, say, a parent. There is no legal decision to this effect, so it does not seem that a parent would have a cause to take legal action in such circumstances.

Having said that, because the nature of some confidences could probably not be kept secret, as a matter of personal ethics it makes sense to ensure that the child knows that you might not be able to keep their secret. Equally, it may make sense to be clear with parents what the school's attitude is likely to be to requests for advice from pupils.

The right of parents to withdraw their child from sex education

A parent of a pupil at a maintained school may request that their child be withdrawn from any sex education lesson (but not a biology lesson in which the scientific aspects of human reproduction are being taught). The guidance reminds schools that parents do not have to give any reason for their decision, but, as with withdrawal from religious education, schools may offer the parents the opportunity to discuss the matter if they so wish.

Drugs

The National Curriculum provides for education about drug use and abuse at various ages as part of the science curriculum. At Key Stages 1 and 2, this is limited to fairly basic information, first about the nature of medicine (good drugs) and then about the potential harmful effects of bad drugs. More detail is required at Key Stages 3 and 4.

The DfEE has issued a circular about drugs education (4/95 – *Drug Prevention and Schools*) and there is also a School Curriculum and Assessment Authority publication entitled *Drug Education: Curriculum guidance for schools*.

Politics

Section 406 of the Act outlaws both the participation by junior pupils in maintained schools in partisan political activities and the promotion of partisan political views in teaching. The expression of political views (by analogy with the expression of certain views about sexuality) is not the same as the promotion of them.

Homework

There is very little law affecting the setting of homework, although there are government policies and initiatives being developed. Home–school agreements will become compulsory under the School Standards and Framework Act 1998 for all maintained schools.

Draft guidance on the effect of these agreements is under review at the time of writing.

The requirement to do homework will be part of home–school agreements. The agreements in themselves will not be enforceable in the courts, although the failure to comply with them may be relevant to other court proceedings about school attendance and in care proceedings. These agreements are just that – a parent is perfectly entitled to refuse to sign one.

Careers education

Under Section 43 of the Education Act 1997 (which came into force in September 1998), governing bodies/proprietors and headteachers and so on must provide careers education for pupils aged 14 to 16. This does not apply to independent schools.

If a careers adviser is appointed, the governing body must cooperate and provide information unless a pupil is over 18 or their parent, if the pupil is under 18, objects. They must also provide access to the pupils at the school, including for purpose of interview, and provide guidance materials and reference materials about careers. See the DfEE circulars 5/98 – *Careers Education in Schools: Provision for Years 9–11* (which has a useful appendix referring to other DfEE publications) – and 5/97 – *Careers Education and Guidance in Schools: Effective Partnership with Careers Services*.

Frequently asked questions

Do I have to teach religious education?

In most cases, no. Under Section 59 of the School Standards and Framework Act 1998, in community/community special, foundation/foundation special and voluntary schools without a religious character, no person may be disqualified from teaching or from promotion and so on by reason of their religious (or irreligious) opinions or because they attend or do not attend religious worship. Nor can they be made to teach religious education. In foundation or voluntary schools with a religious character, preference may be given to those of a similar religious persuasion and voluntary aided schools can refuse to employ someone because of their religious opinions and so on.

Can I tell my pupils what my own beliefs are?

Yes, provided that you do not try to promote your beliefs above all others if they are political. You should ensure that children feel respected for their own values at all times and you should present your views sensitively if appropriate.

Chapter 9

Some of us are more equal than others – equal opportunities in schools and access to education

Specific anti-discrimination laws now outlaw some forms of discrimination on the grounds of disability, race and gender. However, there are other sources of law, such as the employment contract or European law, which may offer additional protection.

Disability discrimination

The Disability Discrimination Act 1995 covers schools as well as other employers and providers of services. The duties do not, however, apply to pupils as such, except when they are being offered a non-educational service.

In 1997, the DfEE produced a circular (3/97) on the implications of the Disability Discrimination Act for schools – *What the Disability Discrimination Act (DDA) 1995 Means for Schools and LEAs*.

The main areas of school activity covered by the legislation are:

- the employment of staff;
- the provision of non-educational services to the public;
- the publication of information about the arrangements for disabled pupils.

Disability and employment

The Disability Discrimination Act 1995 applies to any employer with a total of 20 or more employees. This covers all LEA schools (and pupil referral units), but may also include independent schools, city technology colleges and non-maintained special schools. The employees may be part-time, temporary or contracted and those on maternity or sick leave are also included.

The Disability Discrimination Act says that a disabled person is someone who has 'a physical or mental impairment which has a substantial and long-term adverse effect on his ability to carry out normal day-to-day activities'.

'Discrimination' means treating someone less favourably than someone else for a reason relating to that person's disability and in a manner that cannot be justified.

Employers (and this will mean either an LEA or governing body as in all other contexts) may not discriminate against existing or potential employees who have, or have had, a disability when recruiting, imposing employment conditions, promoting, training or dismissing staff. This covers all staff, including part-time, temporary and contracted staff.

There is also a positive duty to make reasonable adjustments to employment arrangements and premises if their present set-up or layout results in a disabled employee being disadvantaged. The reasonable adjustments do not have to be in place before the relevant employment begins.

Less favourable treatment will only be 'justified' if it is done for a material reason and for a substantial reason. For example, if a teacher is medically unfit to carry out their job by reason of their disability and nothing the employer did would make any difference to this, they will be justified in refusing to employ or continue to employ the teacher.

However, where adjustments can be made in the working environment (by, for example, adapting the premises by providing ramps) or in providing training and the adjustments are not made, this may amount to discrimination. The circular gives some examples of the adaptations that might reasonably be expected in schools and recommends that advice be sought from the Placing, Assessment and Counselling Team of the Employment Service.

Adjustments will not be required if the resulting disadvantage to a disabled person is only a minor one or when an employer does not realize that an employee has a disability. It is also expected that industrial tribunals will consider it proper to take into account the costs of making the adjustment and the resources available to a school in meeting those costs.

The guidance goes into some detail about recommended practice in terms of advertising vacancies and recruitment and in considering the position of an existing employee who becomes disabled or whose disability worsens during the course of their employment.

Rights of access to goods, facilities and services

These rights are being phased in over a period of years. With effect from 2 December 1996, however, a service provider must not refuse to provide a service to a disabled person if it is provided to others or provide a worse service to a disabled person. This will usually include access to premises. In fact, when providing education, schools are exempted from the provisions of the Disability Discrimination Act as it was felt to have been adequately covered by the special educational needs legislation. The Act would probably not cover education being provided in non-school premises either.

What is covered, however, are extra-curricular activities, such as the letting of school premises to outside agencies, meetings held at schools, including meetings of the governing body and education-related hearings, such as exclusion appeals, disciplinary proceedings and the like.

The DfEE does not consider that the right of access will impose an obligation to make physical changes to the premises or that it will have heavy cost implications. In the case of *R* v *Lambeth London Borough Council, ex-parte M* (1995), *The Times*, 9 May, decided before the Disability Discrimination Act 1995 came into force, the court held that the LEA could not be compelled to install a lift for the use of a disabled pupil on the grounds that the lift did not fulfil a special educational need but was a mobility aid.

A service provider may refuse access if there are health and safety reasons for doing so, the disabled person is mentally incompetent or because, in doing so, it would not be able to provide the service to other non-disabled people.

More positive obligations are in the pipeline for future implementation.

Information

See Chapter 10 on the provision of information generally.

Remedies

Remedies for breach of the above requirements are by complaint to an industrial tribunal.

Race discrimination

The Race Relations Act 1976 prohibits discrimination – that is, less favourable treatment – on racial grounds or against members of any racial group. A person will be a member of a particular racial group by virtue of their colour, race, nationality or ethnic or national origins. An ethnic group is characterized by having a long shared history, its own cultural traditions, a common language, literature and religion, a common geographical origin or by being a minority or oppressed group within a majority community. The first two of these criteria are the most significant in legal terms.

According to case law, this definition covers Jewish people, Sikhs and gypsies (Romany people of Hindu origin) and Pakistanis, for example, but not Rastifarians or Muslims. It should be noted that discrimination on the grounds of religion is not in itself unlawful.

Discrimination is outlawed both in terms of employment and in terms of the provision of education.

The fact that an employer did not mean to act in a discriminatory way is unimportant. What is important is the effect of their actions. Nor will it be any defence to rely on the adverse reactions of others if the effect is to discriminate on racial grounds. Thus, 'I would employ them but my customers would not wear it' will not be good enough. In the case of *Hafeez* v *Richmond School* (1981) COIT 1112/38 the judgment was that it is unlawful discrimination to refuse to employ someone to teach English because the pupils wished to be taught by someone of English origin.

Employment

A large body of case law exists on the interpretation of the Race Relations Act in the employment context. The easiest way of summarizing it is to consider the 'but for . . . ' test. Would the employee have been treated any differently but for the fact of their race? If the answer is yes, then there has been direct discrimination and there can be no lawful excuse for it.

More problematical is the question of indirect discrimination. This is defined in the Race Relations Act, but it is not one of the clearest of definitions:

> A person discriminates against another ... if ...(b) he applies to that other a requirement or condition which he applies or would apply equally to a person not of the same racial group as that other but:
>
> (i) which is such that the proportion of persons of the same racial group as that other who can comply with it is considerably smaller than the proportion of persons not of that racial group who can comply with it; and
>
> (ii) which he cannot show to be justifiable irrespective of the colour, race, nationality or ethnic or national origins of the person to whom it is applied; and
>
> (iii) which is to the detriment of that other because he cannot comply with it.

This would include a condition that was discriminatory as to a dress code, language, qualification or area of residence.

Many have criticized the Race Relations Act because of one aspect of an employer's behaviour that remains lawful and is the expression of a preference. For example, in an advertisement, it will not be discriminatory to say that there are some essential requirements, but a candidate will be preferred if they have an English qualification or live in a certain area.

Education

An LEA or governing body has a general duty to provide education without directly or indirectly discriminating against a pupil on racial grounds (Section 19).

An LEA or governing body will contravene the Race Relations Act if it discriminates against a pupil on grounds of race – that is, treats them less favourably:

- in admitting or refusing to admit a pupil to a school or in the terms of offering admission;

- in affording access to any benefits, facilities or services or refusing to offer them;
- by subjecting a pupil to any other detriment, including exclusion from school;
- by victimizing a pupil.

It will be discrimination unless the treatment or condition imposed on a pupil can be justified on non-racial grounds. It is specifically provided that it will not be discrimination to offer pupils from a particular racial group access to educational facilities to meet their special needs.

Here are some cases particularly relevant to the field of education.

- In *Mandla* v *Lee (Dowell)* (1983) All ER 106, it was judged unlawful racial discrimination to refuse to admit a Sikh boy who wishes to wear a turban to school.
- In the *Board of Governors of St Matthias Church of England School* v *Crizzle* [1993] ICR 401, the governors who sought applicants for the post of headteacher who were communicant Anglicans were judged not to be in breach of the Race Relations Act when they failed to appoint an Asian Roman Catholic because the reasons for the failure to appoint related to religion rather than race.
- The case of *R* v *Cleveland County Council ex-parte Commission for Racial Equality* (1992) *The Times*, 25 August [1994] ELR 16 concluded that it is not unlawful for a mother to request that her child be educated at a predominantly white school and the LEA could not refuse to comply with her expressed preference on the grounds that it was racially motivated because an LEA's duty to respect parental choice is absolute and not qualified by the Race Relations Act.
- The case of *R* v *Governors of Small Heath School ex-parte Birmingham City Council* (1989) ILR 3 March found it was not racial discrimination not to provide interpreters at a public meeting on school closures.
- In the case of *Hussain and others* v *J H Walker, EAT* [1996] IRLR 11, the tribunal was entitled to conclude that it was discriminatory to refuse time off to Asian Muslim employees to participate in Eid. Despite the fact that the employer's explanation was that the refusal was on grounds of business efficacy, the tri-

bunal were entitled to conclude that the employer knew that the action would have a racially discriminatory effect.

- The case of *Gwynedd County Council* v *Jones and another* (1986) *The Times*, 28 July found it was not discriminatory to refuse to employ a non-Welsh-speaking person in a retirement home (English-speaking Welsh people do not constitute a racial group).

A useful document to which schools might refer is the Commission for Racial Equality's *Code of Practice for the Elimination of Racial Discrimination in Education* (December 1989).

Sex discrimination

Parallel provisions to the anti-race discrimination laws are found in the Sex Discrimination Act 1975 (as amended), with additional protection being contained in the Equal Pay Act 1970 and regulations made under it. There is also *The Code of Practice for the Elimination of Discrimination on the Grounds of Sex and Marriage and the Promotion of Equality of Opportunity in Employment*. Most of the comments relating to racial discrimination in terms of employment apply equally to sex discrimination.

One particular difference relates to dress code. Tribunals have tended not to consider a dress code prohibiting the wearing of trousers by women to be discriminatory so long as men are also required to meet comparable or equivalent standards of dress (such as having to wear a tie). I am not sure this has a long shelf-life as an approach since even female barristers have been allowed to wear trousers since 1996.

Discrimination on the grounds of pregnancy is dealt with in Chapter 6.

The law in relation to part-time workers often involves aspects of sex discrimination law as so many part-time workers are women. It has been a long hard struggle to change the way in which part-time workers are treated and many cases have to be pursued as far as the European courts.

Unmarried couples

There is no protection offered by English law at present when a couple who are not married or are of the same gender are treated in a different way from couples who are married, for example, in connection with the nomination of a death in service benefit. Attempts are continually being made to seek assistance from the European courts on this, but so far to little effect.

Sexual harassment

In a union survey in 1987, an extraordinary 72 per cent of women teachers in secondary schools reported that they had been sexually harassed at work. This and other forms of bullying are as much a problem for adults in the workplace as children at school. The NASUWT has produced an advisory leaflet entitled 'Stop Personal Harassment'.

Sexual and racial harassment are 'subdivisions' of discrimination, which is less favourable treatment on the grounds of race or sex. Harassment may be a series of actions or just one action if serious. See the more detailed discussion in Chapter 5 on bullying.

Political discrimination

There is as yet no protection in UK law for political discrimination, but this may change with the advent of a Human Rights Act. It may be possible to show that political discrimination amounts to unfair treatment such that a dismissal is unfair.

Most of the reported cases seem to have occurred in other parts of Europe and have involved a refusal to offer or confirm employment. This is a difficulty under UK law as before employment is offered, there is no employment contract and, therefore, no duty to treat a person in any particular way from a political point of view.

Special educational needs

LEAs are given a number of duties, as stated in the Education Act 1996, both to identify and provide suitable education for children with special educational needs. They may meet their duties either by adapting the mainstream provision or by providing specialist schools.

A child is defined as having a special educational need if they have a 'learning difficulty which calls for special educational provision to be made' (Section 312, Education Act 1996). A learning difficulty means that a child:

- has a significantly greater difficulty in learning than the majority of children of the same age;
- has a disability that either prevents or hinders them from making use of educational facilities of a kind generally provided for children of the same age in schools within the area.

The Education Act requires that the first priority should be to educating a child with special educational needs in a mainstream school, provided that this is compatible with the need to give both the child and other pupils the education they need and the efficient use of resources. The *Code of Practice on the Identification and Assessment of Special Educational Needs* states that there is a legal obligation for an LEA to take this into account in making decisions and provision. The Code sets out procedures to be followed, including those to be used in the three stages of school-based assessments. After the Stage 1 assessment, an LEA should provide the assistance of a special needs coordinator to work with the child's class teacher in devising an individual educational plan for the child and in getting more information from parents, doctors and so on about the child's needs. It is not always necessary to go through the motions of following the stages in order. Where it is obvious that a child has a much higher level of need, the assessment can proceed straight to a statement. Equally, the parents of a child can request that an LEA make an assessment of their child and consider whether or not a statement of special needs is required. If the request is refused, the parents have a right of appeal to a special educational needs tribunal (SENT). If an LEA decides not to statement a child, the parents also have the right of appeal to a SENT. The only subsequent appeal that is allowed is an appeal to the High Court, on a point of law only.

There are detailed procedures to be followed in drawing up an educational statement. Ensuring these are gone through is the responsibility of an LEA, not any individual teacher or school. However, of course, a school has a major role to play in providing information for the purposes of completing an assessment and an LEA is under a legal duty to consult schools and seek educational advice. A school's advice must be recorded in a special section of the statement. An LEA also has to consider representations, medical material and so on supplied by parents as well as seek a report from its own educational psychologist. An LEA does not only look at educational needs, it must consider other, non-educational needs.

The first stage is to draw up a draft statement for the parents to consider and to invite them to express a preference for the school their child should attend, which may well include the school the child is currently attending. If the parents and the LEA agree about the school, the school is under an obligation to take the child. If the parents do not agree with the LEA's recommendation, it may take the matter to a SENT. There have been many challenges in which parents have either tried to keep an SEN child in a mainstream school against an LEA's wishes or get their child into a particular special school (sometimes an expensive one and, in a few well-publicized cases, sometimes in another country).

A school should be consulted before a child is imposed on them. However, if a school objects to an LEA's decision, it can only complain to the Secretary of State or consider taking judicial review proceedings on the grounds that the LEA decision is irrational or runs contrary to the school's admission policy, for example (see Chapter 15). One difficulty that faces schools is that they cannot require a child to submit to any medical examination and that will limit their ability to challenge any expert evidence on behalf of the child or LEA. Nor does a governing body have any right to appear before a SENT and will only be able to put forward its views indirectly through the LEA (which might not agree with them). It is therefore important to put forward as much relevant material as possible at the earliest stage if a school does not believe it can cope with the needs of a particular child – either at all or in the light of the proposed support from the LEA.

It seems unlikely that any individual teacher or school could successfully be sued for any failing in the SEN system as such as the principal responsibility lies with the LEA concerned and the special educational needs coordinator. However, it could happen under an extension of the principles arising in the case of *X* v *Bedfordshire*, discussed at the end of Chapter 14. Parents have their own remedies and rights of appeal if requests for assessment are refused. However, there are specific duties imposed on a governing body to:

- use their best endeavours to ensure that special educational provision is delivered;
- ensure that all members of teaching staff are aware of the child's educational needs;

- ensure that teaching staff are aware of the importance of identifying and providing for pupils with special educational needs;
- ensure that any pupil with special educational needs is able to participate in whole-school activities with other pupils who do not have such needs;
- have regard to the Code of Practice.

There are also specific duties to provide information about SEN policies and provision within a school, which are discussed in Chapter 10.

A very useful book on this subject is John Friel's *Children with Special Needs: Assessment Law and Practice: Caught in the Acts*, now in its 4th edition, published by Jessica Kingsley, London. It is particularly written with parents and educators in mind.

Chapter 10

Better informed but not necessarily wiser – information and records

The volume of information that must now be collected and publicized by education providers at every level is phenomenal. Indeed, so much paperwork is involved that a working group was established in 1997 to report to ministers on ways in which it might be reduced. Its report, 'Reducing the Bureaucratic Burden on Teachers', was concluded in January 1998 and a government consultation paper subsequently issued to take forward its recommendations. The DfEE has also issued a circular on the subject – *Reducing the Bureaucratic Burden on Teachers* (DfEE Circular 2/98). In the meantime, it may be helpful for you to know why (in the sense of legal requirements) it is you have to keep certain information and provide it to others on a regular basis and, in the case of personal information, when you should disclose it and when you should not.

Data protection

Any information about an identifiable and living person (whether sensitive or not) that is held on a computer is regulated by the Data Protection Acts 1984. A new Data Protection Act was passed on 16 July 1998, but it is not likely to be fully in force until January 1999 and, even then, there is a phasing in period so that it will not be fully implemented until 2007. One of the most important changes that the 1988 Act makes is that it extends the definition of the data covered. Thus manual records held in a 'relevant filing system' – that is, one where records are structured whether by reference to individuals or criteria relating to individuals – are now included. It is not yet clear just how this will be interpreted and schools will need to await guidance from the DfEE, which, at the time of writing, is being prepared. The Secretary of State also has power under the 1998 Act to make regulations exempting schools from the requirements of the Act, but no such regulations have yet been made.

All users of this data – in a school context, these will usually be the LEA, governing body and headteacher – must be registered as such with the Data Protection Registrar, who will require them to set out the information that is held and for what purpose. As part of the initiative to reduce bureaucratic burdens on teachers, the DfEE and the Data Protection Registrar have devised a pre-ticked standardized registration form tailored to schools' requirements. Further simplification of the process is being developed and up-to-date DfEE guidance on data protection will be issued in the autumn of 1998.

The point of the data protection legislation is to allow individuals (pupils included) the right to see information about them that is held, which they can ask to be amended if it is incorrect.

Information about admissions

An LEA or governing body (of a grant-maintained, voluntary or special agreement school) must collate and supply information about admissions every year. It must be supplied to any parent who requests it, but it is often issued as a matter of routine to any parents with children at primary school who are about to transfer to secondary school. Parents may also request the information from any school. The information that must be provided is as follows:

- the number of pupils to be admitted into school each year;
- information about who makes decisions about admissions;
- the policy that will be followed in deciding admissions;
- information about arrangements that will be made for pupils who do not belong to the catchment area of the particular LEA;
- any other admissions information required by the Secretary of State;

- any other information an LEA or governors think should be published.

Information about a school

School prospectus

Every year, the governing body (of any type of school) must publish a prospectus containing information for prospective parents. The Education (School Information) (England) Regulations 1996 (SI 1996/2585) set out the information that must be contained in a prospectus. See, too, the DfEE circulars *School Prospectuses in Primary Schools 1998/9 Onwards* (DfEE Circular 7/98) and *School Prospectuses in Secondary Schools* (DfEE Circular 8/98).

In primary schools, a prospectus must contain information about:

- a school's name, address and phone number;*
- the names of the headteacher and chair of governors;*
- details of the type of school it is;*
- a statement of its beliefs and values;*
- visiting arrangements for parents considering sending their child to the school;
- details of a school's admissions policy;
- curriculum and secular curriculum policy, including how it is organized, what teaching techniques are used and any optional subjects that are offered;
- arrangements for pupils with special educational needs and any other special arrangements;*
- a summary of policy on special educational needs;*
- a summary of the sex education curriculum and how it is taught (if it is taught);
- the term and holiday dates for the next school year and session times during the day;
- pastoral matters, including school discipline, out-of-school activities and uniform;
- the religious affiliation of the school, if any;*
- the religious education curriculum and the right of parents to withdraw their children from RE and collective worship;*
- a summary of charging policy, if any charges are made for activities;

- how to complain about the curriculum;
- a statement of the school's sporting aims and facilities offered;
- any impending changes to the above;
- pupil absence rates;*
- National Curriculum assessment results (both school-specific and national information);*
- how to get hold of documents that the headteacher must have available for inspection.

* These are the pieces of information that are, more than likely, going to need to be included in prospectuses for the foreseeable future. See the end of the list for secondary schools for other information on this.

Secondary school prospectuses must also contain:

- details of the number of places available at the school, how many applications were received in the last year and how many applicants were successful;
- external qualifications – the courses offered;
- information about careers education arrangements, including work experience;
- information about GCSE A and AS Level and NVQ exam results (school-specific, local and national averages for GCSE and national averages for A, AS Level and NVQ);*
- information about where pupils go when they leave the school.*

* The items marked with an asterisk are those likely to continue to be compulsory to publish in the prospectus. Information about the admissions policy and complaints procedure will probably still have to be published, but not necessarily in the prospectus. Governing bodies may still think it advisable to publish other information in some form or other, in particular information about the curriculum and complaints procedures.

Annual report

Governing bodies in all schools must publish an annual report. This must be presented to parents for discussion at an annual parents' meeting and must be sent to them at least two weeks before that meeting. In primary schools, a report should contain information about:

- the annual parents' meeting – the date, time, place, agenda;*
- a report of progress on items discussed at the last annual meeting;
- the name of each governor and their status, and information about how to contact the chair of governors and the clerk;*
- the next election of parent governors;*
- term, holiday and half term holiday dates;
- progress on the school action plan;*
- action taken to strengthen the school's links with the community and the police;
- a summary of the school's budget and how the money has been spent, including, in maintained schools, any money spent on governors' travel and subsistence;*
- the outcome of the governor's decision whether or not to hold an opting out ballot and the reasons for it;
- school security;*
- whether or not a school's sporting aims have been met and any notable sporting achievements;
- access to a school for disabled pupils and what it has done to promote equal opportunities and treatment for disabled pupils;*
- a school's policy on special educational needs and the implementation of that policy, including an evaluation of the success of its policy and an outline of how resources allocated for special educational needs have been used;
- a summary of the training and professional development undertaken by teaching staff;*
- National Curriculum assessment results (both school-specific and national);*
- pupil absence rates (broken down between authorized and unauthorized absences);*
- any changes to a school's prospectus since its publication.

* These are, most probably, the items that will continue to have to be published in the annual report.

A progress report on action taken between meetings will also have to be published, but not necessarily in an annual report.

In secondary schools, an annual report should also contain:

- information about examination results, as detailed earlier regarding a school prospectus;
- information about pupils' destination after leaving school.

Each governing body should consider whether or not a report ought to be provided in languages other than English, and maintained schools can be made to provide translated reports by their LEA.

See also, the DfEE circulars School Prospectuses and Governors' Annual Reports in Primary Schools (11/96) and School Prospectuses and Governors' Annual Reports in Secondary Schools (12/96).

Information about a school's performance

The Education (School Performance Information) (England) Regulations 1998 (SI 1998/1929, and companion regulations dealing with schools in Wales) came into force on 27 August 1998. They deal with the information that must be supplied by a headteacher to a governing body, and by a governing body to the Secretary of State about their school's performance.

The information that must be supplied relates to attainment levels at Key Stages 1 and 2 (particularly information about pupils who are working towards Level 1) and information about examination and vocational qualification results. The Regulations apply to all maintained schools and to non-maintained special schools. There are slightly different procedures for the transmission of information to the Secretary of State, depending on the type of school. Independent schools must also provide information about examination results and vocational qualifications in respect of pupils over the age of 15 within 2 weeks of being asked for it by the Secretary of State.

In addition, all maintained and grant-maintained schools must provide information to their LEA about the levels of authorized and unauthorized absences. This does not apply to schools providing education for boarding pupils only. Virtually all schools must provide further information set out in Schedule 5 of the Regulations to the Secretary of State within two weeks of a written request. This is basic information about the school – registered pupil numbers, age range and number of pupils over 16, number of pupils with special educational needs (both with statements and without) and other details.

LEAs are further required by these Regulations to publish information about primary schools in a certain format, principally to show the numbers of pupils at the top and bottom ends of the range of achievement.

School policies

There are several different policies that schools are *required* to draw up and publicize and several others that are *recommended*. Table 10.1 sets out details of the different types of policies required in different kinds of schools (both old and new designations of schools are used in this table). There then follow more specific comments about some of those policies.

Table 10.1 School policies that are required or recommended

Policy	Optional or required	Type of school
Action plan following OFSTED inspection	R	All schools
Admissions policy	R	All schools with responsibility for admissions (or LEA if not), except independent schools
Charging policy	R	All schools
Curriculum policy	R O	Community schools Recommended for aided schools
Curriculum complaints procedure	R	Foundation (former GM schools)
Equal opportunities policy	O	All schools
Health and safety policy	R O	GM/aided schools Community schools are encouraged to develop their own version of an LEA policy
Income policy	O	GM schools
Pupil disciplinary policy	R	All schools
School development plan	O	All schools
Staff disciplinary policy	R	All schools
Special educational needs policy	R	All schools
Sex education policy	R	All secondary schools and community and foundation primary schools if sex education is provided
Standing orders	R O	GM schools founded after 19 January 1993 GM schools founded before 19 January 1993

Disciplinary policy

The disciplinary policy headteachers are under a duty to devise (under Section 61 of the School Standards and Framework Act 1998) must be published in written form and drawn to the attention of all pupils, parents, employees and contractors on site at least once a year.

A policy on restraining pupils and the use of force should be drawn up by a headteacher in consultation with governors and teachers (see DfEE Circular 10/98). The policy should be included in the information given by a school to the parents about the school's policy on discipline and standards of behaviour.

Records in schools about pupils

A governing body must make sure that a curricular record is kept for each pupil containing a report of their progress and achievements throughout the year. This is the pupil's main educational record.

According to the Education (Individual Pupils' Achievements) (Information) Regulations 1997 (SI 1997/1368) and similar regulations for Wales (SI 1997/573), this report must contain information about:

- a pupil's progress and achievements in all the National Curriculum subjects, including the results of any national tests taken at the ages of 7, 11 and 14;
- the results obtained in any public examinations sat;
- comments on any other achievements during the year;
- how the pupil's results in national tests compare with the results of other pupils of the same age;
- a general report on progress and attendance;
- information about how to contact teachers about the report and how to make an appointment to see them.

The only people who are entitled to see these records as of right are:

- parents of pupils under 18;
- the pupil if they are over compulsory school age and proposing to leave school (or have already left);

- the pupil, only if they are over 18, unless there are special circumstances that make it appropriate for their parents to have a copy (and it is for the headteacher to decide whether or not there are);
- a headteacher of an independent school or further or higher education establishment or governing body of any other school to which a pupil has applied for admission. Note that assessment results must not be disclosed until after a decision has been made as to whether or not the pupil will be admitted;
- any of the following bodies collating or checking performance information – an LEA, OFSTED, the Qualification and Curriculum Authority (QCA), the Funding Agency for Schools (FAS) and the Teacher Training Agency (TTA).

The DfEE issues regular guidance on reports on pupils' individual achievements. The last published were *Reports on Pupils' Achievements in Primary Schools in 1996/7* and *Reports on Pupils' Achievements in Secondary Schools in 1996/7* – Circulars 1 and 2 of 1997.

School-leavers are entitled to a report containing the following information:

- the pupil's name and the name of the school;
- brief particulars of the pupil's progress and achievements in all subjects in the last year the pupil was at the school (but not exam results).

This information must be supplied not later than 30 September in the year the pupil left the school and should be supplied in the pupil's National Record of Achievement folder.

The educational record must be supplied within 15 days of a written request.

When a pupil changes school, the headteacher of the old school must supply a report to the headteacher of the new school as follows:

- core subject attainment and target levels, including any nationally assessed levels;
- for final year Key Stage 3 pupils, assessed attainment and target levels in design and technology, foreign languages, geography, history and information technology, and a brief summary of achievement in art, music and PE;
- the pupil's exam results.

This report must be supplied within 15 days of the pupil being de-registered (unless, you may be relieved to hear, you do not know, and cannot reasonably find out, which school the pupil has moved to).

A parent or pupil may request that an educational record be amended if it contains inaccuracies or is incomplete (except in relation to the assessments it contains). The governing body must correct the record or attach the parents' statement about the inaccuracies to it.

A school may have other information about a pupil. None of this has to be disclosed and, indeed, the Education (School Information) (England) Regulations 1996 (SI 1996/2585) stipulate that some of it should never be disclosed, except to another educational establishment. This latter would include, for example:

- any information given to a school by someone other than an employee of an LEA or an education welfare officer or a person requesting disclosure or any information that would identify the source of information from those sources;
- any information relating to child abuse, actual or suspected;
- information that might cause serious harm to the child or someone else in terms of their physical or mental health or emotional condition;
- information about another pupil's attainment target;
- references supplied for the benefit of a future employer or other educational establishment;
- reports prepared for a hearing in a juvenile court;
- a statement of a pupil's special educational needs;
- information about a pupil's ethnic origin.

Information about children with special educational needs (SEN)

A school is under an obligation to publish information about its special educational provision under the Education (Special Educational Needs) (Information) Regulations 1994 (SI 1994/1048) as follows:

- the objectives of an SEN policy;
- the name of its special educational needs coordinator;

- the arrangements for coordinating educational provision for pupils with SEN;
- admission arrangements;
- any SEN specialism and any special units within a school;
- any special facilities that a school has that assist access to the school;
- the allocation of resources;
- the arrangements for identification and assessment of SENs and any review procedures;
- arrangements for delivery of the National Curriculum to pupils with SENs;
- how SEN pupils are integrated in a school;
- details of how the SEN delivery is monitored;
- complaints procedure;
- arrangements for training teachers;
- arrangements for the use of non-school facilities and staff;
- arrangements for partnership with parents;
- links with other mainstream and special schools (including details of arrangements for a pupil to change schools or leave school) and links with other relevant organizations.

In addition, a school is required to keep records relating to an individual pupil with SENs with full details of any school-based assessment, recorded views of their parents, health checks and medical advice received, the individual education plan and any reviews and any other relevant material, such as expert reports.

In addition, a school should keep a register of all children at the school who have SENs.

OFSTED inspections

OFSTED is itself under a duty to notify a number of people about the dates it intends to carry out inspections, including LEAs and governing bodies concerned.

A governing body must, in turn, notify the parents of all registered pupils about the date of the inspection and also arrange a meeting so that inspectors can meet any parents who wish to attend. This meeting must be arranged to take place before the inspection and parents should be given at least three weeks' notice. Members of school staff are cordially not invited.

OFSTED reports and school action plans

After every OFSTED inspection, inspectors must prepare a report within five weeks of completion. The school (of whatever type) must send a summary of the report to all parents within 10 days from the date on which they receive it. This must also contain information about how to get hold of a copy of the full OFSTED report. Note that all OFSTED reports are published on the Internet.

In addition, a school must devise and send out a plan of the way in which it intends to respond to the report, both in order to consolidate strengths and eliminate weaknesses (a school action plan). Time limits apply when special measures or re-inspection is recommended, but otherwise a school must respond in this way within 40 days.

Parents who are thinking of sending their child to a school must be given a copy of its OFSTED report on request and may only be charged for the cost of photocopying.

Independent schools

Independent schools in England and Wales are required by the Education (Particulars of Independent Schools) Regulations 1997 (SI 1997/2918) to supply information to the Registrar of Independent Schools. The details of what is required are set out in a Schedule to the Regulations. Certain specified information is required on first registration. Thereafter, an annual report is required, giving details of pupil numbers, staff numbers and so on, and exam results for pupils over 15, together with details about any teacher who has left the employment of the school.

Frequently asked questions

How long should records be kept?

There is very little guidance on this and even less law. The DfEE tends to say that it is entirely up to the school. If you are thinking of preserving records in case they might be relevant to a court case, they would have to be kept for a very long time. You may be aware that there are time limits after which most legal cases cannot be brought. However, in the case of a person under 18, time does not start to run against them until they reach 18. Your LEA may be able to give you guidance on this question. In addition, the Archivist's Society produces a useful booklet entitled *School Records: Their management and retention.*

Chapter 11

A family affair –
children and parents

What is a child?

A 'child' in law is someone who is not over compulsory school age (Section 579, Education Act 1996).

What is a pupil?

In law, a 'pupil' is anyone being educated at a school *except* those who are over 19 and receiving further education and those who are receiving part-time education suitable for a person over compulsory school age. Pupils are divided into 'junior pupils' – those under 12 – and 'senior pupils' – those over 12 but under 19. In the context of admissions and exclusions, the word 'pupil' also includes anyone who would be a pupil if they were admitted or if they had not been excluded (Section 3 of the Education Act 1996, as amended by paragraph 9 of Schedule 7 of the Education Act 1997). There were 8.3 million pupils in school in January 1998.

What is the compulsory school age?

A child begins to be of compulsory school age at 5. A child stops being of compulsory school age at the end of the day that is the school leaving date if they are 16:

- before that date; or
- on that date; or
- between that date and the beginning of the next school year.

The 'school leaving date' has now been permanently fixed as the last Friday in June with effect from 1998 (Education (School Leaving Date) Order 1997 SI 97/1970). The DfEE has issued a circular on the implications of this, including those for work experience, study leave and employment (Circular 11/97 – *School Leaving Date for 16-year-olds*).

What is a parent?

The word 'parent', in law means not only the birth parents of a child, but, under the Education Act 1996, Section 576, includes any person:

- who is not a parent of the child but who has parental responsibility for them; or
- who has care of them.

It has been held by the courts that this definition covers a foster parent (as in the case of *Fairpo* v *Humberside County Council* (1996) *The Times*, 15 August), but it will also cover a relative or friend who has stepped in to look after a child.

The Education Act also says that if a child is being looked after by a local authority (whether as a result of an order or not – see Chapter 12), it must be treated as a parent, except when it comes to eligibility to be a parent-governor, attending annual meetings and voting in opting-out ballots.

In deciding whether or not a person has care of a child, the Education Act specifically states that the fact of the child being away in hospital or at boarding school or for any other temporary purpose is to be disregarded. In other words, although you could describe a hospital authority or boarding school as having care of a child, they are not given the status of 'parent' for the purposes of the Education Act.

What is parental responsibility?

The meaning of 'parental responsibility' is taken from Section 3 of the Children Act 1989:

> 'Parental responsibility' means all the rights, duties, powers, responsibilities and authority which by law a parent of a child has in relation to the child and his property.

Note also Section 3(5) of the Children Act 1989:

> A person who:
> does not have parental responsibility for a particular child; but has care of the child, may (subject to the provisions of this Act) do what is reasonable in all the circumstances of the case for the purpose of safeguarding or promoting the child's welfare.

This might well include a teacher. For example, if a child becomes ill at school and either there is no time to contact the parents or they are unavailable, the teacher is permitted to take the necessary steps to ensure the child is properly cared for until the parents can be contacted.

The scope of parental responsibility

This is not defined in legislation, but the courts have said that it includes the power to make decisions about:

- a child's religion;
- a child's education;
- a child's name;
- where the child should live;
- who the child may spend time with;
- medical treatment.

Who has parental responsibility?

The following have parental responsibility:

- the child's mother;
- the child's father, if married to the mother, whether before or after the child was born;

- any person who has been given a parental responsibility order by the court (this will include any person the court has said the child should live with);
- the local authority if a care order has been made;
- a guardian appointed as such in a parent's will.

Parental responsibility can never be taken away from a mother or married father, except by virtue of an adoption order. However, their ability to exercise their powers can be severely restricted, either by specific orders (such as an order to say that a child's name shall not be changed or that a child cannot be removed from England and Wales) or by the making of a care order.

Parental responsibility may be shared by a number of people, and shared between the parents and a local authority. This means that there may be a number of people the school should liaise with and provide information to.

The definition of 'parent' in the Education Act does not exclude those without parental responsibility. In other words, an unmarried father who does not have parental responsibility is entitled to the same information as a child's mother. A stepfather may also be covered by the Education Act's definition if he is living with the child and sharing care. It is a common complaint – particularly from fathers who are no longer part of the family unit, –that they do not receive information about their children from their school. The fact that a school has not provided information to a person who is entitled to it under the Education Act is highly unlikely to lead to any sort of legal action, but it could give rise to a complaint. If a school failed to give the information after being specifically asked for it, a parent *might* be able to get an order from court requiring that it be produced.

On a practical level, the first problem is likely to be that a school may not have been told that a pupil's parents have separated when it happens. A second difficulty is that much information is sent home to parents via pupil post, which obviously means that the absent parent will not receive it. A school should make sure that information is sent to the absent parent directly. A third, more difficult problem is that the relationship between parents may have deteriorated to the point where a mother wants to exclude the father from her child's life. Unless she has a court order, however, she cannot dictate to her child's school what can and cannot be shared with the father and the school should not allow her to do so.

That said, some discretion should be exercised in circumstances where there are allegations of violence or something similarly serious. See the Frequently asked questions section at the end of this chapter for suggestions on how to deal with this. See also the following sections on other reasons for withholding information.

Information that must be provided to parents

Information about their child

A child's parents are entitled to certain information about their child's educational achievements during the year. Details are set out in the Education (Individual Pupils' Achievements) (Information) Regulations 1997 (SI 1368/97). A charge may be made for the cost of copying this information on a non-profit-making basis.

There are specific exemptions, however, in Regulation 8. A school does not have to pass on any information:

- received from a third party other than an LEA employee or an education welfare officer or the person who is asking for the information;
- if it would reveal the identity of any third party apart from the above;
- if, in the opinion of the headteacher, it is likely to cause serious harm to the physical or mental health or emotional condition of the pupil to whom the information relates or to someone else;
- if, in the opinion of the headteacher, it is relevant to the question of whether or not the pupil has been the subject of, or is at risk of, child abuse;
- if it would disclose the attainment levels of any other pupil.

Information about the school

A pupil's parents are entitled to:

- a copy of the annual governors' report;
- attend the annual parents' meeting;
- access to statements of the school's curriculum policy, including policies on sex education and religious education;

- access to schemes of work, syllabuses, school prospectus;
- notification of the date of any OFSTED inspection;
- attend a pre-OFSTED meeting with inspectors, which the school must arrange;
- a copy of a summary of the OFSTED report free of charge and a copy of the full report on request, for which there may be a charge for copying;
- a copy of the post-OFSTED action plan;
- access to DfEE circulars and statutory instruments;
- access to local performance tables.

Again, a charge may be made to cover the cost of copying any of the above material. However, parents are entitled to inspect a copy of the school prospectus, annual governors' report and full OFSTED report at the school and no charge may be made for this.

Information about complaints

Both LEAs and schools are required to implement complaints procedures, and information about procedures has to be published in their annual reports. From 1999, the information should be made available but not necessarily in an annual report. The Government is still considering its recommendations to schools about this.

Access to pupils at school

For a number of reasons, schools may be asked by parents to allow them to see their children during the course of the school day or at the end of the day. Alternatively, they may be asked by one parent to prevent a child from seeing the other parent. The school will need to handle these situations sensitively.

Much may be obvious from the context in which the request is made. If a parent has parental responsibility, then, unless there is an order preventing contact, in theory, there is no reason for the school to refuse to allow access to the child. Obviously, if a parent is seeking to interrupt their child during lesson time, it may be quite reasonable to refuse, unless there is some sort of emergency. The same would be true, if there is reason to fear violence or other disruptive behaviour. A parent, any parent, is not entitled to go on to school premises as of right. If it is during non-contact time, a school will have to consider whether or not it cuts across the normal end of day handover arrangements.

If there is any doubt about a parent's position, it may be advisable to contact the other parent and/or make enquiries about the state of play between the parents or seek further advice from a lawyer.

Parents' meetings

In theory, any parent (as defined above) can attend parents' meetings and should be invited to them. Schools are under no obligation to make separate arrangements for meetings with parents, but many schools consider it good policy to try and avoid confrontation by offering staggered meeting times or a choice of dates.

The annual parents' meeting is a different matter. If the parents really cannot deal with the possibility of coming into contact with one another (which is primarily their responsibility), it would no doubt promote partnership to try and see if the parents can be given information about the meeting in some other way and to suggest that they channel any views they wish to express through the parent governors.

Registration

Every school must keep two registers in relation to pupils, and every governing body is responsible for making sure that both are kept (Section 434, Education Act 1996). The Education (Pupil Registration) Regulations 1995 (SI 1995/2089) (amended by the Education (Pupil Registration) (Amendment) Regulations 1997) (SI 1997/2624) spell out the details of what must be recorded on these registers.

Admissions register

On the first day a pupil attends school, their name and address must be recorded in the admissions register, together with that of every person known to be a parent of a pupil at the school. The Regulations set out the circumstances in which pupils may be removed from the register, but, as long as a pupil's name is on the register, the school is responsible for that pupil's education.

Attendance register

Schools must also maintain an attendance register for each form or class (except in independent boarding schools where all pupils are boarders). This must record whether or not a pupil has attended for morning and afternoon sessions (the morning register should be taken at the start of the school day, but the afternoon register may be taken at any time during the afternoon session). If a pupil is absent, the reason for the absence must be recorded and the register must show whether or not the absence is an authorized or unauthorized one (see under Non-attendance at school below). If a pupil is away from school for the purposes of an approved educational activity, this should also be recorded, together with the nature of the activity. Work experience in the last school year counts as an approved educational activity and does not require leave of absence, but arrangements should be made to monitor absence from the workplace, which should be recorded as unauthorized in the same way as would absence from school. The attendance register should also include the names and addresses of the pupil's parents or other carer and an emergency contact number.

The DfEE's *School Attendance: Policy and Practice on Categorization of Absence* (May 1994) gives guidance to schools on how to record absences from school. See also the DfEE Circular 11/91 (WO 4/91) – *The Education (Pupils' Attendance Records) Regulations 1991.*

If the registers are kept on computer, this may bring a school under the terms of the Data Protection Act 1984, under which holders of data are required to register with the Data Protection Registrar. See the Circular from the DfEE dated 29 November 1991 – *Data Protection Act 1984: Implications for LEA maintained schools,* which was sent to all LEAs, governing bodies and headteachers.

The attendance register, if handwritten, should be written in ink and in a way that makes alterations obvious. It must be possible to see both the original entry and the corrected entry if a change is required. Registers may also be produced by computer, so long as the register is printed out at least once a month and alterations made are obvious. Printouts of the computerized attendance register for the year must be kept together in one volume for a period of at least three years from the end of the year in which they were produced.

Rates of authorized and unauthorized absence must be published by a school in its prospectus and in its annual governors' report.

School reports to parents on their child's performance must also show their attendance record and the number of unauthorized absences.

Non-attendance at school

The parent of every child of compulsory school age is under a statutory duty to 'cause him to receive efficient full-time education suitable to (a) his age, ability, and aptitude, and (b) to any special educational needs he may have either by regular attendance at school or otherwise' (Section 7, Education Act 1996).

This does not mean that a child has to attend school. If a parent wishes to provide education for their child at home, they are entitled to do so. If a parent informs a school that they wish to do this, the headteacher must take the pupil off the register, but must also notify the LEA within two weeks. The LEA will then investigate to see whether or not the education that is being provided to the child is suitable, as defined above.

The DfEE Circular 11/91 (see above) gives the following guidance about authorizing absence from school:

> In addition to cases itemized in law, there are other situations in which schools might reasonably exercise discretion to grant leave: for example, study leave in the period immediately before public examinations or absence following the death of a close member of the child's family. Schools will be under a continuing duty... to report to their LEA on continuous pupil absences of two weeks or more and on those pupils who fail to attend school regularly, except where such absences are covered by a medical certificate. Schools should be sparing in the exercise of their discretion to grant leave of absence ... Correspondingly, parents should be encouraged to avoid, so far as possible, arranging medical and similar appointments for their children during school hours.

The only person who can authorize the absence of a registered pupil from a school is someone who is permitted to do so by the governing body.

Once a school has notified an LEA that a child has been absent, the LEA should then consider what action to take in circumstances where a child's education may be suffering. Legal proceedings should be a last resort. Efforts should be made to secure a voluntary solution to the problem with liaison between LEA, school and parents and other departments as necessary, such as social services.

The first legal remedy that should be considered by an LEA is whether or not to apply for an education supervision order under the Children Act 1989. It is a statutory requirement that this option be considered before any other step is taken. A court can also direct an LEA to make such an application when dealing with criminal charges for non-attendance. An LEA may decline to make the application, but should give reasons to the court concerned for doing so. If an order is made, a supervisor (who may be an education welfare officer or education social worker) is appointed to advise, befriend and give directions to both the child and their parents with a view to ensuring that the child receives a proper education. For reasons that are not yet clear, despite the availability of these orders, they are not often applied for and few teachers seem to be aware of their existence.

If a child of compulsory school age is registered at a school but does not attend regularly, their parent is guilty of an offence unless the absence is authorized by the school or is due to sickness other unavoidable causes or religious observance. There are also special defences where a child lives more than a certain distance away from their school and transport is not available or when a child's parent has to travel about for trade or business purposes and has no fixed abode.

There is no statutory definition of 'regularly'. It probably means attendance at times prescribed by a governing body. From the relatively few cases that have come before the courts, the following conclusions can be drawn:

- frequent late arrival (after the register is taken) counts as irregular attendance (*Hinchley* v *Rankin* [1961] 1 WLR 421);
- an offence may be committed even if a parent does not know that their child is not at school (*Crump* v *Gilmore* (1969) 68 LGR 56);
- if a parent refuses to ensure that a pupil complies with school rules, such as those relating to appropriate dress, and a school sends the pupil away, this will count as failing to secure regular attendance (*Spiers* v *Warrington Corporation* [1954] 1 QB 61);
- it is not acceptable to keep a child from school to fulfil other

'family responsibilities', such as caring for a sick relative (*Jenkins* v *Howells* [1949] 2 KB 218).

Holiday leave

One particular problem relates to extended holidays. The Regulations allow governing bodies to authorize absence during the school term for up to ten days for the purposes of a family holiday. There is no right to take this or any extra time off – the governing body has complete discretion as to whether or not it should be allowed. A particular problem, especially in metropolitan areas, is that many pupils have family abroad and wish to take much longer holidays to spend time with them. If a school authorizes such absences, it will be difficult for an LEA to take action against the parents. If a school does not authorize such absences, they must be recorded and notified to their LEA. The DfEE guidance suggests that schools should discuss the impact of any proposed holidays on the pupil's education with the parents.

Some writers have suggested that a school should de-register a pupil taking such a long absence and re-register them on their return, thereby maintaining the absence figures at an acceptable level. Others take the view that these absences should not be authorized and pupils who are absent for long periods for such a reason should be de-registered in an effort to discourage parents from doing this as they would then not be guaranteed a place for their child at the school of their choice on their return. Either of these approaches merely shifts the onus back on LEAs, which must be informed about de-registration.

This is really a policy issue that should be discussed between a governing body and its LEA. From a legal point of view, however, it remains the case that if a pupil is on the register and takes a long holiday, their parents are arguably committing a criminal offence unless they can argue that they are providing education of a suitable nature during the child's time away.

Enforcing attendance

There are also criminal offences relating to failure to comply with a school attendance order. This is an order that an LEA can serve on a parent requiring the parent to satisfy the LEA that their child is receiving suitable education under Section 437, Education Act 1996).

A child's school attendance record may also be relevant in care proceedings. Although a care order can no longer be made on the grounds of non-attendance at school (an education supervision order being the alternative to this), a child's poor attendance record may be evidence of poor parenting or of a child being out of the control of its parents, which can be grounds for a care order. The attendance record may also be relevant in disputes between parents as to which of them should look after their child on a day-to-day basis.

For all these reasons, and for reasons of health and safety, the school registers are extremely important documents and may be needed as evidence in court.

Parents' choices about education

Admission to a school

The law on school admissions is in transition at the time of writing in anticipation of changes to be introduced as a result of the School Standards and Framework Act 1998. Intakes from September 2000 admissions will be governed by a statutory Admissions Code of Practice. For the year before that, the DfEE has issued an interim guidance document that, to a certain extent, foreshadows the changes that the new legislation will make. Admissions authorities are also encouraged to voluntarily implement the new systems from September 1999.

The law allows parents to express a preference as to the school they wish their child to attend and the LEA or governing body (whichever is the admission authority, as to the guiding principles for this, see below) must make arrangements to allow them to do so and publicize the way in which they can do so. The DfEE guidance encourages LEAs to try and ensure that parents do actually express a preference when applying for a school place and are told of the possible consequences if they do not. There must also be an appeals procedure in place. At the time of writing, an appeals panel can include councillors and school governors, but this will change. There is currently a further right of appeal to the Secretary of

State, but this will be replaced by the independent adjudicator, except in respect of appeals relating to religious denominational criteria.

Each school has a designated standard number and an LEA cannot set a lower limit on the number of places at a school and cannot refuse admission to any pupil until that number has been reached. From September 1999, applications to vary the standard number will be decided locally, but any variation will have to take account of new requirements to reduce class sizes.

As the law stands, parental preference may be ignored if arrangements for admission are based on selection by reference to ability or aptitude with a view to admitting only pupils with high ability or aptitude (Section 10, Education Act 1997, amending Section 411(3)(c) of the Education Act 1996). Partial selection by ability has been permitted in some schools by previous legislation. If a school already operates a system of partial selection, it will be allowed to continue with it, subject to the views of an independent adjudicator, but schools that do not already operate such a system will not be allowed to introduce one. What will be allowed are systems to ensure a fair 'banding' of pupil ability and for schools with a specialism to give priority for admission to up to 10 per cent of children in a relevant age group based on their aptitude for the subject concerned.

Where a child has been permanently excluded from two or more schools, in the two years following the date of last exclusion, parental preference may be ignored (Section 411A, Education Act 1996, inserted by Section 11, Education Act 1997). There is no appeal against a decision to refuse to admit a child to whom this applies, but the governing body of a school may appeal against an LEA decision to admit them.

As far as most county schools are concerned, admissions policy is a matter for their LEA, but the governing body of a school has a right to be consulted on their arrangements each year. They must also publish information about the admissions policy. For voluntary aided and special agreement schools and most grant-maintained schools, the governing body is the admission authority and must consult the LEA about the school's intended policy on admissions.

For the September 2000 intake, the new admissions arrangements must be implemented. These include:

- a statutory Code of Practice giving practical advice on admissions;
- a requirement for admissions authorities to consult with local forums as to admissions policies and arrangements;
- an independent adjudicator to determine disputes between admission authorities over admission policies and practices, including partial selection;
- a requirement for LEAs to publish information about admission arrangements;
- an independent system of appeals against admission decisions.

Home–school agreements

From the beginning of September 1999, Section 110 of the School Standards and Framework Act 1998 requires all maintained schools and city technology colleges to draw up home–school agreements and associated parental declaration. Home–school agreements must set out the school's aims and values, the school's responsibilities towards its pupils, the responsibilities of the pupil's parents and what the school expects of its pupils. The parents will also be expected to sign a declaration to the effect that they acknowledge and accept the parental responsibilities set out in the document.

The DfEE is currently consulting on draft guidance regarding the implementation of home–school agreements that was issued on 29 July 1998. This explains the purpose of the home–school agreement, gives advice about its contents and how to go about introducing them.

The School Standards and Framework Act requires that, before a home–school agreement document is adopted or revised (as it should be at least every two or three years), a governing body must consult the parents of all registered pupils. The guidance refers to case studies of schools that have successfully used a home–school agreement that have also involved consultation with the pupils themselves, and the guidance recommends this practice. It also recommends that the pupils should be encouraged to sign the agreement as well as their parents.

A home–school agreement will not have the status of a contract and the School Standards and Framework Act specifically provides that there can be no liability in contract or tort based on the agreement. In other words, if either a school or parent fails to live up to the terms of the document or their declaration, it will not be possible to take any action in court. Nor should the document contain any terms or conditions that would be unlawful or unreasonable, such as requiring a parent to make a financial contribution to a school or attend an excessive number of meetings.

The guidance gives examples of the sorts of issues that should be covered in an agreement, such as the ethos of the school, punctuality and attendance, discipline and behaviour, homework (there is separate guidance on this last aspect that is due to be finalized in the autumn of 1998) and a procedure for complaints (the complaints procedure is the subject of regulations due to come into force in September 1999).

Essentially the document is a statement of intent. Although a governing body is under a duty to take all reasonable steps to ensure that parents sign the parental declaration, it has no power to compel a parent who is not willing to sign. In particular, it will not be possible to exclude a child or refuse to admit a child to a school because their parents refuse to sign the document.

Preferably both parents should sign the document, but where this is not possible, the parent or other carer who has parental responsibility (as explained earlier in this chapter) should sign it. However, the School Standards and Framework Act specifically allows that a governing body does not have to seek the signature of a parent where they consider that there are special circumstances relating to the parent or the pupil in question that would make it inappropriate to do so. An obvious example is a parent who has abused the child.

What a child is taught

LEAs are under a duty to take account of parents' wishes about their children's education so far as this is compatible with the efficient provision of education and what constitutes reasonable public expenditure (Section 9, Education Act 1996).

Parents also have the right to withdraw their children from religious education and sex education (see Chapter 8).

Frequently asked questions

A father has asked for copies of his child's school reports. The mother has told the school not to let the father see the child or have any information. What should we do?

Tell the father that you intend to speak to the mother and will let him know whether or not there is any legal objection to him having the requested information. Ask the mother to come in to school to discuss the matter and see if there are any relevant court orders and why she objects to the father having information. She may be more concerned that the father does not find out her address than in stopping him from seeing how the child is progressing. You could get round this by providing the report without the address (but do not just use correction fluid or it will probably still be visible).

You should explain to the mother that the father is legally entitled to the information and that you intend to provide it within a certain number of days. She then has the opportunity to go to court if she wishes. It is not your job to give her legal advice – she should go to a lawyer for that. If she has a lawyer already, it may be a good idea to write to them and tell them about the request and what you intend to do unless you hear from them as to why you should not do so within a certain period of time. If the 'parent' requesting the information is not the child's birth father and does not have parental responsibility, you do not have to give him any information at all and you should not do so without the consent of the mother or under a court order.

Chapter 12

Protecting children

Child abuse has a long history. There have been laws passed since mediaeval times to criminalize certain behaviour towards children. As one historian has put it, 'The history of childhood is a nightmare from which we have only begun to awake. The further back in history one goes, the lower the level of child care, and the more likely children are to be killed, abandoned, beaten, terrorized and sexually abused' (Lloyd de Mause, *The History of Childhood*, J Aronson, 1974).

> We have learnt during the Inquiry that sexual abuse occurs in children of all ages, including the very young, to boys as well as girls, in all classes of society and frequently within the privacy of the family.

This was one of the conclusions of the *Report of the Inquiry into Child Abuse in Cleveland 1987*. It is an unfortunate fact of life that children suffer serious harm on a daily basis, most often at the hands of those we would normally expect to care for them best.

Whether or not incidents of child abuse are more frequent than they seemed to be earlier this century is a moot point, and it is not one to be debated in this book. However, Department of Health figures show something of the current nature of the problem. There are approximately 12 million children and young people under the age of 18 in England and Wales. It is estimated that about 160,000 of them are annually the subject of some sort of social services investigation (about 1.3 per cent). During the year ending March 1997, about 43,600 children (about 0.36 per cent) were the subject of child protection conferences and 29,000 (67 per cent) of them were subsequently put on the Child Protection Register. This represented a 3 per cent increase over the previous year's figures (it should be noted that approximately the same number of children came off the Register during the year). Just over half of the children placed on the register were girls. A third of the registrations were made because of risk of physical injury and 21 per cent because of the risk of sexual abuse (60 per cent of children in this category were girls). In terms of organized sexual abuse, it is estimated that this affects some 250 children a year.

In the same year, about 2200 children were made the subject of a supervision order (a decrease of 12 per cent). On 31 March 1997, about 33,500 children were living in foster care and a further 7000 in children's homes.

These figures do not take into account the statistics relating to criminal offences perpetrated on children that do not result in them being separated from their families.

During a teaching career, therefore, you will inevitably encounter children who are suffering abuse in its many forms and there is bound to come a time when it will fall to you to take some sort of action to deal with its consequences.

The Children Act 1989

In terms of your professional responsibilities towards children, it is easiest to think of child abuse in the way it is defined in the Children Act 1989 (referred to as 'the Act' in this chapter). The Act is the main piece of legislation that governs disputes about children, both in terms of disputes between parents and other family members and in terms of disputes between parents and social services about whether or not their care of their children is adequate.

The Act places the main responsibility for protecting children on local authorities, but local authorities may request help in carrying out their protective functions from other authorities, including any LEA. Such a request must be complied with, so long as it is compatible with its own statutory duties and does not unduly prejudice the discharge of its functions. A local authority must consult an LEA and other school representatives in its area before settling its child service plan, setting out how it intends to provide help for children in need in its area.

The Act gives a local authority a number of different ways in which they can both investigate whether or not a child is being properly looked after and take steps to remove a child from a harmful environment if their parent or carer will not cooperate.

Investigation

A local authority must investigate a child's circumstances whenever either a child is made the subject of an emergency protection order or is in police protection or has reasonable cause to suspect that a child in its area is suffering or likely to suffer significant harm. At the conclusion of its enquiries, it must decide whether or not to apply to court for further orders to protect the child. It is specifically required to consult its LEA if appropriate and anyone asked to assist the local authority must do so.

The local authority can also apply to court for a child assessment order in similar circumstances. This is a useful power when a local authority finds a child's parents are uncooperative in having a child medically examined, for example.

Emergency protection

In real emergencies, the police have powers to remove and accommodate a child who would otherwise suffer significant harm, but must notify the local authority at the earliest opportunity that this has been done.

A local authority can apply to court for an emergency protection order if it has reasonable cause to believe that a child will suffer significant harm if not removed or taken away from local authority accommodation after being placed there voluntarily. These orders are very short term and can only last a maximum of eight days, with a possibility of one seven-day renewal.

Care and supervision orders

The local authority can, ultimately, apply to court for a supervision order or a care order. Typically, under a supervision order, a child will remain living at home with their family, but subject to the supervision of the local authority for 12 months and other appropriate conditions. Under a care order, a child is often removed from their family and placed with foster carers and possibly adopted. However, in certain cases, a child continues to live with family members, but the local authority shares parental responsibility and keeps a very close eye on the situation. This often happens when there are tensions within the extended family such that the person caring for the child cannot manage without local authority assistance.

Education supervision orders

These orders can be made in favour of an LEA if a court is satisfied that the child concerned is of compulsory school age but is not being properly educated, which means not receiving efficient full-time education suitable to their age, ability and aptitude and any special educational needs. Under an education supervision order, an LEA's duty is to advise, assist, befriend and give directions to the supervised child and their parents in order to secure that the child is educated. It is a criminal offence for a parent to consistently fail to comply with the directions given.

These orders are surprisingly uncommon and not applied for uniformly throughout the country. It is not clear why this should be, although they did not receive much publicity when they were introduced and knowledge of their existence is patchy. The orders themselves envisage a cooperation from the parents and it may be that that is already being sought outside the context of court proceedings.

Reference has been made above to the notion of 'significant harm', which is the 'entry-level' test for applications to court. 'Significant harm' is defined in the Act as follows:

'harm' means ill treatment or the impairment of health or development;
'development' means physical, intellectual, emotional, social or behavioural development;
'health' means physical or mental health; and
'ill treatment' includes sexual abuse and forms of ill treatment which are not physical.

Where the question of whether or not harm suffered by a child is significant turns on the child's health or development. Their health or development shall be compared with that which could reasonably be expected of a similar child.

Secure accommodation orders

Local authorities also provide secure units that may be used for any child being looked after by an authority and not solely to accommodate young offenders or alleged offenders on remand. They are provided for young people who have a history of absconding from other types of accommodation and are likely to suffer harm if they do abscond or are likely to injure themselves or others if kept in any other form of accommodation.

On 31 March 1997, there were 348 places in secure accommodation units and 290 children securely accommodated. In total, 895 children were admitted into secure accommodation during the preceding year, of whom 9 per cent were re-admissions.

Teachers and inter-agency cooperation

The role of the teaching profession in dealing with child abuse is acknowledged in *Working Together Under the Children Act 1989: A guide to arrangements for inter-agency cooperation for the protection of children from abuse* (Home Office, Department of Health, DfEE 1991). It should be noted that this guidance is under review at the time of writing.

4.35 The education service does not constitute an investigation or intervention agency, but has an important role to play at the recognition and referral stage. Because of their day-to-day contact with individual children during school terms, teachers and other school staff are particularly well placed to observe outward signs of abuse, changes in behaviour or failure to develop. Education welfare officers and educational psychologists also have important roles because of their concern for the welfare and development of children. Youth workers have regular contact with some children, and will therefore also be in a position to help.

4.36 All staff in the education service – including those in grant-maintained and independent schools, sixth-form and further education colleges, and the youth service – should be aware of the need to alert the social services, the NSPCC or the police when they believe a child has been abused or is at risk of abuse. They should refer cases according to the locally established procedures. For the institutions they maintain, local education authorities (LEAs) should seek to ensure that all staff are aware of this and know what the proper procedures are. Social services departments (SSDs) should ensure that educational establishments not maintained by the LEA are aware of the local inter-agency procedures, and the governing bodies/proprietors of these establishments should ensure that appropriate procedures are in place, seeking advice as necessary from the SSD. For all educational establishments, the procedures should cover circumstances where a member of staff is accused or suspected of abuse.

4.37 The key element essential to ensuring that proper procedures are followed in each educational establishment is that the headteacher or another senior member of staff should be designated as having responsibility for liaising with SSDs and other relevant agencies over cases of child abuse. For establishments maintained by them, LEAs should keep up-to-date lists of designated staff and ensure that these staff receive appropriate training and support.

4.38 The relevant school, including nursery school, should be promptly notified by the social services department of the inclusion of a child's name on the Child Protection Register. The details notified should include the care status and placement of the child, the name of the key worker and where possible what information has been made known to the parents about any allegations or suspicions of abuse. Schools will wish to pay particular attention to the attendance and development of such children and the designated teacher should report any cause for further concern to the social services department. The social services department should inform the school of any decision to remove the child from the Child Protection Register and of termination of a care order as well as any change in the status or the placement of the child. The social services department should inform the school when a child who is already on the Child Protection Register starts school. When a child on the Child Protection Register changes school, the information should be transferred between schools immediately and the custodian of the Child Protection Register informed.

4.39 Schools and further education colleges have a role in preventing abuse, not only by adopting sound policies and procedures on the management of situations where there is suspected abuse, but also through the curriculum. They can help pupils and students to acquire relevant information, skills and attitudes, both to resist abuse in their own lives and to prepare them for the responsibilities of their adult lives, including parenthood. Some schools include specific teaching about the risks of child abuse and how pupils can protect themselves, within their personal and social education programmes.

4.40 A number of publications relating to health education and the development of a personal and social education curriculum are already available in schools and address issues related to child protection. More recently, the National Curriculum Council has advised that children aged five years and above should begin to develop skills and practices which will help them to maintain personal safety. It has also identified family life, sex and safety education as three key components of school health education, and has included family life education as a key topic in its advice to schools on education for citizenship. Its Guidance to schools on both health and citizenship suggests ways in which these issues can be integrated into the wider curriculum and topics appropriate to different key stages.

Research by Christine Hallett (*Inter-agency Co-ordination in Child Protection*, HMSO, 1995) shows that teachers and GPs are the professionals who are most 'rarely involved and frequently not well informed' and whose role in inter-agency coordination is the least clear to the other agencies (although they are well respected). Clearly, there is still room for improvement in terms of promoting coordination and training teachers to take up their role fully. It was also noted in the research that care plans (which local authorities must produce to the courts setting out their plans for a child, including where they will live, what medical or psychological provision will be made and what will happen about their education) contained very little information about schooling.

Schools' responses to suspected abuse

Further guidance on the role of teachers in protecting children can be found in DfEE Circular 10/95 – *The Protection of Children from Abuse: The role of the education service.*
In summary:

- every school should have a policy on dealing with situations raising child protection issues and a clear procedure for the referral of concerns to other agencies with responsibility for investigation;
- a named teacher should have responsibility for child protection issues in a school and for coordinating with other agencies, such as social services and the Area Child Protection Committee

(ACPC), which is a coordinating committee set up in each local authority area consisting of representatives from social services, health, police, probation and relevant voluntary-sector bodies;

- priority should be given to attendance at, and reporting to, child protection case conferences and supply cover arranged to enable this;
- proper records should be kept in relation to any child it is suspected has been abused and their progress at school kept under review;
- each local authority should produce local guidance on how child protection procedures work in their area;
- every member of staff should have easy access to the documents setting out the procedures to be followed;
- every member of staff (not just teachers) should know which teacher is responsible for overseeing child protection matters;
- all teachers should receive training in child protection issues on a regular basis;
- records in relation to individual children should be securely stored as there is a greater than usual need to preserve confidentiality;
- the curriculum should include the teaching of materials that will promote children's abilities to keep themselves safe.

Children who are being abused will often exhibit emotional and behavioural disturbance, although this is by no means the only explanation for challenging behaviour. Educational under-achievement may be the explanation as well as the symptom. Clearly it is easier to identify a potentially abused child when their behaviour changes over a short period of time than where this occurs gradually over a period of time, although in the former case this may simply be the result of adolescence and relationship turmoil of a much more innocent variety.

One of the key points arising from the Cleveland Report and other reports on child abuse investigation procedures is that there is a particular technique involved in questioning children in such a way as to maintain a balance between taking the child seriously and acting in a supportive way and carrying out a full and thorough investigation. Recommended practice is set out in the *Memorandum of Good Practice* (HMSO, 1992). This is a long and detailed document. However, teachers are specifically reminded by *Working Together* that they are not an intervention or investigation agency.

In practice, what this means is that teachers must respond carefully and sensitively to any confidential disclosures from children that indicate they are being abused or exploited in some way. f you observe any physical signs indicating that a child has been injured, it is preferable to speak to the named teacher first before seeking any explanation from the child.

Further, if a child volunteers information to you, generally speaking, they must be made aware that there are certain confidences that cannot be kept. There may be a bit more room for manoeuvre when it comes to older children (those aged around 14 or 15), depending on what it is they are telling you. See the discussion on confidentiality in Chapter 8. Government guidance suggests that teachers should err on the side of disclosure rather than preserve confidences. My personal view (and I am not alone) is that a little more discretion can be applied. Revelations of a sexual relationship with a boy their own age might be considered to be in a rather different category from revelations of sexual relations with a much older person or family member, particularly if they are unwanted. In the first circumstance, it may be more appropriate to use persuasion to get the child to talk to someone in the family or a doctor or to give you permission to do so. However, you need to ask yourself why the child is telling you about this if there is no cause for concern.

In most circumstances, all a teacher can promise is that they will tell the child if they have to take matters further and consult them about how this is to be done. It is not easy to get this message across in a sensitive way while at the same time showing empathy. The most important thing to do is to listen attentively and not try to ask a lot of questions. If you do need to ask questions, keep them as open as possible, avoiding putting suggestions into the child's mind. 'Who is it who is upsetting you?' rather than 'Is it your dad who's been doing this?' Stop the conversation as soon as you feel you have understood the gist of the child's problem.

As soon as any apparent disclosures have been made, a teacher should contact the named teacher responsible for child protection issues in the school (or a member of senior management if the named teacher is not available) who can advise on how best to follow the matter up. Do not delay or you will risk forgetting to do it altogether or some vital details.

You may feel apprehensive about starting the wheels of an express train in motion, but this is not an inevitable consequence of telling the named teacher what has happened. It may be enough simply to note the concern and ask other members of staff to keep a special eye on the child. Also, just because social services become involved with a family does not inevitably mean that this will lead to care proceedings and criminal charges.

On a practical note, you should make a note of what was said to you at the earliest opportunity, sign it, date it and put it on file. Information about abuse does not have to be revealed to parents along with the rest of the file (see Chapter 10).

Allegations about colleagues

Such allegations may be particularly difficult to deal with on a personal level, but you must make a special effort to put aside any feelings that might cause you to minimize the significance of what a child is telling you. A DfEE survey in 1994 concluded that about 46 per cent of complaints made by children about staff members had some basis in fact, but a far lower percentage resulted in any court action. There are all sorts of reasons for a child not to be telling the truth in the context of the school (particularly a residential school) environment, but, equally, some abusers can be very convincing and charming to other adults.

Allegations about staff members should be treated in just the same way as any other allegation of abuse and the exact same procedures should be followed. Especially if the allegation is a serious one, you must resist the temptation to talk to your colleague about what you have been told and leave it to the normal channels to decide how to respond.

The *Working Together* guidelines specifically encourage those in residential establishments to make sure that children know who they can talk to when they have any worries about staff members or other problems. This is an issue that should be dealt with in all schools as part of their overall pastoral care responsibilities. A school must also ensure that teachers' own observations of inappropriate behaviour are treated seriously and that those reporting concerns are not victimized in any way.

Most importantly, a school policy should deal with this issue so that staff are clear about what is expected of them and what is likely to happen.

Clearly it is sensible, given the amount of contact between teachers and children, for you to give some consideration to your own behaviour to ensure that it is appropriate. This does not mean that you can never touch a child or be alone in a room with them, but you should exercise good judgment in school, just as you would in your personal lives.

In Chapter 6, I referred to the maintenance of List 99. Schools and LEAs are required to check against this list before employing a teacher or other member of staff. From 1 August 1998 it has also been necessary for teacher employment agencies and businesses and organizations that provide services involving regular contact with young people under 19 (such as catering, cleaning, school maintenance and transport) to make the same checks (Education (Teachers) Regulations 1993, as amended). Even volunteers have to be checked.

Bullying

In a 1998 survey, about 10 per cent of pupils in a sample of secondary schools reported being bullied in the last year and 17 per cent admitted to having picked on others. Childline reports that 1 in 4 of all its calls (about 10,000 a year) are from children suffering from bullying. It is obviously a serious problem that is blighting the lives of children and they are particularly vulnerable at school (of course, so are teachers and this is dealt with in Chapter 5).

Bullying can take many forms, from threats to actual violence, to merciless 'teasing'. It is a significant factor in truanting (30 per cent of children in one survey claimed to be put off going to school because of bullying). It may cause as many as 12 young people a year to commit suicide. It can be a problem both within schools and between schools or between current and former pupils.

While the subject is given only a passing reference in Circular 10/95 on child protection, it is dealt with more fully in a separate DfEE publication produced in conjunction with Sheffield University – *Don't Suffer in Silence* (DfEE, 1994). In December 1995, the Home Office also produced a resource pack for schools – *Preventing School Bullying: Things you can do*. There are various excellent publications about what schools can do to deal with bullying, including a BBC booklet – *Bullying: A survival guide* – and a great deal of information is available from voluntary-sector organizations such as Kidscape, the Anti-Bullying Campaign and Childline. Information about relevant publications and the addresses of these organizations is given in the Useful addresses and Further reading sections at the back of the book.

It is now a specific statutory requirement that a headteacher should determine measures that, among other things, prevent all forms of bullying among pupils (Section 61(4)(b) of the School Standards and Framework Act 1998).

Typically, the recommended strategies include:

- surveying children to find out what their current experience of bullying is in order to identify key areas for improvement;
- developing systems for improving security at certain flashpoints, such as the school gate and quiet areas on site;
- outlawing the bringing of certain items into school.

There should be a well-publicized written policy and children should be clear about who they should talk to when they have a problem – this could perhaps be a nominated confidential contact. It is widely accepted that the whole school needs to be involved, as with most strategies concerning behaviour and safety. It can be addressed in lessons, too, both to raise awareness and promote the children's self-confidence to use self-help measures. It will also be necessary to improve teacher training on intervention in violent incidents and the discussion above about restraining pupils is relevant.

In the last two years, there has been a wealth of publicity concerning cases in which children have recovered damages from LEAs because they have been psychologically damaged by their experience of bullying at school. Unfortunately, it is not easy to give clear guidance on what schools or LEAs need to do to prevent court action in this area. One thing is clear – you must be doing something.

Bullying is now a well-documented and researched problem about which there is no shortage of advice. In my view, any school that does not have a policy and strategy for dealing with it will be at risk. It will not be enough to demonstrate simply that there is a written policy. A court will expect to see real efforts being made to implement it, not just a big bang followed by the usual fizzling out of interest. Systems must be monitored and revised as appropriate.

Any strategy should cover the recording of complaints. The extent of a problem may not be apparent until two or three pupils complain about the same individual. A judgement will need to be made in all cases, however. Some sorts of behaviour will need to be met with immediate action.

The most likely cause of litigation occurs when teachers or schools ignore any specific complaints made by pupils. A pupil who is the victim of bullying is already frightened and vulnerable and will be terrified about the consequences of speaking out and they need to be reassured about what will happen to them if they pursue a complaint. They may be tempted to minimize the problem so that they are not seen to be getting the bully into too much trouble. Efforts should be made to find out just how much of a problem it has been. Often, by the time a pupil speaks out, they may be at the end of their tether. It is vital to have a good follow-up procedure as well to ensure that the problem really has been dealt with and that worse recriminations have not followed.

A particularly tricky area is the need to balance protection for the bullied against the provision of education for the bully, particularly given the governmental pressure to reduce exclusion rates. Advice and help may need to be enlisted from an education welfare officer, educational psychologists, social workers, police and so on as to whether or not the behaviour can be contained within the school or the pupil must go elsewhere. Any disagreement between a teacher, school and local education authority should be carefully recorded.

It may be tempting for a school to try and cover its position in all circumstances by recommending a child's removal from the school. I think this is unnecessarily defensive. If court action did arise, a court would hear evidence about all the factors that went into the decision-making process and should be made aware of the rock and the hard place between which educators have to steer. Equally, a court should be made aware of any resource difficulties, if these are pertinent.

From 1 April 1998, LEAs have been obliged by law to develop a written behaviour support plan, setting out, among other things, what provision they make of advice and resources to schools for promoting good behaviour and discipline and dealing with pupils with behavioural problems (The Local Education Authority (Behaviour Support Plans) Regulations 1998 (SI 98/644). Every school is to be consulted about the plan. A behaviour support plan is expected to cover all sorts of problem areas – truancy, exclusions, bullying, racism, inter-agency liaison, training and so on.

Your school should have a copy of the plan and whoever is responsible for child protection issues should be completely familiar with the local policy and resources available.

Children in employment

There have been restrictions on the employment of young people since Regulations made in 1933 that, over the years, have been tightened up, including the development of new regulations – the Children (Protection at Work) Regulations 1998. These came into force on 4 August 1998 and implement a European directive. From now on, children may only be employed if:

- they are over 14, unless they are:
  - employed by a parent or guardian;
  - in light agricultural or horticultural work on an occasional basis;
  - employed in work specifically permitted as suitable by local authority by-laws (children above 13 only) and the by-laws must themselves comply with the European directive.
  - they are only employed to do light work, which is work that is not likely to be harmful to the safety, health or development of children and will not be harmful to school attendance or their ability to gain from education received or other work experience;
  - the employer has obtained a licence from the LEA to employ a young person – this applies to all children of compulsory school age, whether or not the work is paid, if it is work done for a commercial enterprise.

The hours of work are also restricted:

- if under 15, children may only work for a maximum of 5 hours in any non-school day (not including Sunday when they may only work for 2 hours) and may only work for a maximum of 25 hours in any non-school week;
- if under 18, young people may only work for a maximum of 8 hours on any non-school day and for a maximum of 35 hours in any non-school week;
- no young person should have to work for more than four hours without a break;
- children cannot be expected to start work before 7 am or work for more than an hour before school or finish after 7 pm.

Children must also be allowed to have at least two consecutive weeks in which they are neither employed nor attending school.

There are special rules relating to children who work in the entertainment field, which includes working in advertising, cabaret, film, modelling, musicals and other theatrical shows and cultural events, sports and television and performing arts. Schools are subject to special regulations. All such work must be licensed by an LEA. Participation in dangerous performances (performances endangering life and limb) of any kind are prohibited. A chaperon must accompany a child undertaking this sort of work and there are specific requirements as to working hours and breaks.

Research carried out by the Low Pay Unit in 1998 found that some children are working as much as 29 hours a week during school time, some being paid as little as 33p per hour. Also that 25 per cent were employed before the minimum age allowed (then 13) and nearly half had suffered some kind of injury at work in the previous year – 10 per cent had needed medical treatment as a result. Extrapolating from these figures to gauge what the national situation is, as many as 1.5 million children could be working illegally out of a total of 2 million children who work.

A survey carried out by Save the Children in 1998 estimated that around 80 per cent of children who work do so illegally, which is very much in line with the Low Pay Unit's research. The majority of employers had not obtained licences and many children started working before the age of 13 (the age is now 14) and before 7 am.

A major problem is that local authorities say they simply do not have the resources to enforce the law in this area. However, it is recognized that if pupils are working for more than ten hours a week, this has a damaging effect on their ability to make the most of school. In some cases, the flouting of the law has much more serious consequences. Employers who do not apply for a licence may find that their insurance policies do not cover the young people they employ, as happened in the case of a 14-year-old boy who was knocked off his bicycle when delivering newspapers. Children may be working in workplaces that are not appropriate for their abilities and injuries may occur.

Further improvements to the law in this area are being considered, but there are doubts as to what their potential effectiveness will be unless more resources are allocated to enforcement measures. An LEA can serve a notice on employers banning them from employing a child, which can result in criminal proceedings if breached. In the meantime, schools have an important contribution to make in supporting children as best they can and making sure they are not exploited. In particular, schools can ensure that pupils do not absent themselves from school in order to work and can report any information about unreasonable working hours or conditions to their LEA.

If an employer does employ a young person (for this purpose, a 'young person' is anyone under the age of 18) the Health and Safety (Young Persons) Regulations 1997 (SI 1997/135) provide that an employer must either make or review their normal risk assessment of the workplace to take into account any special risks that might be posed to, or result from, the employment of a young person. Special factors to consider are:

- the inexperience, lack of awareness of risk and immaturity of young persons;
- the fitting out and layout of the workplace and workstation;
- the nature, degree and duration of exposure to physical, biological and chemical agents;
- the form, range and use of work equipment and the way in which it is handled;
- the organization of processes and activities;
- the extent of the health and safety training provided or to be provided to young persons;
- the presence of a particular list of dangerous substances or processes set out in an EU directive (94/33/EC), which includes radiation, high pressure, carcinogenic substances, lead, asbestos and so on and dangerous or poisonous animals.

The conclusions of a risk assessment should be provided to the child's parents (that is, parent with parental responsibility).

In addition, an employer should ensure that any young person is protected at work from a risk due to their lack of experience, awareness or immaturity and should not employ a young person for work that:

- is beyond their physical or psychological capacity;
- involves harmful exposure to toxic agents or radiation;
- involves the risk of accidents that the young person would not be likely to foresee due to lack of attention to safety issues, lack of experience or lack of training.

There are some excepted types of employment to which these Regulations do not apply – domestic work in a private house and non-dangerous work for a family business, for example.

Work experience

Work experience is specifically exempted from the Regulations mentioned above and does not count as employment as such. Rather, it is considered part of a pupil's educational provision. The Secretary of State is to use powers to allow amendments to the National Curriculum at Key Stage 4 (to drop up to two subjects from modern languages, design and technology or science) to enable individual students to take more advantage of work-related training opportunities, and the Qualifications and Curriculum Authority is coordinating the initiative. It has published a booklet – *Learning from Work Experience – A guide to successful practice*.

DfEE Circular 11/97 – *School Leaving Date for 16-year-olds* – also refers to work experience as follows:

> A child may participate in approved work experience activities during the last four terms of compulsory schooling, i.e. from the summer term of Year 10 .... Under proposals recently sent out for consultation, approved work experience placements would come under a new registration category of 'approved educational activity' and no longer count as authorized absence. Other supervised activities such as field trips, educational visits, approved sporting activities and link courses would also come under the category.

It also reminds schools:

> While children are of compulsory school age, they may not be employed full time. They are, however, free to undertake a range of part-time jobs. All children of compulsory school age who choose to work part-time must be registered with the local education authority. For further details consult your Education Welfare Service.

Work experience placements should not involve any activity for which there is an age restriction, such as that using certain types of factory machinery (Section 558, Education Act 1996).

Although work experience does not count as employment as such, Regulations provide that the Health and Safety at Work Act 1974 (and, therefore, Regulations made under that Act) shall apply as if the child was an employee (Health and Safety (Training for

Employment) Regulations 1990 (SI 1990/1380)). This means that if any of the Regulations are breached and an injury to a child results, an action may be brought against an employer. The question of whether or not an employer might be liable under common law would depend on whether or not a court accepted that the employer owed a duty of care in this situation (even though the child was not technically an employee). In my view, a court would be likely to do that, but it would not preclude a liability also being owed by the school. There are as yet no authoritative reported cases where a child has been injured during work experience, so it is not entirely clear whether or not the courts would place the primary responsibility for the pupil's safety with the school or the 'employer'. There is a case of an accident in 1997, when a child on work experience on a farm fell into a grain silo and was killed. A Health and Safety Executive investigation is underway, but has been temporarily suspended pending the possible bringing of criminal proceedings against the employer. The investigation report may give a clue to how the division of responsibilities will be perceived at law.

As indicated earlier, it seems likely to me that schools could be liable, in principle, for negligence if an injury occurred, so best practice would be to act as if a school might be primarily liable. A school should certainly monitor an employer's health and safety practices carefully, inspect the workplace (or get the LEA to do so) and follow the guidelines given in the literature below, taking advice from the education welfare service, local TEC and the HSE as appropriate.

Another point to bear in mind is insurance. Work experience will generally be covered if the placement is for a period of up to two weeks – anything longer might not be and a check should be made with the insurance company. It is important to notify the insurance company of any planned placements on every occasion. As a result of an agreement with the Association of British Insurers and others, pupils and teachers on placements will be treated as if they were employees for the purposes of insurance against personal injury – that is, they will be covered by an employers' liability policy, provided the insurer has been notified about the activity.

Further guidance is contained in two DfEE booklets – *Work Experience: A guide for schools* and *Work Experience: A guide for employers*, both published in 1996. A useful book produced with DfEE support is *Work Experience and the Law* by Anthony Johns, Centre for Education and Industry, Warwick University (for address, see the Useful addresses section at the back of the book).

For other matters relating to a child's safety in school, on school trips or in the workplace, please refer to Chapter 14.

Frequently asked questions

A child in my class has made a strange remark in an essay about not liking his PE teacher because he says funny things and touches him. What should I do?

A very tricky situation. On the surface of it, this remark could either concern quite innocent behaviour and a misinterpretation on the child's side or something more sinister. You need to try and see the remark in the fullest possible context. What do you know about the teacher concerned? Have you heard anything along these lines before? Do you know anything about the relationship between the teacher and that particular child? Does the child enjoy PE? Is there any cultural background that might make any sort of touching offensive to that particular child? Is the child generally reliable? Are there any other features of the child's behaviour that worry you?

Once you have thought all this over, there are several options and you will have to use your judgement to decide which one you will take. You might say nothing, but keep an eye on the child and on the teacher. You might want to take someone else into your confidence to see if they have any concerns about either the child or the teacher. You might want to let the named person know so they can at least file it at the back of their mind for future reference. What you should probably not do is tackle the teacher concerned. If they have done nothing to reproach themselves with, they are simply going to be offended, no matter how sensitively you approach them. If they are up to no good, then you will simply be forewarning them so they can start preparing a defence. You might consider making sure the child concerned has an opportunity to discuss matters with you or someone else in private, but bear in mind all that has been said about confidentiality and tainting evidence.

Chapter 13

An assault course – assault, punishment and discipline

Threats and physical assault

Before looking at assaults in a school context it is necessary to examine the general law relating to assaults.

First, an assault may be both a criminal and a civil wrong (tort).

Criminal assault

In terms of criminal law, there are two main types of offence – assault and battery.

A common 'assault' can be defined as any act by which the perpetrator intentionally or recklessly causes the victim to apprehend immediate and unlawful violence.

A 'battery' is any act by which the perpetrator intentionally or recklessly inflicts unlawful personal violence on the victim.

In other words, an assault may not actually involve physical touching – it is enough if the victim thinks they are going to be hurt in some way, whereas a battery involves actual touching and injury. If you threaten to hit someone and then you do so, you have committed two criminal offences. It is not, however, an offence 'just' to insult someone. Nothing short of a threat to harm will do (in fact, there is also a separate offence of 'threats to kill') and probably nothing short of a face-to-face threat – in other words, a threat over the telephone would not be an assault (although it could be a different criminal offence).

In practice, the offences are often treated and referred to inter-changeably.

The word 'reckless' has been the subject of much case law. In some cases (usually where, for the offence to be proved, an element of maliciousness must be proved), for a person to be guilty of an offence, they must have known that there was a risk of some sort of harm but taken the risk anyway for reasons that are not considered by the law to be justifiable. In other cases, a court will say that someone is reckless when the risk would be obvious to any reason-able person and the accused either takes the risk for some legally unjustifiable reason or does not stop to think about the risk at all. An example of recklessness that for some reason springs to my mind in 1998 is suggested by Glanville Williams in an elderly text-book on criminal law. It is that of the man who lies on the ground (say a football pitch) and kicks out at random towards other people around him. 'He may have hoped to hurt someone, but anyway is reckless.'

The sort of physical act that is required for an offence of assault or battery to be proved is an intentional touching of another person without the consent of that person and without lawful excuse. It need not necessarily be 'hostile, or rude, or aggressive'.

The courts have, however, decided that quite a lot of touching is lawfully excusable because it is impliedly consented to by society. For example, in the case of *Collins* v *Wilcock* [1984] 3 All ER 375, Lord Justice Goff said:

> Generally speaking, consent is a defence to battery; and most of the physical contacts of ordinary life are not actionable because they are im-pliedly consented to by all who move in society and so expose themselves to the risk of bodily contact. So nobody can complain of the jostling which is inevitable from his presence in, for example, a supermarket, an underground station or a busy street; nor can a person who attends a party complain if his hand is seized in friendship, or even his back is (within reason) slapped.

Jostling in a school corridor would therefore clearly come within the range of legally acceptable behaviour! So will tapping a pupil on the shoulder to attract their attention.

There are a number of other reasons courts have decided will amount to an excuse for behaviour that might otherwise constitute an assault:

- actual consent – although this will not amount to an excuse for extremely violent behaviour or behaviour that the courts consider to be morally reprehensible, such as some forms of sado-masochistic sexual practices;
- reasonable actions – those necessary to prevent some (usually more or apparently more) serious evil, such as personal injury, such as pushing someone out of the path of an oncoming bus;
- lawful correction of children (more on this later);
- actions to protect yourself from harm;
- the use of reasonable force to prevent a crime or assist in a lawful arrest.

The last example begs the question 'What sort of force or action is reasonable?' You do not use jewellers' scales to measure reasonable force. What is reasonable will depend on all the surrounding circumstances, such as:

- whether or not a person should and could have opted for flight rather than fight;
- the seriousness of the harm that the assault was designed to prevent – violence is much more likely to be justified if it occurred as a means to prevent greater violence than to prevent damage to property;
- how much time there was to think about the response options;
- what other options were available – for example, help from others, distraction.

Response time is an important factor. As Lord Morris put it in the case of *Palmer* v *R* [1971] 1All ER 1077:

> If there has been an attack so that defence is reasonably necessary it will be recognized that a person defending himself cannot weigh to a nicety the exact measure of his necessary defensive action. If a jury thought that in a moment of unexpected anguish a person attacked had only done what he honestly and instinctively though was necessary, that would be the most potent evidence that only reasonable defensive action had been taken.

There are several other specific criminal assault charges – threats to kill, malicious wounding with intent to cause grievous bodily harm, maliciously wounding or inflicting grievous bodily harm and so on.

The charge that is brought will usually depend on the prosecution's perception of the deliberateness of the action that resulted in the injury. Did the person carrying it out intend serious injury all along? Were they 'merely' trying to frighten someone and the situation got totally out of control? For example, D is in the middle of an argument with V and making threats to harm V. V jumps out of a window in order to escape the threatened attack. Even though D did not lay a finger on V, there are a number of assault charges that might be brought against D.

There are also several other related criminal offences that may be committed and involve injury to the person without any deliberate effort to cause or threaten injury. An example of this would be failing to comply with various requirements of the Health and Safety Act 1974, the Regulations under it and related health and safety legislation, and manslaughter.

Civil assault

The same sorts of act that constitute criminal assault and battery will usually amount to civil wrongs – the tort of trespass to the person – as well. As such, they may be the foundation for an action for damages being brought in a civil court. It has to be said that such actions are rare and, generally, where there are criminal proceedings for the same offence, civil proceedings cannot be pursued. Trespass actions, for example, have most commonly been used in quasi-family situations in order to get a court to award an injunction, but new law on domestic violence should make this even less common. The civil remedy is sometimes used where a prosecution is not pursued for some reason, perhaps because the evidence is not quite enough to meet the higher standard of proof required in the criminal courts.

Children and crime

Until July 1998, children below the age of 14 were given special protection in criminal courts. The law presumed that a child below the age of 14 was incapable of committing a crime because they were considered too young to form an intention to commit a criminal act. If the prosecuting authority wanted to take action against a young person, it had to be able to prove, beyond a reasonable doubt, that the particular child knew that what it had done was seriously wrong.

With effect from 31 July 1998, that rule was abolished so that any child above the age of 10 is presumed to be capable of criminal acts (Crime and Disorder Act 1998, Section 34). This does not mean that they will always be deemed capable. In the same way that the prosecution can attempt to prove that a child knew what it was doing (and they will still have to in relation to a child below the age of 10), a child's lawyers can attempt to prove that a particular child, although aged 10 or over, was not sufficiently mature to understand the consequences of their actions. In order to do this, they will only have to meet the civil burden of proof – that is, the balance of probabilities.

This will obviously make it easier to prosecute children aged between 10 and 14. It will also help in situations where an adult uses force against a child in order to prevent a crime being committed as there is much less scope than in the past for arguing that as a child could not commit a crime, it could not be reasonable to use force against them (not that this was ever a well-respected argument).

If a pupil does commit a crime, they are susceptible to proceedings, just as a teacher is, although they will usually be dealt with in a special court called a youth court where proceedings are relatively informal and powers of punishment are limited. The authorities may also consider responding by a number of other means, such as by initiating care proceedings or applying for secure accommodation orders (for more on these, see Chapter 12).

Assault or lawful punishment?

Corporal punishment
Since 1987 (at the latest), corporal punishment has been banned in any State school or one receiving financial assistance from the State or towards any pupil in a fee-paying school, the fees for which are met from public funds.

The Education Act 1996 restricted corporal punishment in independent schools, but has now been amended to completely outlaw it in all types of school (Section 548, as amended by Section 31 of the School Standards and Framework Act 1998). This has come about largely because of pressure from the European courts in the wake of one or two well-publicized cases.

It is no longer acceptable for a teacher or other member of staff to administer corporal punishment (that is to say, any degree of physical contact that is deliberately intended to punish a pupil or primarily intended to cause pain, injury or humiliation), either in a school or in any place where the child is being educated. This will not apply to parents educating or otherwise dealing with children at home (the Government is consulting on the issue of parental chastisement, but has indicated that smacking will not be outlawed). In other words, it will not affect how teachers punish their own children in a home environment.

'Corporal punishment' includes any type of punishment that would amount to a battery (see above). It is specifically stated that it will not include any act done with a view to avoiding personal injury or danger to property.

Restraining pupils

The defences referred to above, in which avoiding danger by the use of reasonable force and so on has always been available to teachers, just as they are to anyone else acting in this way. For some reason, teachers in the past 20 or so years have felt vulnerable about any behaviour involving touching a pupil, some even believing it had been forbidden by law. No doubt the sense of vulnerability is partly a consequence of the job itself, as there are few situations in which children and adults are thrown together so regularly and in such quantities. In fact, it has never been the case that any touching in a teaching context is unlawful, although touching should never be inappropriately sexual or unreasonably forceful. In fact, there have been very few (and certainly very few successful) prosecutions of teachers.

In an attempt to clarify the position, the Education Act 1997 (Section 4) adds a new section to the Education Act 1996 – Section 550A – dealing with the power of members of staff to restrain pupils in appropriate circumstances. This Section has been in force since 1 September 1998. It allows any member of staff (defined as meaning any person who has lawful control of the children, so could include classroom assistants, midday supervisors, caretakers and so on) to use such force as is reasonable in the circumstances to prevent a pupil from:

- committing any offence;
- causing personal injury to anyone;
- causing damage to anyone's property;
- engaging in behaviour prejudicial to the maintenance of good order and discipline at the school or among the pupils.

This applies on or off school premises.

It is specifically stated that in talking about the use of force to prevent an offence being committed, it does not matter whether a child is below the age of criminal responsibility (now 10) or not, although it is to be hoped that it would rarely be an issue in practice. It is likely that the younger and smaller the child concerned, the less force will be considered reasonable, except in extreme situations.

In addition, the DfEE in July 1998 published new guidelines on this subject after consultation with the unions and others (Circular 10/98 – *Section 550A of the Education Act 1996: The use of force to control or restrain pupils*). They emphasize that in taking action to restrain pupils, it is essential that a teacher does not appear to lose their temper or act out of anger or frustration to punish a pupil (so it seems likely that any form of slapping or striking of the face or head should be avoided). Restrictive holds are considered acceptable only in 'extreme' circumstances. The methods of restraint more usually acceptable include blocking the pupil's path, holding, pushing, pulling, leading the pupil away by the hand or arm, or with a hand at the centre of the back. methods to be avoided include holding a pupil around the neck, twisting or forcing limbs against a joint, tripping a pupil up, holding or pulling a pupil by the hair or ear and holding a pupil face down on the ground. Ideally, a teacher should tell a pupil to stop the offending behaviour and let them know what will happen if they do not. Any restraint technique should stop as soon as the offending behaviour stops or the immediate danger is past. It should not be used in a situation where a pupil is trying to leave the classroom or school, unless they could be at risk from doing so.

The NUT has supported this guidance, but the NASUWT has been a little more cautious, fearing that more intervention by teachers will actually provoke violence rather than prevent it. The obvious risk is that a teacher may end up getting hurt. Indeed, the guidance specifically reminds teachers that there may be times when a teacher should not intervene without help and suggests that, in those circumstances, help should be summoned and other pupils removed from the scene. The guidance also suggests that a written record should be kept of any incident in which a teacher has had to use force, unless of a trivial nature.

This new guidance will not do away altogether with the threat of misplaced complaints or prosecutions against teachers, with all the stress that will entail, but it marks a public recognition of what, in my view, has been the law for some time. A teacher's response to violent incidents is much more likely to be an issue in considering whether or not the offending pupil's exclusion is justified than to result in criminal proceedings. Further guidance on strategies for restraining pupils is expected, with a consultation draft to be issued in spring 1999.

False imprisonment

As with assault, false or wrongful imprisonment may be both a civil wrong and a criminal offence.

It is commonly defined as the unlawful and intentional or reckless restraint of a person's freedom. Some forms of false imprisonment may be obvious. A police officer who locks someone in a cell when they have done nothing wrong and are not in any danger will be guilty of false imprisonment. However, it can be much less obvious. In theory at least, it does not even matter whether or not the 'prisoner' knows that they are being restrained. It can be false imprisonment simply to leave someone with the impression that they are not free to leave in some situations or to pretend that they are locked in when they are not.

In the school context, it is most relevant to the question of whether or not a detention is lawful. Detentions, like all punishments, must be reasonable and moderate. To hold someone in detention for an excessively long time or for a trivial misdemeanour may be a false imprisonment. In one County court case, a judge found that it was not lawful to detain the whole class when only one unidentified pupil had actually done something wrong (*Terrington v Lancashire County Council* 1986).

To avoid falling foul of the law on false imprisonment, schools have had to devise elaborate systems for obtaining parental consent to detentions, which have not always met with parental approval.

In an attempt to put an end to the constant threat of legal action that schools have faced over detentions, a new section has been included in the Education Act 1996 – Section 550B, inserted by Section 5 of the Education Act 1997. It came into force on 1 September 1998. As Lord Henley put it in the Lords debate on the subject on 14 February 1997:

> Schools will for the first time be given explicit statutory authority to detain badly behaved pupils after school without their parents' consent. That will ensure that detention as a sanction is more readily available, free of the potential risk of legal action against the school for false imprisonment.

It is true that this is the first time the written law has authorized detention, but Section 550B is not much different from the guidance that the DfEE had previously issued on the subject of detentions.

Needless to say, it is not quite as simple as Lord Henley seems to suggest. The law now allows a pupil (at a maintained, grant-maintained or grant-maintained special school or city technology college) to be kept at school after the end of the normal school day without specific consent from the parents if:

- the headteacher has notified both parents and pupils in advance in general terms that detention is a punishment that may be imposed on pupils;
- the headteacher or someone else authorized by them has imposed the detention as a punishment;
- it is reasonable in all the circumstances;
- the parent has been given at least 24 hours' notice in writing that the detention will take place.

The DfEE guidance referred to suggested that 24 hours' notice should be given in the case of any detention lasting over 30 minutes. The new law means that even a shorter period of detention will only automatically be lawful if 24 hours' notice is given unless the parents' consent to a lesser period has been obtained.

Further qualification is added to explain when a detention will be considered reasonable:

- it has to be in proportion with the circumstances of the case;
- before imposing it as a punishment, consideration has been given to any special factors relating to the pupil's age, special educa-

tional needs, religious requirements and arrangements to travel home.

Like all other documents, notice to the parents in writing may either be hand delivered, sent by post or left at the parent's address. The Section also says that any other effective method could be used. In theory, it could be sent by pupil post, but there is always the risk that it will not be delivered. I would recommend that if pupil post is used, the school should make sure that the letter has come to the parents' attention. Sending the notice by fax, where possible, would also probably be accepted. One case has held that court documents are considered to be served from the moment they enter the memory of a fax machine, but that was in the context of service in a solicitors' office – that is, in a legal/commercial environment. In a school context, however, it may be as well to seek some sort of confirmation that the parent has actually received the fax. Communications by e-mail are not yet generally approved by the courts. It might be acceptable to send an e-mail to a parent, but I would not recommend relying on it without asking the parent to confirm receipt.

Confiscation of property

The waters of the law on when a teacher might be justified in confiscating a pupil's property are much muddier. There are some items that must be taken from a pupil, for example, any dangerous items or unlawful materials, such as drugs or pornography and they should be handed over to the police as soon as possible.

Taking someone's property away might be considered to be theft, although, in my view, this would be difficult to prove in a school context. Theft is defined as the dishonest appropriation of property belonging to another with intention to permanently deprive that other and it seems unlikely that all the elements would be proved, as they would have to be. Even if a teacher were to take away an annoying toy from a pupil, intending never to give it back, it would be difficult to see how this could be construed as dishonest behaviour on the teacher's part.

As with assault, there is a civil equivalent to theft called 'trespass to goods', which might be described as a wrongful physical interference with them and will most obviously be proved when someone else's belongings are taken and the person who took them refuses to give them back. It may also be actionable to allow goods to be damaged or destroyed when you are looking after them for someone.

In any event, punishment by confiscation must be reasonable and moderate, as for all other punishment.

For all these reasons, it is not a good idea to take property away and keep it for too long, particularly if it is valuable. Some have suggested that property should be returned at the end of the school day. I think this is too rigid, although it may be best practice. In some circumstances, it will be necessary to involve the pupil's parent and that may take a little time to set up. It is obviously sensible to make sure that parents are told whether or not certain items should not be brought to school at all and what is likely to happen if they are or even to seek their specific consent to confiscation of prohibited articles. It is equally advisable, although it may not always be practical, to set aside a safe place at the school where confiscated items can be kept (especially mobile phones).

In practice, I suspect that this is one of those issues that causes a huge headache on a day-to-day basis, but rarely results, if ever, in any legal action being taken. However, with the implementation of complaints systems in schools it is not a headache that is going to be easily cured. It is likely to be further complicated by the introduction of human rights law into the arena.

Searches

Since September 1996, it has been an arrestable offence to carry a knife or other offensive weapon on school premises (Section 4, Offensive Weapons Act 1996). The Act also extends police powers of search in respect of weapons on school premises. Further guidance on police/school liaison was being prepared during the course of 1998 by the DfEE.

There is no reported case that sets out clearly whether or not a teacher is entitled either to search a pupil or their property, such as a locker. If a pupil will not consent to show a teacher the contents of pockets and the like, I would not suggest forcing the issue without involving their parents, unless there is a suspicion of possession of something dangerous, in which case the police should be involved. The risk is that there may be an allegation of assault.

Searching property is less risky in theory. If a school has allowed a pupil the use of a storage space, it may be possible to argue that it is a condition of the use that the pupil is deemed to consent to searches (so long as they are reasonable and provided damage is not done to property). Personal belongings are trickier as getting hold of them without consent may involve an assault. These matters should be dealt with in the school's behaviour/discipline policy, but in general terms a teacher would be extremely ill-advised to resort to force. In time, this may become a 'rights' issue when there is a Human Rights Act, but, at the time of writing, there is no recognized 'right' to privacy.

Exclusions

More than 2 million school days are lost each year as a result of exclusions. Out of a total school population of 8.3 million pupils, there were 12,500 permanent exclusions in the 1995/96 school year and 12,700 permanent exclusions in the 1996/7 school year. Overall, there were 137,000 temporary exclusions during 1996–97.

The law relating to exclusions is now contained in Sections 64ff and Schedule 18 of the School Standards and Framework Act 1998. Exclusions may only be fixed or permanent. Parents (or the pupil if over 18) must be informed about the exclusion, its length and the reasons for it without delay and they must be specifically told of their right to a review by the governing body. If a pupil is either permanently excluded, excluded for a total of five days in any term or will miss an exam as a result of the exclusion, a headteacher must inform both the governing body and the LEA without delay, giving the reasons for the exclusion.

If a parent asks a governing body to review an exclusion decision, the governing body listens to representations from the school and the parent. A representative of the LEA is entitled to be present. The governing body will either uphold the exclusion or direct that the child be reinstated, either immediately or on a particular date. If the governing body directs reinstatement, that is the end of the matter. If they do not, then they must follow a similar procedure as the headteacher and they must specifically tell the parent about their right to appeal to the LEA and the procedure for doing so.

Appeals are heard by a specially constituted panel of the LEA, which has similar powers to a governing body to order reinstatement or not. Schedule 18 sets out the appeals procedures in more detail, giving the time limits and details of the membership of the appeals panel, the hearing procedure and so on. Appeal hearings are normally held in private, although an LEA observer and an observer from the Council on Tribunals may attend. Parents may be represented by a friend or nominated advocate.

DfEE Circular 10/94 – *Exclusions from School* – expands on the procedure and the operating principles to be applied in dealing with exclusions. It deliberately steers away from giving examples of the sorts of behaviour that might justify exclusion as the whole emphasis is on taking into account a whole range of factors and weighing them in the balance before coming to a conclusion. The Circular also stresses the desirability of involving other agencies, particularly where a child has special educational needs. The panel Chair has a wide discretion on how the hearing is conducted, but should follow the Code of Practice and ensure that a clerk is present for the hearing.

One of the important things to remember about the hearing is that the principles of natural justice apply. This means that the person involved in the incident that gives rise to the question of exclusion should not be the one who makes the decision. Indeed, one exclusion decision was quashed on judicial review because a teacher governor who was in a position to speak as a witness on some relevant matters sat on the review panel (*R* v *Governors of Stoke Newington School, ex-parte M* [1994] ELR 1). It also means that the pupil should be given a proper opportunity to know what the allegations are so that they can make full representations. This can cause difficult management problems as other 'informant' pupils may be reluctant for their names to be known. If a pupil or parent or other person chooses not to attend a hearing (assuming they have been given adequate notice and do not have a good reason for not attending), then it is perfectly acceptable to go ahead in their absence.

At the governing body review or local authority panel stage, it is important that the pupil does not get the impression that there are private discussions going on between the panel governors and the headteacher or others. Thus, a local authority panel hearing should not take place on school premises. Equally, any information given to the governors should also be given to the pupil or representative, preferably at the same time. Any relevant documents should be copied and given to the representative in advance. Some teachers report that parents ask for vast amounts of documents to be copied, even at this stage. The governing body review should be relatively informal and not turned into a formal court hearing. Only a core of relevant documents needs to be provided. If they have had a significant influence on the decision to exclude, then it is not unreasonable for the representative of the pupil or parents to ask to see them. This should highlight the need to make accurate (albeit brief) contemporary notes of the incident or incidents in respect of which the child is being disciplined.

Although neither a governing body nor an LEA panel needs to carry out searching enquiries involving oral evidence on every occasion, they should identify any crucial issues and then investigate those reasonably thoroughly and, more importantly, even-handedly. In the case of *R* v *Camden London Borough Council ex-parte H* (a minor) (1996), *The Times*, 15 August, the governors recommended reinstatement of two pupils. One of them had fired an air gun (of the type that could be bought in a toy shop) at H, who lost consciousness for several hours as a result. H was a child with special needs who suffered from impaired hearing and had been bullied at his previous school. He was described as being emotionally vulnerable. Neither H nor his parents were invited to attend the governor's review and the governors therefore had little to go on that challenged the excluded pupils' story that the injury had been accidental. They also made assumptions about the effect of their reinstatement on H without further investigation. Nor did they consider the overall impact on discipline in the school of reinstating the pupils. The court was not impressed and said that the governors should have investigated more comprehensively once they had decided that the issue of whether or not the firing of the gun had been deliberate was critical. The court also said that the effect on discipline was a proper consideration for the governing body and should have been taken into account. The decision to reinstate was quashed and the matter sent back for a rehearing.

On the other hand, in the case of *R* v *Cardinal Newman's School, Birmingham and another, ex-parte S* (1997) *The Times*, 26 December, the governors erred in the other direction in not investigating the evidence against a pupil carefully enough. The pupil had been excluded after an alleged assault on another pupil that had been witnessed by a classroom assistant. The assistant had identified the pupil from a witness, but two other members of staff had named the pupil to the assistant when the identification was made. The governing body had not made any enquiries about the nature of the identification and the court held that they should have done.

The normal method for challenging exclusion appeal decisions is by way of judicial review, which is described in Chapter 15. The most important lessons to be learned from the reported cases are that it is important that the hearings follow the correct procedure and that the principles of natural justice are followed.

It is becoming increasingly common for teachers to have to give evidence before appeal panels dealing with exclusions. Chapter 15 also gives advice on giving evidence and preparing for hearings. In many cases, it may be advisable for a school to be represented by a lawyer at the appeal to the LEA.

Discipline

Under Section 61ff of the School Standards and Framework Act 1998, governing bodies have responsibility for ensuring that schools have policies in place that are designed to promote good behaviour and discipline. They must direct a headteacher as to the principles they should follow, taking into account any guidance from the Secretary of State, the headteacher and parents of pupils on the register of the school. A headteacher is required to determine measures with a view to:

- promoting among pupils, self-discipline and a proper regard for authority;
- encouraging good behaviour and respect for others on the part of pupils and, in particular, preventing all forms of bullying among pupils;
- securing that the standard of behaviour of pupils is acceptable;
- otherwise regulating the conduct of pupils;

and, in so doing, they must take into account the directions of the governing body.

The measures devised by a headteacher must be publicized in writing and at least once a year drawn to the attention of all pupils, parents, employees and contractors on site.

If discipline breaks down completely, an LEA may step in and take such steps as it considers necessary to prevent the breakdown or further deterioration in disciplinary standards.

Chapter 14

Can I have your attention please – negligence

Introduction

You will have gathered by now that there are more than a few other legal remedies that may be used against an incompetent teacher and their employers than a negligence law suit. Some have already been referred to earlier in this book. A teacher may face disciplinary measures, including, ultimately, dismissal. Special measures may be imposed on schools. Some kinds of wrongdoing in schools may attract criminal penalties. The equivalent of special measures can now be imposed on LEAs.

This chapter, however, deals with the reasons teachers and their employers may face actions for 'negligence'. The vast majority of the cases that have been reported have involved allegations of a failure on the part of the teacher, school or LEA to keep children safe from physical harm, rather than allegations of failure to provide an adequate education. For some subject areas, such as PE and practical science, this may be a distinction without a difference, but, on the whole, the professionalism of teachers as such has not been challenged by negligence actions, which it has been for doctors and nurses, for example.

There are wide-ranging reasons that could be suggested for this – a golden age when teachers were more respected, a less litigious society and so on. The climate appears to be changing as far as negligence actions are concerned as in other areas of law. In an important decision by the House of Lords reported in 1998 (of which more later), it was made clear (if it needed to be) that, in certain circumstances, there is no magic shield available to teachers, any more than for any other professional and, in theory at least, they may be sued for bad teaching and certainly for bad educational advice. In fact, in my opinion at least, the particular case about which much fuss was made in the press will not have any great immediate impact.

For some years to come, the average teacher is most likely to run into trouble because of physical injury caused by lack of supervision, failure to maintain equipment or failure to follow health and safety guidelines. Therefore, most of this chapter will deal with these cases.

Negligence – a whirlwind tour

If you stand by the side of any busy junction and watch the traffic go by, unless you are a traffic police officer, you are probably a very sad person. However, *if* you do, you will see that many drivers are driving rather badly and a surprising number of them are breaking the law. Near accidents are frequent, but, fortunately, mostly avoided. You may be tempted to describe these drivers as negligent in the legal sense, but they are not (although they may be careless or inconsiderate in a criminal sense, that is another story).

In order for the civil courts to find that someone has been negligent, at least three factors are involved:

- there must be a duty of care owed by one person to another in the particular context;
- the guilty party must have fallen below the standard of behaviour expected of them in exercising that duty of care in the particular context; and
- damage must have been caused as a result of the breach of the duty of care.

It is also possible to be negligent by:

- not doing something;
- doing something badly;
- doing something badly even though you did not mean any harm or were not personally aware that it would cause any harm;

- failing to warn someone of potentially dangerous consequences of a particular act;
- failing to stop someone causing themselves harm by doing something stupid.

It is also possible for several people to be responsible for the consequences of a negligent act or series of acts. An employer will be liable for the actions of an employee who is acting in the course of their employment or for the failure to ensure that there was an appropriate system or training scheme in place to prevent harm from happening. This will not extend to every act of an employee. Indeed, in the case of *Trotman* v *North Yorkshire County Council*, 14 July 1998, CA, the court held that the LEA could not be said to be liable for the actions of a Deputy Headteacher who sexually assaulted a pupil during the course of a school trip abroad. The teacher merely had the opportunity to commit the assault by reason of his employment – it was not an unauthorized way of doing what he was employed to do. The person who is harmed may also share legal responsibility (this is called contributory negligence). The person who steps in to help may end up making things worse and thus be held partly to blame.

There are two other important points about negligence. First, it must be reasonably foreseeable that if X does Y, A is likely to get hurt in some way before A can recover damages. Furthermore, it must be obvious that A will get harmed in a particular way. To give an example, in the case of *Jolley* v *London Borough of Sutton* [1998] 3 All ER 559, some boys found a rickety old boat on wasteland owned by a local authority. The boat had been left there for some time and the council should really have taken it away. Two boys decided to jack the boat up and work underneath it. Even though the boat was an obvious allurement to children in a way that would normally give rise to liability to negligence, the court decided that it had been impossible to predict that they would jack the boat up and be injured as a result.

The courts have decided that a duty of care will be owed to anyone who might be described as your legal 'neighbour'. There are many common relationships to which this neighbour principle applies – doctor and patient, employer and employee, car driver and other road users and, of course, teacher and pupil.

The law of negligence has been developed by the courts and continues to be developed. A court will not step in and hold someone to blame for an accident in every circumstance. The logic of when it will do so or not do so will not always be obvious. As Lord Justice Stephenson said in the case of *Porter* v *City of Bradford MC* (1985) CA 901:

> It is quite clear what the duty of an education authority and of its teachers is; the difficulty is to apply the law correctly to the facts of any particular case.

The basic view of the courts is that teachers are expected to be as careful with the pupils in their charge as a reasonably careful parent would be. This was rather well put in a case that was decided in 1937 – *Hudson* v *the Governors of Rotherham Grammar School and Selby Johnson* [1937] LCT 303. The playing field at Rotherham Grammar School was out of bounds to pupils. Mr Selby Johnson inspected the field and made sure that there was no one on it. After he left, two boys went onto the pitch and started pushing a roller. The plaintiff (Hudson) joined them and the roller was pulled over him, causing injuries that included a fractured skull. The court dismissed the claim that the school had been negligent. The judge said:

> What has a reasonably careful parent to do? Supposing a boy of yours and some other little boys who are friends of his, coming to tea on a Saturday afternoon, and you see them all playing in the garden. Suppose your garden roller happened to be there. Would you consider you had been neglectful of your duty to the parents of those other boys because, for five minutes, you had gone into the house and two of them had managed to pull the roller over the third?
>
> Would you think that, in those circumstances, you had failed to exercise reasonable supervision as a parent? These things have got to be treated as matters of common sense, not to put on Mr Johnson any higher standard of care than that of a reasonably careful parent.
>
> If boys were kept in cotton wool, some of them would choke themselves with it. They would manage to have accidents: we always did, members of the jury – we did not always have actions at law afterwards.
>
> You have to consider whether or not you would expect a headmaster to exercise such a degree of care that boys could never get into mischief. Has any reasonable parent yet succeeded in exercising such care as to prevent a boy getting into mischief and – if he did – what sort of boys should we produce?

As Mr Micawber put it in *David Copperfield,* 'Accidents will occur in the best regulated families'.

In the case of *Williams* v *Eady* (1893) 10 TLR 41 CA, the court found against the school. Phosphorus was kept in a locked room in the school, but, unfortunately, the pupils had easy access to the key. One boy got hold of a bottle and set light to it. The bottle exploded and the Plaintiff was burned. The school was found to be negligent and the judge commented:

> The school master was bound to take such care of his boys as a careful father would take of his boys, and there could be no better definition of the duty of a school master.

Little seems to have changed by 1980 when in *Myton* v *Wood and Essex County Council* (1980) CA 646, *The Times* 11 July, the court said:

> The duty of a local education authority in the provision of transport for children attending schools in accordance with its statutory duty under Section 55 of the Education Act 1944, is to take such care as a reasonably careful father would take for his own children.

The LEA had arranged for a taxi to take two boys with learning difficulties to and from school. On one occasion, the driver dropped one of the children off on the wrong side of the road, in a dangerous place and the child was injured while crossing the road. The LEA was not vicariously liable for the driver's negligence because a reasonable parent would not have supervised the driver.

However, the approach has been refined a little to take into account the fact that teachers do not operate in a home environment, dealing with a small number of children. In the case of *Nicholson* v *Westmorland County Council* (1962) *The Times* 25 October [1962] CLY 2087 CA, the court said that the test of reasonable care was that of a reasonably careful parent, but one who had 20 children. In the *Lyes* v *Middlesex County Council* (1962) 61 LGR 443 [1962] CLY 2425 case, too, the court said that the prudent parent principle must take account of circumstances of school life, including how pupils generally behave and the state of the school premises. A 15-year-old schoolboy was playing when his hand went through a glass panel in a door. The panel was too thin and therefore not 'efficient', which put the defendants in breach of the statute law and regulations that applied at the time. The standard of care required was that of a careful parent applying their mind to school life, where there was more larking, rather than to home life.

Although the test is, essentially, that of a reasonably careful parent, a court will also consider whether or not a teacher in any given situation has followed recommended practices and, in particular, whether or not a significant number of competent teachers would have acted in the same way. In the case of *Meehan* v *Lancashire County Council* (1988) CA 1006, the judge said:

> If a teacher can say 'in all that I did, I followed the approved practice generally adopted throughout the land'... he is in a position of considerable strength to answer the charge of negligence.

A number of different organizations offer advice to employers and schools on health and safety matters. One of the easiest ways to prove negligence is to show that good advice has not been followed. Of course, not all the advice is consistent, nor is it all of equal status. It has therefore to be read with a critical eye. Union advice, for example, tends to emphasize practices that protect teachers. I do not mean to suggest that this is a bad idea. In a general sense, if you watch out for yourself, your organization and your clients (in this case pupils), in that order, you will probably not go too far wrong. However, as the courts have emphasized, eliminating all risk may be incompatible with an all-round education ('it is better that a boy break his neck than allow other people to break his spirit'). Advice from commercial organizations may be influenced by motives more related to marketing products than to promoting good practices. Again, this is not necessarily a bad thing, but it may mean that the material tends to put forward an image of the school environment as a combat zone. Resources are limited and material has to be categorized into what is essential and what is merely desirable or an interesting way of getting a point across.

The courts say you must follow an approved practice. This does not mean every approved practice. You cannot be expected to keep up to date with every research development or safety product. You can, however, be sure that if a practice is recommended by the DfEE or the Health and Safety Executive and you or the school does not follow it, you risk somebody taking legal action for negligence if a pupil is injured as a result. There are also certain products or practices that, if not used or followed (or not avoided, such as asbestos) after a certain date (usually when official advice is published), give rise to negligence actions. The HSE has produced a number of useful publications for schools that are noted in the Further reading section at the back of the book and Chapter 5. Relevant DfEE circulars are also listed in the Further reading section.

In essence, a school should:

- carry out a safety audit and assess the risks arising to pupils in all areas (taking advice as appropriate);
- identify areas for improvement and prioritize between them;
- institute a system for reviewing the risk assessment;
- ensure that critical repairs are carried out as a matter of priority;
- institute a system for reporting problems in the school that affect health and safety;
- institute and monitor a system for reporting school accidents.

In addition, each school should have written policies covering:

- security;
- health and safety;
- reporting accidents.

As with all such policies, they are no good if they are locked away in a headteacher's office. They must be publicized. Teachers must be trained in health and safety and clear about what their individual responsibilities are.

What follows is a review of negligence cases in schools, grouped under headings that relate to particular areas of operational concern – teachers' helpers, trainee teachers, supervision, playground supervision, PE, science, pupil assault, equipment, premises, leaving school, medical needs and other special needs. Some of the cases are now rather elderly and might be decided differently now in the light of changing legislation on health and safety, and different attitudes towards the care and supervision of pupils at school, but they still give some idea of the approach that will be adopted by the courts.

Teachers' helpers

Will it be negligent if a child is asked to do something that is not directly related to subjects taught in the classroom? Essentially the courts have answered this question with a 'no'.

In the *Smith* v *Martin and Kingston upon Hull Corporation* [1911] 2 KB 775 case, the court said:

> The Education Acts are intended to provide for education in its truest and widest sense. Such education includes the inculcation of habits of order and obedience and courtesy: such habits are taught by giving orders, and if such orders are reasonable and proper, under the circumstances of the case, they are within the scope of the teacher's authority, even though they are not confined to bidding the child to read or write, to sit down or stand up in school, or the like. It would be extravagant to say that a teacher has no business to ask a child to perform small acts of courtesy to herself or others such as to fetch her pocket handkerchief from upstairs, to poke the fire in the teachers' room, to open the door for a visitor or the like: it is said that these are for the teacher's own benefit and to save herself trouble, and not for the child's benefit, but I do not agree: not only is it good for the child to be taught to be unselfish and obliging but the opportunity of running upstairs may often avoid punishment: the wise teacher, who sees the volatile child become fidgety, may well make the excuse of an errand for herself an outlet for the child's exuberance of spirits very much to the benefit of the child. Teachers must use their common sense, and it would be disastrous to hold that they can do nothing but teach.

The facts of the case were that the teacher had asked a child of 14 to go and attend to a fire that was being used to cook the teacher's food. The LEA could not escape liability just because the instruction given by the teacher was for her own benefit. The fire was dangerous and the child should not have been asked to perform the particular task.

In the *Cooper* v *Manchester Corporation, The Times*, 13 February, 1959 [1959] CLY 2260 CA, case, a girl of 14 was carrying a half gallon pot of tea to the staff room (all older pupils took turns at this). A boy unexpectedly ran out of a room into her path and she was burned by the hot tea. The court said that it was perfectly reasonable to ask a child to perform an ordinary domestic operation – it was not being carried out in dangerous circumstances so no special duty of care arose. Note that it might have been negligent if the teapot was too big for the particular child to manage or for a younger child or if she had been burnt because the tea-making equipment was defective.

Trainee teachers

Does it make any difference if an accident occurs when children are in the care of a trainee teacher? If you think of them as being on the same level as learner drivers and junior medics, probably not. A learner driver is just as liable as a fully qualified driver. Because a trainee teacher does not have the experience of a fully qualified teacher, from an employer's point of view, there is a greater need for a trainee to be supervised in the school environment as there is a greater likelihood of them being unable to control a situation or anticipate a problem than would be likely with an experienced teacher.

You may remember reading of the mock armed robbery that a trainee teacher allowed pupils to stage and the ensuing press reports. I do not know whether or not any legal action followed. In fact, I do not think anyone suffered any injury as a result. No doubt the trainee acted from the best of intentions, however naively. It does show, however, why supervision is essential and schools will be liable if the supervision is inadequate.

The same would go for a newly qualified teacher who was not given plenty of support and supervision in the early years. They cannot possibly be expected to carry out their full teaching schedule and supervise children safely without more back-up than an experienced teacher would need. Care should also be taken with teachers who are new to a school. Even the most experienced teacher who has done as much as humanly possible to familiarize themselves with the new environment and the nature of their new charges is not necessarily going to be aware of the potentially lethal dynamics of a particular badly behaved class or faction within it.

Supervision

Possibly the greatest source of negligence actions has been in the area of supervision of pupils.

In the *Clark* v *Monmouthshire County Council* (1954) 52 LGR 256 CA case, Lord Denning said that what amounted to reasonable supervision will depend on the particular circumstances.

> The duty of a school master does not extend to constant supervision of all the boys all the time. That is not practicable. Only reasonable supervision is required.

The facts involved a pupil of 13 bringing a knife into school and, in a scuffle with another pupil, injured his leg, which, ultimately, had to be amputated. Even though at least one of the teachers knew that pupils sometimes brought knives into school, this did not mean that the school was negligent in not supervising the boys at every moment.

In the *Harris* v *Guest, The Times,* 25 October 1960 [1960] CLY 2146 case, the court said that a school was not liable when a boy of 16 was shot with an air pistol by another pupil during an unsupervised period. It is not necessary to supervise a class of 16-year-olds constantly (there were about 20 pupils in the class). In the case of *Jacques* v *Oxfordshire County Council*(1968) 66 LGR 440 [1968] CLY 2727, a pupil was hit in the eye when another pupil fired a pellet at him while they were on the school bus. The bus driver was the only adult on board and prefects were expected to supervise the other pupils. The court said this was acceptable and the LEA was not negligent.

More recently, in the case of *Wilson* v *Governors of the Sacred Heart Roman Catholic School* (1997) *The Times,* 28 November, a six-year-old boy was injured by another pupil as they were leaving school. Although the children were supervised at lunchtime, they were not supervised at the end of the day and there had never been any reason to think that this was necessary. The boy was to go home on his own and it could not be said that this was a failure on the part of his parents to exercise their duty of care. Equally, it could not be said that the school was under a duty to provide supervision for the short time that the boy was walking from the door of the school to the exit gate.

However, in the case of *Porter* v *City of Bradford MC* (1985) CA 901, a boy of 16½ on a geology expedition was told to stop rolling boulders down a path. When the teacher was out of sight looking after another group, he threw them off a bridge into a river, hitting another pupil and fracturing her skull. The court said:

> ... looking at the admitted facts of this case and looking at what [the boy] did such a short time before, I think ... that on this occasion [the teacher], faced with the difficult task of trying to instruct pupils, some of whom were keen and some of whom were obviously not, failed in his duty to supervise this particular set of pupils. In my judgment, he ought not to have relied on the obedience of [the boy] as negating any reasonable possibility that he might try something of the same sort again; he ought to

have kept the pupils, willing and unwilling, together and he ought not to have gone out of sight and sound of this group, including as it did the boy although I sympathize with him and appreciate the difficulty of the task.

Playground supervision

There is no general expectation that children must be supervised in the playground at all times and the courts have repeated this time and again. In the case of *Rawsthorne* v *Otley* [1937] 3 All ER 902, for example, the court held that staff were not negligent in leaving boys in the playground without supervision. In the *Jeffrey* v *London County Council* (1954) 52 LGR 521 [1954] CLY 2241 case, a child of nearly 6 climbed from the playground up a water pipe on to a glass roof, through which he fell and died. He should have been waiting in the playground for his mother to collect him, but, unfortunately, she was a little late in arriving.

The judge said:

> School authorities, when they are considering the care of children, must strike some balance between the meticulous supervision of children every moment of the time when they are under their care, and the very desirable object of encouraging the sturdy independence of children as they grow up, and the ability to get on without detailed supervision must start at quite an early age ... it is better that a boy break his neck than allow other people to break his spirit.

Numerous other cases have followed suit.

- *Pettican* v *Enfield LBC* (1970): the court said that, as far as lunchtime supervision is concerned, staff are not expected to act as 'policemen or security guards'. It will be sufficient supervision if there is 'the implanting of the feeling that there is authority about, that is, that there is some control and sanction'. There is no need to have a teacher on duty in every classroom when the children were indoors on wet days (a pupil had thrown a piece of chalk into the eye of another pupil).
- *Murrell* v *Bexley Borough Council* (1979): a boy was injured by a heavy trolley that a group of older boys was playing about with in the playground. A teacher was supervising the playground but she was away inspecting another part of the school. The court said that all reasonable care had been taken. It was impossible to

expect all parts of the school premises to be under constant supervision during breaks and the school was under no obligation to impose a regime that suppresses ordinary high spirits.

- *Ricketts* v *Erith Borough Council* (1943) 42 LGR 471, 2 All ER 629: the teachers in the school would patrol the playground, but not continuously. The gates were closed, but not locked. A 10-year-old pupil left school at lunchtime without permission and brought back a bow and arrow, which he fired at another pupil. Her glasses broke and a splinter of glass entered her eye. The school was not liable as continuous supervision was not required of a reasonable parent and therefore it was not required of a teacher.

- *Newton* v *East Ham Corporation* (1963) *The Guardian*, 11 July 1963: a four-year-old boy was injured by a piece of coke thrown at him by another pupil. A teacher was supervising, but she was looking somewhere else. The LEA was under no obligation to provide efficient supervision to watch all parts of the school playground at the same time.

- *Ward* v *Hertfordshire County Council* (1969) 114 Sol J 87 CA [1970] 1 All ER 535: schoolchildren were allowed into the playground before the start of day without supervision. An eight-year-old crashed into a wall during a race and suffered a head injury. Staff knew that children raced in the playground, but they would not have stopped it had they been present. The wall that the child ran into was a jagged flint wall, but the court said this was not inherently dangerous because it was a common type of wall of its period and common in the local area, at both schools and private homes. The accident occurred in the ordinary course of play and the court said that the authority was not liable. Moreover, it was said to be wrong to try to protect children against all injuries 'by forbidding them the ordinary pleasures which schoolchildren so much enjoy ... It often happens that children run from one side of the playground to the other. It is impossible so to supervise them that they never fall down and hurt themselves. I cannot think that this accident shows any lack of supervision by the school authorities.'

- *Mays* v *Essex County Council* (1975) *The Times*, 11 October: a child was injured five minutes before the start of the school day from slipping on some ice in an unsalted playground that was not supervised. The school gates were open early, but parents were specifically asked not to send their children to school too early.

Most of them had arrived 10 minutes before the start of school. The court felt it was perfectly reasonable for children of 14 to be allowed to play on ice unsupervised – this was an innocent and healthy amusement. The court said, 'Life is full of physical dangers which children must learn to recognize and develop the ability to avoid. The playground is one of the places in which to learn.' Two other comments were made. First, it was impractical to salt the whole playground every time there was a frost. Second, the school could not be made responsible for something that had happened outside school hours unless they specifically accepted that they should be, and in asking the parents not to let children arrive too early they clearly had not.

A court will be particularly unwilling to hold a school responsible when pupils who are old enough to know better disobey instructions they have been given or themselves act in a foolhardy way, as the following judgments demonstrate.

- *Peters* v *Hill* (1957) *The Times*, 29 March [1957] CLY 2367 CA: a pupil of seven climbed up a ladder into a tree, but, instead of climbing back down again, he jumped and was injured. The court said that it was not necessary to supervise him to make sure that he came down in the same way he had gone up.
- *Price* v *Caernarvonshire County Council* (1960) *The Times*, 11 February 1960 CLY 2145 CA: pupils used a bat to play rounders, despite having been told not to. The headteacher had looked in on the game shortly before the injury and no bat was being used. This was not negligent.
- *Good* v *ILEA* (1980) 10 Fam Law 213 [1981] CLY 1830 CA: after school, some pupils were taken to the playground where they would be collected by their parents. A child of 6½ went with some others to a play centre nearby. The play centre was not quite complete and there was a pile of building sand roped off. The pupils were told to keep away from it. However, the child and a friend went to play in the sand and the friend threw sand in the child's eye. No staff were supervising. The LEA were considered to be under no duty to keep an eye on children every minute of the day.

By contrast, in the case of *Beaumont* v *Surrey CC* (1968) 66 LGR 580; [1968] CLY 2726, the LEA was liable. In a mixed secondary school of 900 pupils, aged 11 to 18, 2 teachers were in charge of clearing classrooms and supervising the playground. While they were in the classrooms, a child found a piece of elastic (9 feet long and powerful) that had come from a trampoline and which the PE master had thrown away in an open waste bin. Two other boys started playing around with it and flicked it into the child's eye. The school was held liable for inadequate supervision and for leaving the elastic in an open bin.

> The duty of a headmaster towards his pupils is said to be to take such care of them as a reasonably careful and prudent father would take of his own children. That standard is a helpful one when considering, for example, individual instructions to individual children in a school. It would be very unwise to allow a six-year-old child to carry a kettle of boiling water – that type of instruction; but that standard when applied to an incident of horseplay in a school of 900 pupils is somewhat unrealistic, if not unhelpful.
>
> In the context of the present action, it appears to me to be easier and preferable to use the ordinary language of the law of negligence, that is, it is a headmaster's duty, bearing in mind the known propensities of boys and indeed girls between the ages of 11 and 17 or 18, to take all reasonable and proper steps to prevent any of the pupils under his care from suffering injury from inanimate objects, from the actions of their fellow pupils or from a combination of the two. That is a high standard.

Again, in the case of *Blasdale* v *Coventry CC* (1981) unreported (*TES*, 13 November 1981), a pupil was awarded £7500 damages for injury to his eye caused when another pupil fired a paper-clip from an elastic band at him when they were inside on a 'wet' day. Only one dinner lady was supervising two classrooms and this was found to be inadequate when there were over 30 pupils aged 8 in each classroom.

However, in the *Mullin* v *Richards & Birmingham City Council* [1998] 1 All ER 920 case, the court held that neither the school nor the LEA could be held liable when a couple of 15–year-old girls were having a mock sword fight with plastic rulers and one of the rulers shattered and a piece flew in one of the girl's eyes. This was nothing more than a schoolgirl game and it could not be said that the school should have anticipated the sort of injury that arose or that they should have been supervising to the extent that would have stopped the game from being played in the first place.

Leaving the school's premises

Even when a pupil has left the premises, a school may still be responsible for their actions if they have managed to get themselves into a dangerous situation due to lack of supervision. The following is an example of a case where the court found an LEA to be liable.

- *Barnes* v *Hampshire County Council* [1969] 1 WLR 1563: at an infant school, the arrangements at the end of the school day were that the children were usually collected from the school gates at 3.30 pm. They were instructed to report back to a teacher if their parents were not waiting for them at the gates. The plaintiff, who was five, was let out with the rest of her class five minutes early. The main road was very near the school. The child's mother had not arrived when she was let out and the child (who was said to be somewhat unpredictable) walked out of the gate and was knocked over by a lorry as she crossed the road. The court said that both the LEA and the teacher were negligent.

The LEA (but not the teacher) was also held to blame in the following case.

- *Camarthenshire County Council* v *Lewis* (1955) AC 549, 1 All ER 565: a teacher was going to take two four-year-old pupils at a nursery school for a walk. She got them ready and left them in the classroom to wait for her while she went to the lavatory. On her way back, she was detained because she had to see to another child who had been injured in a playpen and had cut himself. She was not sure whether or not the cut was sufficiently serious that the child needed to see a doctor, so she took him to the headteacher's office. She was away from the other two pupils in all for about ten minutes. The pupils she had left were known to be fairly well behaved. However, in this time, the pupils had wandered off, gone into the playground and through unlocked school gates. A lorry driver swerved to avoid one of them who was crossing the road and the driver was killed when the lorry crashed into a telegraph pole. The court held that the LEA was negligent as it was too easy for four-year-olds to escape through the gates. This may have been partly because they did not put any evidence before the court as to how the children had managed to get themselves out onto the road. The teacher herself was not deemed negligent, however.

Her duty was that of a careful parent. I cannot think that it could be considered negligent in a mother to leave a child dressed ready to go out with her for a few moments, and then, if she found another of her children hurt and in need of immediate attention, she could be blamed for giving it, without thinking that the child who was waiting to go out with her might wander off into the street. It is very easy to be wise after the event and argue that she might have done this or that; but it seems to me that she acted just as one would expect her to do, that is to attend to the injured child first, never thinking that the one waiting for her would go off on his own.

However, in the following case, the LEA was not judged to have been negligent.

- *Nwabudike* v *London Borough of Southwark* [1997] ELR 35: a pupil ran out of his primary school playground at lunchtime and was run over by a car. The court found that the school was not negligent. A balance has to be struck between maintaining security and turning a school into a fortress. A pupil who was determined to disobey the rules as this one had seemed to be would probably always be able to find a way.

Off school premises

Tragedies have occurred when children have been away from school at outdoor activity centres and the like and, in response, these centres are now heavily regulated. The DfEE have also now issued guidance to schools – *The Health and Safety of Pupils on Off-site Visits: A good practice guide* – a draft booklet due to be finalized during the course of 1998. This supersedes the previously issued circulars on this topic.

School trips

As with other aspects of pupil safety, any activities in which they are involved outside the school premises must be carefully organized and supervized as they would be by a reasonably careful parent. There are many sources of detailed advice on what needs to be considered, including permissions from parents, arrangements for emergencies, anticipated medical problems, equipment required, sleeping arrangements, night-time supervision and so on. Incidentally, the fact that a parent has given permission for a trip and even signed a 'waiver' form will not assist a school if a child is injured as a result of its negligence. Liability for personal injury or death cannot be excluded in this way. Consideration should be given to the need for insurance, both on the part of the school or trip organizer and the parents.

Activity centres that have been at the heart of much bad publicity are now affected by statutory requirements under the Activity Centres (Young Persons' Safety) Act 1995 and the Adventure Activities Licensing Regulations 1996 (SI 1996/772). See also the Safety in Outdoor Activity Centres House of Commons Paper 178 Session 1994–5 (HMSO).

Transport

If transport is provided by a school or LEA, the provider is responsible for aspects of the children's safety while in transit. The courts will expect there to be some level of supervision adequate to the circumstances (which may involve supervision by older pupils). Any vehicles used to transport children (including the teacher's own) should be fully insured and comply with all safety standards. See in particular *School Transport Safety* (RoSPA), *Advice to Users and Operators of Minibuses and Coaches Carrying Children* (VSE 1/96, Department of Transport) and the *Advice on Retro-fitting Seat Belts to Minibuses and Coaches* (VSE 2/96). Seat belt provision is now required by the Regulations in all vehicles registered after October 1988 and, from February 1998, they are required for all vehicles registered before October 1988.

If a child is involved in an educational activity or *en route* to school under the care of the LEA, similar precautions and supervision are expected of the school and the LEA as would be the case when they are in school. This applies even where there is no legal requirement to provide the service or educational activity.

- *Shrimpton* v *Hertfordshire County Council* (1911) 104 LT 145: an LEA provided transport to and from school. On one occasion, a child was injured while getting out of the vehicle because there was no one to help the children get in and out. The particular child should not have been on the bus in the first place, but the court still held the LEA to be liable. The operation of a school transport system by the LEA must be safe and it was held that it did not matter that the child was not legally entitled to the transport as the LEA had impliedly given permission for the use of the transport.

However, in the following cases, on the facts, there was no liability.

- *Atherton* v *Bentley* (1970) CA 212: some cub scouts were on a treasure hunt in small groups – one group dashed across a suburban road.
- *Murphy* v *Zoological Society* (1962) *The Times*, 14 November [1962] CLY 68: some cub scouts were on a trip to Whipsnade Zoo. There were 35 boys and 3 adults in charge. Three of the boys wandered off on their own to the lions' cage and climbed in between the fences. One was badly injured by a lion. The zoo was not liable (because the boys were trespassers and the lion had not escaped) and nor was the Scouts Association. There was no negligence by the supervisors in allowing boys to split off into unsupervised groups.
- *Mason* v *Essex County Council* (1988) CA 295: a volunteer was driving a minibus to a youth camp even though he knew he was not supposed to be driving it. He knocked down the plaintiff and injured him. The court held that the accident did not occur while the driver was acting in the course of his employment, so the LEA could not be held liable.

PE

About two thirds of accidents to pupils happen in PE or sports activities, so this is a particularly critical area for schools to monitor regarding their health and safety practices. The DfEE has produced guidance for schools in conjunction with the British Association of Advisers and Lecturers in Physical Education – *Safe Practice in Physical Education* – as have many other accident prevention organizations (see the Useful addresses section at the back of the book) and other professional bodies. The most typical findings of negligence involve inadequate supervision of a dangerous activity and the use of inadequate safety equipment.

Cases in which a teacher or school were not found to be negligent include the following.

- *Wright* v *Cheshire County Council* (1952) 2 All ER 789 CA: 40 boys were taking part in a PE lesson, with one group vaulting over a buck. The teacher was moving between groups. Each boy vaulted over the buck, and stopped to provide support for the next one. The boys had done this before and were reasonably good at it. The boy who should have supported the plaintiff ran off to the changing room when the bell went instead of waiting to catch him and the plaintiff fell and was injured. The court decided that the school was not negligent as the teacher had followed a general and approved practice – the boys had been trained in the method and the teacher was supervising adequately. 'There may well be some risk in everything one does or in every step one takes, but in ordinary everyday affairs the test of what is reasonable care may well be answered by experience from which arises a practice adopted generally, and followed successfully over the years so far as the evidence in this case goes.'

- *Van Oppen* v *Clerk to Bedford Charity Trustees* (1990) 1 WLR 235 [1989] 3 All ER 389 CA: a pupil suffered a serious spinal injury when playing rugby. He alleged that the school had been negligent in failing to advise his father of the risks attached to playing rugby, not carrying insurance to cover this type of injury and in not alerting him to the need to get the boy insured. This is how the judge explained the decision:

It is fundamental to the relationship between school and pupil that the school undertakes to educate him in as wide a sense as it reasonably can. This involves the schools having the pupils in its care and it involves the pupils in various activities in the classroom, in the chapel, in the gymnasium, on the sports field and so on. There are risks of injury inherent in many human activities, even of serious injury in some. Because of this, the school, having the pupils in its care, is under a duty to exercise reasonable care for their health and safety. Provided due care is exercised in this sphere, it seems to me that the school's duty is fulfilled.

While it might be desirable to take out insurance or inform parents that they should do so, this did not amount to a legal obligation on the part of the school. Generally speaking, a school does not have a duty in such circumstances to have regard to the pupil's economic welfare. However, it might be liable if it had told the parents that there was insurance cover but then failed to renew it.

There had been an allegation earlier in the last case that the school might have been negligent in the standard of coaching it had provided. This is what the judge had to say:

> It is accepted on all sides that the Bedford School, being in *loco parentis*, owed a general duty to the plaintiff and to all pupils to exercise reasonable care for his and their safety, both in the classroom and on the games field. It is also accepted that injury is more likely if the correct techniques are not followed by the players, particularly in tackling. It follows therefore that it was the school's duty by teaching or coaching or by correction to take reasonable care to ensure that the plaintiff in playing the game of rugby football applied correct techniques while tackling ....
>
> I am satisfied that the defendants, through staff 'taking' rugby, were well aware of the inherent risks in playing rugby football and of the need for the application of correct techniques and the correction of potentially dangerous errors and lapses. I am also satisfied that the standard of supervision was high, that the refereeing was vigilant and strict and that ... there was at the school an emphasis on discipline, which meant playing the game correctly. There is therefore no substance in the allegations of negligence.

This is another example of the need to follow approved practices.

- *Porter* v *Barking and Dagenham LBC* (1990), *The Times*, 9 April: failure to supervise two 14-year-old boys who were practising shot-putting was not negligent.
- *Conrad* v *ILEA* (1967) 111 SJ 684, *The Times*, 26 May 1967 CA: during the course of a first class in judo with an experienced instructor, pupils were shown how to do a particular throw. At the end of the class, the pupils were told to practise the throw and specifically warned to yield to their opponents if they achieved domination to avoid injury. The instructor used the expression, 'Get your man down' and the pupil tried to argue that he understood this to mean 'in any way possible'. The pupil's arm was broken. The court said that looking at all the circumstances and everything that had been said by the instructor, he had not been negligent. In any event, the pupil had caused the injury by failing to yield as he had been advised.
- *Hopkins* v *Birmingham Corporation* (1974) CA 351: it was not necessary to supervise a girl of 15 playing tennis in a gym.
- *Walters* v *Liverpool City Corporation* (1983) CA 609: a ten-year-old child walked along one of the parallel bars in a gym instead of using both of them as he had been instructed. He fell

and injured himself. The court held that the supervising teacher was not negligent for not having seen that the child was disobeying instructions.

- *Morgan* v *Avonhurst School Educational Trust Ltd* (1985) CA 982: during the course of a properly conducted demonstration of an Army assault course for cadets, the plaintiff lost his grip on the rope, fell and broke both wrists. The defendants were deemed not to have done anything wrong.
- *Webb* v *Essex County Council* (1954) *TES*, 12 November: a pupil aged five jumped from a stool during an exercise class. The stool was surrounded by rubber mats. The court held that the equipment was sound and the teachers were not negligent – it had been a pure accident.

Cases in which the court has found that the teacher or employer was negligent include those in the following list.

- *Affutu-Nartoy* v *Clarke and ILEA* (1984) *The Times*, 9 February (1984 CLY 3391): a teacher was playing rugby alongside the pupils and tackled one of them. It was a perfectly proper tackle according to the rules, but the court decided it was too dangerous in the circumstances. It concluded that the teacher should not have been joining in in a way that gave rise to physical contact with the boys, although it was perfectly all right to join in the game to keep the game and the ball moving and to demonstrate the skills of the game.
- *Smolden* v *Whitworth* (1996) *The Times*, 18 December: a 19-year-old was injured when a scrum collapsed. The referee had repeatedly failed to enforce the scrum rules and a more than usually high number of scrums had collapsed. It was obvious that serious spinal injury could result, as it unfortunately did, and the referee was liable. That is not to say that he would have been liable for every single error of judgement – rugby is by nature a fast-moving game and decisions have to be made on the hoof.
- *Moore* v *Hampshire County Council* (1981) 80 LGR 481 CA: a 12-year-old girl who was disabled persuaded her teacher to let her play games despite the fact that the teacher had been told from two different sources that the pupil should not play because she had congenital dislocation of the hips and walked with a limp. The teacher then compounded the error by failing to watch her when she started her exercises. Not surprisingly, the court held

the school negligent when the girl tried to do a handstand and broke her ankle.

- *Povey* v *Rydal School* (1969): pupils were exercising in a group on rings and the teacher was moving from one group to another. A pupil fell and was very badly injured, resulting in permanent paralysis. The court found that the school was negligent because of the poor standard of the safety mats in the gymnasium.
- *Gibbs* v *Barking Corporation* [1936] 1 All ER 115 CA: a male pupil fell when vaulting because the teacher did nothing to catch him or prevent him from falling. The school was held to be liable as 'The games master does not seem to have acted with that promptitude which the law requires'.
- *Fowles* v *Bedfordshire County Council* (1955) *The Times*, 22 May [1996] ELR No. 1: the local authority was found to be in breach of statutory duty when a university student (aged 21) who was attending a youth centre to take part in gymnastics was injured. He had been taught gymnastics at school (but not forward somersaults because they were considered to be too dangerous). He was instructed at the youth centre to do forward somersaults, but by an unqualified member of staff. Mats were freely available. He attempted a forward somersault onto a mat that was too close to the wall. The court said that there was no duty to remove or secure the mats to the floor, but there was a duty to supervise and warn. The university student was also found to have contributed to the accident and was held to blame to the extent of two thirds – any intelligent young man in his situation would have appreciated the risks of his conduct. It may have been influential that it seemed the young man had performed the somersault in the hope of impressing some watching girls!

Science and design and technology lessons

The Association for Science Education is a registered charity with the aim of promoting, supporting and developing primary- and secondary-level science education and produces a number of useful publications on good practice in science education and health and safety issues. These include *Be Safe!* (produced in consultation with the HSE), *Safety in the Lab*, *Safeguards in the School Laboratory*, *Topics in Safety* and a collection of safety articles and notes from *School Science Review* and *Education in Science* entitled *Safety*

Reprints 1996, which will be regularly updated.

The DfEE has also issued guidance – *Safety in Science Education* – (to which the ASE has contributed) aimed at secondary schools. For primary schools, safety guidance on design and technology issues has been issued by the National Association of Advisers and Inspectors in Design and Technology in the form of *Make it Safe*. Many other organizations produce relevant and helpful material, including RoSPA and the Safety Association for Education.

It should be remembered that there may be criminal consequences for failing to comply with the Health and Safety at Work Act 1974. According to the ASE, the only known prosecutions relating to school accidents (about one third of which occur in science lessons) have been of science teachers who had failed to follow safety procedures required by the employer. Two of the prosecutions involved a failure to use control measures, such as eye protection and safety screens, in situations that clearly required them. The ASE reminds teachers that they are more likely to win the National Lottery than be prosecuted for an accident in a science lesson, but you will increase the odds if you contribute to preventable accidents by failing to follow obvious safety precautions.

In fact, there are relatively few reported civil cases. I do not think this is because accidents do not happen as the above paragraph indicates, but,possibly, because the cases settle out of court and I would hazard a guess that it is the LEA or the school that has had to accept liability.

The schools and LEAs were not found to be negligent in the following cases.

- *Shepherd* v *Essex County Council and Linch* (1913): a 15-year-old boy in a chemistry lesson was told to collect pieces of phosphorus to use in an experiment. He put a piece in his pocket. All the boys in the class had been warned about the danger of phosphorus. The piece in the pocket caught fire and burned the pupil;
- *Crouch* v *Essex County* (1966) 64 LGR 240: a group of 15-year-old pupils were doing an experiment involving the use of caustic soda. They were told clearly about the reaction of caustic soda with water and that it was dangerous. Two girls squirted some caustic soda in the eyes of another pupil with a teat pipette, thinking that it was water. The beaker from which they had taken the caustic soda was not labelled. This was held not to be negligent as there was nothing else the caustic soda could have been mistaken

for. Nor was the teacher to blame for not keeping better discipline in the class. He had done the best he could to maintain safety standards – the pupils were behaving irresponsibly and should have known better.

However, in the following case the court found against the teacher:

- *Noonan* v *ILEA* (1974) *The Times*, 14 December: if a dangerous substance is being used in the laboratory, the teacher must explain exactly how and why the substance is dangerous. It is not enough to say 'don't touch'.

Pupil assault

The circumstances in which a school will be liable to one pupil for the assault of another are usually related to the age of the child (the younger the child, the more likely the court will say that the defendants should take special care to supervise), the level of supervision, whether or not the child or children are known to be violent or generally unreliable and how predictable the type of behaviour was. The older the child, the more likely it is that he will have to accept responsibility for his own actions, especially if he is disobeying instructions.

On the whole, in the reported cases, the court has absolved the school of blame. Here are some actual examples.

- *Staley* v *Suffolk County Council and Dean Mason*, 26 November 1986 (unreported): a boy of 12 threw a tennis ball into a classroom. He had aimed at another boy, but hit the dinner lady, who was injured. He was held liable, not the dinner lady;
- *Suckling* v *Essex County Council*, *The Times*, 27 January 1955 [1955] CLY 1844: one pupil attacked another with a scoring knife used for handicrafts that he had taken from an unlocked cupboard.
- *Rich* v *London County Council* [1953] 1 WLR 895, 2 All ER 376 CA: a pupil was injured when another pupil threw a lump of coke at him. The coke was in an unfenced pile on the playground. The judge repeated the maxim that the school's duty was to take such care 'as a careful father would take of his boys' and said that the supervision was adequate – a careful father would not have fenced off the coke.

- *Driscoll* v *Grattan Wilson* (1954) CLY 2239 CA: one pupil was attacked by another with metal bars from a playground shed.
- *Smith* v *Hale* (1956) *The Times*, 27 January [1956], CLY 5940: a pupil in an approved school attacked another with a home-made arrow. It was concluded that the school had taken all reasonable steps to prevent arrow throwing.
- *Ellesmere* v *Middlesex County Council* (1956) *The Times*, 12 December [1956], CLY 2367 CA: one pupil attacked another with scissors during a handicrafts class.

However, see the case of Porter (under the heading 'Supervision' earlier in this chapter) where a teacher was held liable when one pupil threw a boulder at another. There has also been a case in which the LEA was held liable when a teacher had been assaulted by a pupil as the LEA had been requested on several occasions to remove the boy from the school. If one pupil were injured by another in similar circumstances today, the LEA would also be likely to be held to blame. It would have to weigh up the competing duties owed by the LEA to provide sufficient and suitable education for the pupil who committed the assault and their duty to keep other children and staff at the school safe. This is a most difficult balancing exercise.

Equipment

Equipment is an obvious source of hazard in the school environment. Good practice requires that it should be regularly inspected and maintained, that its use in the classroom should be regularly reviewed (including consideration of age appropriateness) and that any operating advice should be followed. Protective clothing should be worn, if appropriate, and it is important to inspect this regularly to ensure that it is still up to the job.

The courts have found schools to be liable in the following circumstances.

- *Black* v *Kent County Council* (1981) *The Times*, 23 May: a pupil aged seven was injured with scissors being used in an art class because a chair was jogged by another pupil. The court criticized the use of pointed scissors as well as the fact that the staff allowed the child to go home without getting proper medical advice. The court said that it was reasonably foreseeable that the use of sharp, pointed scissors as compared with blunt-ended ones involved quite a degree of risk where children of this age were concerned (particularly as it went against the advice of the Department of Education and Science) and awarded damages of over £13,000.

- *Barnes* v *Bromley LBC* (1983) *The Times*, 16 November: a male pupil was taking a rusty bicycle apart in a metalwork class. He was using an old and brittle riveting tool that splintered on contact with the bicycle. The school was held to be negligent because of the condition of the tool, but the pupil was also contributorily negligent in the way in which he was using the tool.
- *Hoar* v *Board of School Trustees* (1984) 6 WWR 143 [1985] CLY 2333 British Columbia: a pupil hurt himself on a woodworking machine. He had been away from school when the teacher had shown the class how to use it. The school was found to be negligent, but the court held the pupil also to be 50 per cent to blame.

No negligence was found, however, in these cases:

- *Butt* v *Cambridgeshire and Isle of Ely County Council* (1970) 68 LGR 81: a class of 37 girls between the ages of 9 and 10 were given pointed scissors to cut out pictures, but told to put the scissors down when they were not using them. While the teacher was facing one way talking to a pupil, another girl waved her scissors about and poked the plaintiff in the eye, blinding her in that eye. The court dismissed the action for negligence as, although it was a large class, the use of the scissors was normal and the supervision adequate.
- *Smart* v *Gwent County Council* (1991) Lexis: a girl of three was playing in the home corner at her nursery school. She trapped her hand in the door of the house and lost the tip of her thumb. The judge said that, although the risk of this sort of injury was foreseeable, the LEA could not be said to be negligent – the risk was no greater than it would have been in the child's own home. The judge specifically rejected the argument that the risks of using a home corner at school were greater because of the number of children involved (30). The judge said he was 'wholly unpersuaded that the risk in this nursery school, supervised as it was by a competent teacher, was significantly greater than in an ordinary home'. The risk of injury was:

not an unacceptable risk, that as it was one to which a prudent parent would not say that it was unreasonable to expose this child to, notwithstanding the fact that they were in a class of 30 rather than in their own home ... Drawers, cupboard doors, and windows can be a source of trapped fingers and can from time to time cause quite nasty injuries. Injuries from falling off chairs, tables and other common or garden everyday objects are foreseeable risks to small children, but no-one would suggest that they should not be subjected to them, providing, of course, that they are properly supervised according to their age.

- *Smerkinich* v *Newport Corporation* (1912) 76 JP 454: a youth of 19 was injured while using a circular saw at a technical institute. The court found that the local authority was not liable, but the judge commented that they might have been had the plaintiff been a child. The plaintiff had admitted in evidence that he knew there was no guard and that it would have been safer to use a guard, but had not suggested this or discussed it with the instructor.
- *Watson* v *Mid Glamorgan County Council* (1989) CA 971: a 15-year-old pupil injured his right wrist on a band saw machine in the wood workshop. He had been shown how to use it and was being supervised in its use – it could not be said that the defendants had done anything wrong.

The state of school premises

The health and safety requirements relating to school premises are discussed in Chapter 5. Numerous organizations, including the Health and Safety Executive produce further guidance on particular topics, such as safety glazing and so on. From the cases mentioned below, it will be obvious that glass is a particularly important source of potential accidents and a school should ensure that any glazing complies with the relevant standards. For example, any glass in a 'critical' location – doors at shoulder height or below (including doors with glass panels) and windows at waist height must be fitted with safety glass, of which there are several different types. Schools should seek advice on whether the current glazing meets the requirements.

Other obvious sources of injury include the passageways and floors. Floors and passageways should be regularly inspected to ensure the integrity and cleanliness of the surface area, and that access is not being obstructed.

Another key issue in the light of the tragedies occurring in Dunblane and the death of Philip Lawrence is the security of the premises. The Suzy Lamplugh Trust has done a lot of useful work in this area (see its publication *Personal Safety for Schools*) and initiatives for cooperation between schools and police are growing. Research shows that most assaults on staff are likely to be carried out by parents, while most assaults on pupils are likely to be perpetrated by pupils in other schools.

Of course, the need to keep the premises secure must be balanced against promoting a comfortable and happy atmosphere in schools, which is not always an easy balance to strike. Equally, the already stretched school budget may snap under the strain of some of the recommended security equipment. Although some security measures might, strictly, be the responsibility of the LEA, it may be a long time before resources are actually available from the LEA to implement them, so the school needs to consider whether or not there are measures that have to be paid for from the budget. Some extra money has been made available by the DfEE for the provision of CCTV cameras in schools, together with other funds to improve school security. The UK Schools Administration web site contains some useful advice about security measures and the approach schools should adopt. The DfEE have also produced guidance – *Improving Security in Schools*.

In rather more of the reported cases in this area than the others we have been looking at so far, courts have found schools or teachers to be negligent.

- *Ralph* v *London County Council* (1947) 63 TLR 546 CA: pupils were playing a game of touch in a large assembly hall, divided from the dining hall by a large partition, with glass panes at a height of three feet. The plaintiff ran into the panes of glass and was badly injured. The court found the teacher, and therefore the authority, negligent in allowing the game to be played at all and certainly for not supervising it sufficiently.
- *Cahill* v *West Ham Corporation* (1937) 81 SJ 630: during an indoor relay race, a boy put his hand through a glass partition.
- *Gravestock* v *Lewisham Hospital Management Committee* (1955) *The Times*, 27 May [1955] CLY 1853: a patient aged nine was left unattended temporarily and ran into glass swing doors.

- *Refell* v *Surrey County Council* [1964] 1 WLR 358, 1 All ER 743: a pupil put out her hand towards a swing door as it was coming towards her. The glass panel was an eighth inch thick and not toughened. The court said that this was an obvious danger.
- *Lyes* v *Middlesex County Council* (1962) 61 LGR 443 [1962] CLY 2425: a 15-year-old pupil put his hand through a glass door while playing. The glass was too thin, contrary to the Regulations then in force.
- *Martin* v *Middlesborough Corporation* (1965) 63 LGR 385 [1965] CLY 2735 CA: a child fell in the school playground and cut her hand on a broken milk bottle. The children put the bottles back in the crates after their mid-morning break, which were then left in the playground for collection in the afternoon. The caretaker swept up twice a day, but said that there was often broken glass and empty bottles by the crate. The court was not satisfied with the existing arrangements for disposal of milk bottles.
- *Butt* v *ILEA* (1968) 66 LGR 379 [1968] CLY 2724 CA: a child was injured by an unfenced printing machine.
- *Fryer* v *Salford Corporation* [1937] 1 All ER 617: an 11-year-old girl's apron was set on fire by an unguarded gas cooker. The judge said that it was natural for children to crowd round the oven to see the final results of their efforts, so the danger should have been anticipated and a guard installed (even though it was not normal practice at the time, because the danger was so obvious).
- *Woodward* v *Mayor of Hastings* [1944] 2 All ER 505 CA: a pupil slipped on frozen snow on a step that had not been cleared.
- *Murphy* v *Bradford Metropolitan Council* (1991) ICR 80, *The Times*, 11 February CA: a pupil slipped on a notorious, sloping, frozen path to school that had not been gritted. The caretaker cleared and salted the path at regular intervals, but the court said that cinders or grit should have been put down.
- *Ching* v *Surrey County Council* [1910] 1 KB 736: there was a hole in the surface of the playground and a child was injured.
- *Morris* v *Caernarvon County Council* [1910] 1 KB 858: a child caught her fingers in a door that was heavy and too highly sprung, representing a danger to young children.
- *Moualem* v *The Council of the City of Carlisle* [1995] ELR No. 1 QBD: the operator of a commercial play centre was convicted of an offence under the Health and Safety at Work Act 1974. He tried to argue that the Act did not provide protection to children using the centre, only to workers. The court found against him –

lawful visitors who were not workers were to be protected under Section 4 of the Act. The same would obviously apply to schools and local authorities.

- *Allen* v *London Borough of Barnet* (21 November 1997, CA): a teacher recovered damages when she slipped and broke her leg on a wet floor. Just before slipping, it had rained heavily and the floor had become wet as a result of rainwater being brought in when the children came inside from the playground. On the particular facts of the case, the judge concluded that there should have been a mat on the floor to absorb the moisture. The Court of Appeal upheld the judge's decision but emphasized that it turned on the particular facts and had no wide-ranging implications for schools' health and safety practices. This was despite the evidence on behalf of the LEA that a mat might have been more slippery rather than less and that the floor's coefficient of friction was above safety levels, whether the floor was wet or dry.

Schools and other organizations have escaped a finding of liability in the following circumstances.

- *Gillmore* v *London County Council* [1983] 3 All ER 31 DC: a young man taking part in an exercise class slipped on a highly polished floor of a local authority hall that was usually used for dancing. He was wearing rubber-soled shoes. The court held that the floor was not suitable for the sort of exercises that were being performed. It took note of the fact that there had been discussion about whether or not the floor should have been covered. Although it would not have been reasonable to cover the floor, it showed that the organizers of the class were aware of the danger.
- *Chilvers* v *London County Council* (1916) 80 JP 246: a child was injured when the lance on a toy soldier poked his eye. It was common practice for children to be allowed to play with such toys in schools.

Medical attention

There have been calls for teachers to receive better training in ministering to the medical needs of pupils, while others say that this should be left to those who are properly expert. However, staff in school, unless specially employed for the purpose, are under no legal obligation to administer medicine. Indeed, the Medicines Act 1968 restricts dealing with, and administering, medications, and only a qualified practitioner should administer injections, for example, except in the case of an emergency (a life or death emergency). As part of the common law duty of care, a teacher should do whatever a reasonably prudent parent would do in the same circumstances. This may include the administration, or supervision, of the taking of medicine and certainly the seeking of appropriate medical attention. A school is required to have an area for the purpose of medical examination and treatment by the Education (School Premises) Regulations 1996. Although this need not be exclusively used for this purpose, it must always be readily available.

The DfEE has issued guidance on medical needs – *Supporting Pupils with Medical Needs in School* (DfEE Circular 14/96) – which advises, as usual, that the school should have clear policies on dealing with medical needs, medical emergencies and medicines. It has also issued further, more detailed, guidance – *Supporting Pupils with Medical Needs: A good practice guide*.

Precisely because a teacher is not a doctor, the courts are reluctant to find teachers liable for any mistakes in terms of medical treatment or response to a medical situation, as the following cases show.

- *Davies* v *Cornwall County Council* (1962) CA 308: a girl of six fractured her leg when she fell at school. The staff did not realize she had been seriously injured – the girl was crying, sweating and complaining of pain – her leg was examined, but the girl was allowed to walk to her aunt's shop nearby. The court held that it was not negligent of the school not to have taken further steps, such as contacting her parents or doctor. This case might have been decided differently now, especially if the school policy was to contact parents in the event of any accident of a more than trivial nature.
- *Hippolyte* v *Bexley London Borough Council* (1994) *Ed. Law Monitor*, July 1995: in 1986, a 16-year-old pupil had a severe asthma attack at school. The teacher failed to call an ambulance, but suggested that the pupil went home. The girl suffered brain damage. The court said that the LEA had a duty of care to get medical help, even if a pupil was over the age of 16 if health problems developed at school. However, it could not have foreseen at the time (1986) what the consequences might have been, so they were not liable on the facts. Asthma is now much better under-

stood and a similar response in 1998 would probably give rise to being found negligent.

Children with special needs

It may seem obvious, but a court will expect a higher degree of care in relation to children who, for some reason, are not well-equipped to look after themselves. In the case of *Ellis* v *Sayers Confectionery* (1963) 61 LGR 299 (1963) CA 56A, a deaf and dumb pupil of eight was run down while crossing the road, having just got off a school bus. The woman in charge of the bus was held 20 per cent liable for not making sure the pupil was safe to cross. The driver of the car that ran the pupil over was judged 80 per cent liable because they were going too fast.

Negligence in the provision of education or educational services

> Upon the education of the people of this country, the fate of this country depends.
>
> Disraeli, *Hansard*, 15 June 1874

This remark neatly encapsulates a not uncommonly expressed sentiment showing the importance society places on a good education. For many years, Parliament has required LEAs to provide both sufficient and efficient education. The duty to cause a child to receive efficient education is also imposed on parents. For the first time, in the School Standards and Framework Act (which became law on 24 July 1998) there is a requirement that LEAs provide education 'with a view to promoting high standards' (Section 5). This is one among many measures proposed both by the new Labour Government and the previous Conservative one to raise the standards of the education provided to children in the United Kingdom.

In fact, despite the bad press that teachers and LEAs have suffered recently with regard to their abilities to provide (or at least deliver) a good (or no less than adequate) standard of education, in the field of negligence, teachers as professionals have not received the same level of unwelcome attention from the courts as have other professionals.

A court decision has shown that the winds of change may be blowing in the direction of the teaching profession – *X* v *Bedfordshire County Council*, etc [1995] 3 WLR 152, 2 FLR 276, a batch of six cases. The following is the passage that best summarizes the court's approach to the issue of negligence:

> The question therefore is whether the headmaster of any school, whether private or public, or a teaching adviser is under a duty to his pupils to exercise skill and care in advising on their educational needs? ...
>
> In my judgment a school which accepts a pupil assumes responsibility not only for his physical well-being but also for his educational needs. The education of the pupil is the very purpose for which the child goes to the school. The headteacher, being responsible for the school, himself comes under a duty of care to exercise the reasonable skills of a headmaster in relation to such educational needs. If it comes to the attention of the headmaster that a pupil is underperforming, he does owe a duty to take such steps as a reasonable teacher would consider appropriate to try to deal with such underperformance. To hold that, in such circumstances, the headteacher could properly ignore the matter and make no attempt to deal with it would fly in the face, not only of society's expectations of what a school will provide, but also of the fine traditions of the teaching profession itself. If such a headteacher gives advice to the parents, then in my judgment he must exercise the skills and care of a reasonable teacher in giving such advice.
>
> Similarly, in the case of the advisory teacher brought in to advise on the educational needs of a specific pupil, if he knows that the advice will be communicated to the pupil's parents must foresee that they will rely on such advice. Therefore in giving that advice he owes a duty to the child to exercise the skill and care of a reasonable advisory teacher.

The House of Lords was considering this batch of six cases together – three about social services and three about education. In the 'Dorset' case, there was an alleged breach of discretionary statutory powers given to the LEA to make statements and provision for special educational needs and negligence in the provision of such services. In the 'Hampshire' case, there was an alleged breach of a common-law duty in advising about educational needs. In the 'Bromley' case, there was an alleged failure to provide suitable education and place a pupil in a special school.

In summary, the court found in the Dorset case that there was no separate common-law duty of care in the LEA's exercising of its discretionary statutory powers. The statute provided its own remedies and that put an end to any other rights there might otherwise have been. However, the court decided that there was a duty of care to exercise care in the provision of a service authorized under the discretionary statutory powers. An LEA will therefore be vicariously liable for any breaches of that duty of care.

It was in the Hampshire case that the judge made the remarks quoted above. It also said that the standard of care expected would be decided by reference to the advice that would have been given by reasonably experienced and competent members of the teaching profession at the time.

In the Bromley case, the court said that there was no private-law right to damages for breach of an LEA's statutory duty to provide education – it was for the Minister of State to enforce the statutory duties under the acts. Again, the judge commented that the acts said clearly what remedies were available to the dissatisfied parent or pupil so that, by implication, there were no other remedies. There could only be a claim against the authority if what they actually provided was provided negligently.

The gist of this is that if an LEA fails to exercise its statutory powers, no private individual can do much about it, except by using any statutory machinery, such as by taking a case to the SENT and above or by complaining to the Secretary of State. However, if they purport to carry out their duties under the statutory powers, they may be liable if they do so negligently.

In fact, although there was a great deal that was not decided by the court as it was looking only at the preliminary issue of whether or not there could be theoretical liability imposed on an LEA. What it did not decide in these cases was whether or not the facts supported a finding of negligence and, if so, what damages might be recoverable for the alleged impairment of personal and intellectual development.

Since these cases were decided, the courts have had to deal with two claims of negligence in which they have had to decide on these other issues. In the *Phelps* v *Hillingdon Borough Council* (1998) *The Times*, 9 November case, the court had originally decided that an educational psychologist was negligent in failing to diagnose dyslexia. The plaintiff underachieved at school. Once she found out that she was dyslexic (several years later), she received proper teaching and this led to a marked improvement in her ability to read and write. The Court of Appeal overturned this decision saying that damages were not recoverable on public policy grounds. The educational psychologist had not assumed a duty of care towards the plaintiff but even if she had done so, she was not in breach of that duty, nor had her 'failure' caused damage to the plaintiff.

Some of the batch of cases in *X* v *Bedfordshire* have gone before the European Court of Human Rights for a decision on whether or not there has been a breach of the Convention on Human Rights. The cases have passed the first hurdle, but it is likely to be a considerable time before a final decision is available and it is not yet possible to anticipate its likely effect on domestic law.

In conclusion, therefore, although the door has now firmly been declared to be open in theoretical terms, it is not yet clear whether or not the decision will have any major impact and how much litigation will follow. Sound advice, however, is to ensure that insurance policies cover liability for damages for negligent advice or omissions.

Chapter 15

Brief encounters – legal remedies

Reasons for being in court

In Chapter 2 we saw an outline of the main court structure and hierarchy.

There are some, admittedly fairly rare, situations when you may find yourself actually having to give evidence to a court or tribunal. These include, for example:

- because it is said that you, a colleague or the school have been negligent;
- when a court is trying to decide whether or not to place a child in care;
- when a court is considering what sentence to impose on a child;
- when a court is considering whether or not to make an education supervision order;
- when a court is deciding which of a child's parents they should live with;
- governors or an LEA panel are considering whether or not to uphold an exclusion decision;
- you have witnessed a road traffic accident;
- you have witnessed an assault on school premises.

Table 15.1 shows the main types of cases you are likely to be involved in as a teacher and the court or tribunal that most often hears that type of case. Sometimes a case starts in one court and is transferred to a higher court (in some instances, a case may be transferred down to a lower court, but this is rarer) and this is also shown in Table 15.1.

Table 15.1 The types of cases teachers may be involved in and where they are heard

Types of cases	Court or tribunal
Care proceedings.	All start in a magistrates' court as civil cases, but may be transferred up to a County court or the High Court.
Residence/contact disputes between parents.	Usually in a County court, but may be a magistrates' or the High Court.
Juvenile crime.	Youth court, which is a special informal court in a magistrates' court for criminal matters involving young people.
School attendance order.	Magistrates' court exercising criminal jurisdiction.
Education supervision order.	As for care proceedings.
Action for negligence/breach of statutory duty.	County court, but may be the High Court.
Road traffic accident.	County court, but may rarely be the High Court.
Criminal assault.	Magistrates' court, but may be a Crown Court.
Application for an injunction.	County court, but may be the High Court.
Exclusion appeal.	Special panel of an LEA.
Admissions appeal.	Special panel of an LEA (or independent panel called by an aided or GM school).
Challenge to decision on special educational needs.	Special educational needs tribunal (or the High Court at judicial review stage.)
Challenge to a decision of an LEA appeal panel about admissions or exclusions.	The High Court, by way of judicial review.

| Disputes over employment contracts. | Industrial tribunals. |
| Applications for a licence to sell alcohol. | Licensing justices – special panel of magistrates. |

Legal remedies

Some of the types of cases shown in Table 15.1 have already been discussed in earlier chapters. Special educational needs are dealt with in Chapter 9, admissions in Chapter 11 and exclusions in Chapter 13. Disputes between parents are discussed in Chapter 11. Other family proceedings (such as care orders), education supervision orders and school attendance orders are discussed in Chapter 12. Employment matters are discussed in Chapters 4 to 6, assaults and similar criminal proceedings in Chapter 13 and negligence actions in Chapter 14.

The main legal remedy that has not been discussed so far, but to which there has been reference throughout this book is judicial review. This is a vast subject and there is only room for a relatively brief summary here. Judicial review is the main method anyone with sufficient interest in a decision – for example, a parent who is not happy with an LEA's decision about its policy on schools – can use to challenge the decision of any public authority.

A judicial review is not quite the same as an appeal against a decision. It is an attack on the way in which a decision was arrived at rather than a direct attack on the decision itself, although it may result in the decision being quashed or overruled. The main grounds for challenging a decision by means of judicial review are that it is:

- illegal – the decision maker has applied a law incorrectly or acted outside it altogether, for example, by making a decision it did not have the power to make or using a power to make a decision that was not the sort of decision Parliament intended it to be used for;
- irrational – the decision maker's decision was wholly unreasonable – 'so outrageous in its defiance of logic or accepted moral standards that no sensible person who had applied his mind to the question to be decided could have arrived at it';
- procedure improper – for example, failing to follow the rules of natural justice, failing to act fairly and failing to follow the rules

set out in legislation, disciplinary procedures and so on, failing to take into account relevant considerations or taking into account irrelevant considerations.

An example of an illegal decision was that of Liverpool City Council to dismiss all its teachers because it had run out of money. It was illegal for all sorts of reasons, including that it failed to comply with the legal requirement about making decisions for educational reasons. Examples of procedurally improper decisions are found in the cases referred to in Chapter 13 on exclusion appeals – for example, where a teacher governor who was a potential witness participated in an exclusion decision.

Applications for judicial review must be made very promptly after the decision has been made and certainly within three months of it. It is a two-stage application. First, some cases are screened out without a hearing as being without merit. If a case proceeds to a full hearing, the court has a number of options if it agrees that the decision that has been challenged was not correctly made. It can make a declaration (a legal statement of someone's status or entitlement or power to do something), grant an injunction (to stop something from happening or order that it should happen), quash the decision altogether (wipe it out as if it had never been made), make an order that a decision should not be made at all (or only if conditions are fulfilled) or order an authority to take certain steps to make sure it fulfils its legal obligations. In very rare circumstances, a court can also make an award of damages. What a court does not do is substitute its decision for that of the body that has been challenged, although the effect of a court's decision may end up being the same thing as making a new decision. It is completely up to a court as to whether or not to grant any remedy at all. It will not do so, for example, if it agrees that there has been some procedural impropriety, but thinks it would not have made any difference to the eventual decision or that there has been no unfairness.

The law of judicial review in the education context is complicated and specialized. It is a remedy frequently used to challenge the decisions of an LEA (particularly about exclusions and admissions) and SENTs. It cannot normally be used against independent schools, unless they are in some way funded by, or controlled by, the State (such as a city technology college or some voluntary aided schools).

Generally speaking, applications for judicial review do not involve the giving of any oral evidence and are decided on written evidence and legal argument. This is one tribunal where you, as a teacher, can at least sit back and relax and leave it to the lawyers.

Local government ombudsmen and the Commission for Local Administration

There are three local government ombudsmen for England and one for Wales who can investigate complaints of injustice arising from maladministration by local authorities and certain other bodies. Their remit includes educational matters, unless they relate to the internal affairs of an individual school. Nor can the ombudsmen investigate any complaint if there is some other provision or right to appeal or review by another tribunal, court or Minister of State.

In the main, in the educational context, they deal with complaints about admissions, special needs and exclusions. Complaints have to be made within 12 months of the matters alleged in the complaint being known to the complainer. Investigations by the ombudsmen are held in private and reports of their decisions do not usually identify any individuals, unless there is a finding that a councillor has been guilty of maladministration. Their reports must be published by the local authority. The ombudsmen usually make a recommendation as to any need for policies or practices to be revised and may recommend the payment of a (usually modest) amount of compensation to the complainant.

Giving evidence

In many of the other situations referred to in Table 15.1, you might be called on to give live evidence. The reason for your being asked to give evidence will affect the way you are treated in a courtroom by the various parties. In some cases, you will have the status almost of an expert witness. In most cases, your views will be treated with a great deal of respect. Even when one party is hostile to your evidence, they are unlikely to give you too much of a mauling in court because it will not find favour with the tribunal. However, there will be times when your professionalism is called into question and you can expect an uncomfortable experience.

Before you go into court, you may be asked to produce a summary of your evidence in a written statement or affidavit. You may also be asked to produce documents to the court. Some documents may be automatically accepted by the court without anyone having to attend to formally explain their origins and produce them in evidence. Which these are is set out in Section 566 of the Education Act 1996:

- any document signed by the clerk or chief education officer of an LEA or by any other officer authorized to sign it;
- any extract from the minutes of a governing body of a county or voluntary school if signed by the chairman or clerk to that governing body;
- any document setting out the attendance of a child at school signed by the headteacher;
- any document signed by a medical officer of an LEA.

Other documents may have to be disclosed to a court and the parties in the proceedings. Some information is given in Chapter 10 about records that are private and confidential. Some documents are covered by public interest immunity – that is, it is in the public interest that they be kept confidential. If you are in any doubt about whether or not a document should be disclosed to anyone, you should seek legal advice.

In court proceedings, your duty is to tell the truth, the whole truth and nothing but the truth. You will be asked to swear an oath or make an affirmation to the effect that your evidence will be truthful. Even in more informal proceedings, you are, of course, expected to be honest.

Before you go to court, it will be helpful to find out why you are being called to give evidence if it is not obvious. For example, in disputes between parents, teachers may be being asked to give evidence to show that a child is undisturbed by contact with one of its parents or, conversely, upset and badly behaved after contact. In care cases, you may be asked to describe a child's behaviour, how they are usually dressed or what they have said to you about the way they have been treated at home. In this sort of situation, you will not be represented by a lawyer of your own. You will usually be called (asked to come to court) by one side or the other. You may even have been ordered to come to court under a witness summons or subpoena and you may be asked to bring certain documents with you. The lawyer representing the person who calls you will probably be able to tell you what the case is about and why your evidence may be relevant. Your duty, though, is not to win the case for one side or the other, but to tell the truth as you know it. For example, if you disagree with a colleague's actions, you must say so.

What no lawyer is allowed to do is to tell you how to give your evidence. Coaching a witness is not allowed. There is nothing wrong, however, with a lawyer telling you whether or not your evidence is accepted by all parties and, if not, what particular matters are likely to be in dispute.

Before you go into court, make sure you read through your written statement and any notes that you have made for yourself. You will usually be asked to confirm that the statement was made and signed by you and that it is true to the best of your knowledge and belief. You should tell the court if there are any mistakes in the statement or anything important you want to add.

While you are giving your evidence, you may want to refer to your own personal notes that you made at the time of an incident. The court will usually let you do this, although they may want to know when you prepared them and insist that the originals are shown to all parties.

You may be asked questions by a number of different lawyers. You will give your version of events first in answer to questions from the lawyer acting for the person who asked you to come to court. Afterwards there comes the cross-examination. You may be asked questions to clarify how much you could see of an incident or test out the accuracy of your memory of an event or challenge your evidence. This type of questioning may feel quite hostile. On the other hand, you may be asked questions designed to get you to say something positive in someone's favour. You may also be asked questions by the tribunal members. Finally, the lawyer who started the questions off can ask some further questions to clear up any misunderstandings that may have arisen or to get you to emphasize a point.

Addressing a court – what to call the judge or tribunal member

Table 15.2 shows what you should call the judge or tribunal member to whom you are giving your evidence. Most courts will not mind very much if you get this a bit wrong (particularly not if you accidentally promote the judge!), so long as you are polite. However, you might feel more at home knowing you are using the right terminology.

Table 15.2 How to address the judge or tribunal member when you are giving evidence

Judge or tribunal member	Direct	Indirect
Tribunal chairperson, such as at exclusion appeal, industrial tribunal, magistrate, coroner, district judge.	Sir or madam.	You (and your colleagues).
Clerk to tribunal or magistrates.	Sir or madam.	Your learned clerk.
Master in the High Court.	Master	You
Circuit judge in a County court and Crown Court (also recorder or assistant recorder (part-time judge in these courts).	Your honour.	Your honour.
High Court judge, Court of Appeal judge, judge at the Old Bailey, House of Lords.	My lord or lady.	Your lordship or ladyship.

When you have finished your evidence, the court will usually let you know that you can leave. You may not do so until you have formally been given permission.

If your evidence is interrupted by a break for lunch or overnight, you may not discuss your evidence with anyone during the interruption. This can be very frustrating, but it is an important rule designed to stop lawyers and others from trying to improve the evidence or tell a witness what to say. A court will usually remind you about this when they send you away.

Some proceedings are entirely confidential and you should not discuss what went on with anyone. Cases under the Children Act 1989 are an example of this.

It is impossible to give a blueprint for giving evidence in all the situations when you might be called as a witness, but I can offer you a few golden rules to observe.

Don't

- get into an argument with the person asking you questions;
- use too much jargon;
- try to work out why you are being asked the question before you answer it;
- take things too personally;
- let yourself be pressured into simply answering 'yes' and 'no' when more detail is required.

Do

- explain any educational jargon if you need to use it, such as individual education plan, key stage;
- listen to the question you are asked and answer it;
- dress reasonably formally – you do not have to wear sober or dark clothing, but you will probably feel more comfortable if you are not too colourful);
- be as even-handed as possible – for example, if there are positive things that can be said about a parent, remember to mention them as well as the bad things;
- give your answers to the person who has to make the decision – that is, not to the person asking the question;
- speak slowly enough and with enough pauses to allow your audience to make notes about your evidence.

It helps to get to court a bit early so that you can ask any questions you want to, such as what do I call the tribunal, where do I stand, what is the procedure? It will also give you time to find the toilet and the nearest source of tea or coffee. There is almost always a great deal of waiting around, so bring something to do while you are waiting.

Finding a lawyer

If, for some reason, you need to instruct a lawyer yourself, there are various ways of finding one, including the *Yellow Pages*, although I would not necessarily recommend this!

The first port of call will usually be your union or professional body or else your employer's legal department. Depending on the circumstances, you may have the benefit of legal expenses insurance, in which case, the insurance company will usually instruct a solicitor for you. Even if you cannot get help from any of these sources in terms of providing you with a lawyer, they may be able to recommend someone suitable. Some lawyers, believe it or not, do work for nothing if there is an interesting point involved and special circumstances that mean you cannot fund the litigation and are not eligible for legal aid. It is also becoming increasingly possible for work to be taken on under a variety of agreements for payment depending on the type of case, such as deferred payment, payment by instalments, payment on success. These options are governed by strict professional rules and the US style of 'no win, no fee' does not operate in the UK.

Failing that, you can get a list of solicitors in your area who specialize in the relevant area of law from the Law Society (see the Useful addresses section at the back of the book). Friends and colleagues may also be able to help with recommendations. There are also numerous professional directories that can give you information about the experience, background and specialisms of particular lawyers. These are often available in public libraries and some are published on the Internet, such as the *Butterworth's Law Directory* and the *Waterlows Directory*).

Types of lawyer

There are many different types of lawyer you may encounter during the course of a legal dispute or court case. These are set out in Table 15.3.

Table 15.3 Types of lawyers and what they do

Solicitors	<ul><li>90 per cent of lawyers.</li><li>Must have degree in law or diploma.</li><li>On-the-job training for 2 years – can take instructions during that time, but supervised by qualified solicitor.</li><li>Employed (until become partners).</li><li>Work in firms (partnerships).</li><li>Can be directly instructed by clients.</li><li>Can represent clients in some courts (and in higher courts if have advocacy certificate.)</li></ul>

- Can refuse to take instructions.
- Can sue for unpaid fees.
- Are regulated by the Law Society.

Barristers

- Also called 'counsel' (fat cat, brief, hired gun and numerous unpublishable insults).
- 10 per cent of lawyers.
- Must have degree in law or diploma.
- On-the-job training as pupil for 12 months – first 6 months cannot accept instructions.
- If in independent practice, self-employed (but may be employed, say, by a company or an LEA's legal department).
- Work in Chambers (offices/cooperatives).
- Cannot be directly instructed by clients (except by certain professions – accountants and surveyors – and then only for non-court work.)
- Cannot refuse to represent for personal reasons, unless this is because they are insufficiently experienced/competent in the particular area of law (cab rank rule).
- Specialist advocates.
- Cheaper than solicitors.
- Cannot sue directly for unpaid fees.
- Regulated by the Bar Council.

Legal executives

- Members of the Institute of Legal Executives (22,000 members) and and subject to the ILEX Code of Conduct.
- Entry qualifications –: 4 GCSEs or 2 A levels and 1 GCSE or BTEC or GNVQ.
- Qualification by part-time course over 4 years.
- Usually specialize in a particular area of law, often probate, wills, debt collection, and tend to carry out routine/procedural work
- Also known as 'paralegals'.

Paralegals and clerks

- May be legal executives.
- Work for firms of solicitors or in-house.
- Otherwise, general term covering many types of legal support staff.
- May be intending lawyer gaining work experience or being tried out before training contract offer.
- May be member of National Paralegals Association, which runs training courses.

Licensed	• Specialists qualified to deal with conveyancing
conveyancers	work only.
	• Regulated by the Council of Licensed Conveyancers.

What to expect from a lawyer

Any solicitor or barrister is subject to the Professional Code of Conduct, which regulates the ways in which they should deal with their clients. This includes giving estimates of the costs of proceedings, keeping information about clients confidential, treating them with courtesy, responding to letters and telephone calls in a timely way and so on, as well as giving you competent legal advice.

It is the job of a lawyer to give you advice. It is for the client to give instructions and make the decisions about whether or not to take action, when to settle and on what terms. A lawyer will often point out all sorts of unlikely consequences and risks. That is part of the job. They should also be able to tell you how likely a consequence is so that you can decide whether or not it is a risk you are willing to run in order to achieve some sort of other benefit, such as an end to the litigation.

It is also part of the job of a lawyer to act for a client in such a way that there is no conflict with any other clients. A barrister, for example, has at least two clients – the lay client and the professional client, usually a solicitor. For a barrister, this means that the lay client comes first. If a solicitor or barrister has done something wrong, both the barrister and the solicitor are under a duty to tell the client so that they can consider their options, which include taking advice from another lawyer.

There can be other clients, too, who are more or less obvious. For example, if you have the benefit of legal expenses insurance, your insurer is also a client and entitled to information about the likely prospects of success of the case and the likelihood of recovering damages. The insurer can ultimately decide whether or not to continue funding the litigation process. If the union is funding litigation, the same applies to the union.

It should also be remembered that, in many cases in teaching, both the employer and the employee may be jointly sued. Typically, it is the employer who funds the litigation and is the client, not the teacher or other member of staff. In most cases, there will not be any, or barely any, conflict between the two in practice, but they can arise and the teacher should be aware that the lawyer for the employer owes a first duty to the employer.

If, for any reason, you become involved in litigation and are not happy with any aspect of your lawyer's behaviour, you have the right to complain about it to the relevant professional body – In the case of a solicitor, this is the Office of the Supervision of Solicitors; for a barrister, the Professional Conduct Committee of the Bar Council; for legal executives, the Institute of Legal Executives; and for licensed conveyancers, the Council for Licensed Conveyancers (see the Useful addresses section at the end of the book). If possible, you should discuss your concerns with your solicitor before taking this step and give them the opportunity to offer you an explanation or apology or other appropriate remedy. There is a special protection granted to any lawyer in respect of the work they do in the court room, which means they cannot be sued (although a complaint can still be made). This protection is strictly limited to the courtroom (in order to avoid duplication of trials and hearings) and would not apply to any advice about a settlement, for example. It is far from a blanket immunity.

In addition to the professional bodies, there is also the Legal Services Ombudsman to whom complaints can be made about the professional bodies themselves, including about the manner in which they have dealt with any complaints made to them (see the Useful addresses section at the back of the book).

If you are unhappy with any aspect of your treatment by court staff, you should address your complaint to the chief clerk of the particular court in the first place. If this does not produce a satisfactory response, then you can take the matter up the line to the courts administrator and then the court service customer service unit of the Lord Chancellor's Department. If you are still not satisfied, you can refer the matter to your MP and ask for a reference to the Parliamentary Commissioner for Administration (Ombudsman). If your complaint concerns the way in which a judge has treated you in court, you can write to the Judicial Appointments Group of the Lord Chancellor's Department.

Frequently asked questions

I was assaulted at school by the parent of a pupil, but the school management do not want to pursue any action? What can I do?

If you have a personal legal remedy, which is likely in these circumstances, you are perfectly entitled to take action yourself. In the case of a criminal prosecution, it is normally the police who decide whether or not to pursue proceedings, but you can take out a private prosecution if you really want to. Of course, the problem with taking any proceedings yourself is that they cost money.

On a practical level, you may wish to invoke the grievance procedure and talk to your union to see whether or not it can help with litigation or at least persuade the governing body to do so (you may have an employment remedy if it refuses to back you in some circumstances). You need to watch your objectivity. Management may be reluctant to take action for reasons of resources (which would probably not be a terribly proper consideration), but it may be that there is no likelihood of a successful outcome to litigation. This might be to do with the quality of evidence that you would give or because you did something wrong or questionable yourself – for example, by inflaming a situation instead of calming it. There might also be compassionate grounds to do with the personal circumstances of the parent or pupil.

In the main, unless the incident is minor or trivial, you should be able to expect support. Be clear, however, about whether or not what you want is a day in court. I enjoy it, but thousands would not. Proceedings are stressful and sometimes unpleasant (particularly being a witness in criminal proceedings, despite the support that is available through the Victim Support Scheme). You may be better off with an apology and some sort of embargo on the parent attending the school or approaching you.

Appendix I

Summary of relevant legislation

The Education (No. 2) Act 1986

The main relevant provisions of this Act that remain in force concern appraisal of teacher performance in maintained and grant-maintained schools. Under the Act, the Secretary of State has the power to make provision to require LEAs or others to secure the regular appraisal of teachers, governors to ensure that this happens and allow disclosure of the results of performance appraisal to teachers themselves and them to make representations about their appraisals. This is also the Act that gives the Secretary of State power to make regulations governing grants for teacher training.

The Education Reform Act 1988

The remaining important provisions of this Act give the Secretary of State power to make regulations as to the qualifications a teacher is required to have and other related matters, such as probationary periods, the keeping of records and health standards. It is under this Act that the Secretary of State can bar certain persons from being employed as teachers. This Act will be repealed by the Teaching and Higher Education Act 1998 when the relevant sections of that Act come into force.

The Children Act 1989

An Act to provide for the hearing of disputes about children, both within families and between families and their local authority. The Act also sets out the duties of a local authority in meeting the needs of children and families, the responsibility of social services departments for the regulation of voluntary homes and registered children's homes and daycare provision for pre-school children who are in need.

The School Teachers' Pay and Conditions Act 1991

Under this Act, the statutory pay and conditions of employment of teachers are determined following recommendations from the School Teachers' Review Body (STRB), a body appointed by the prime minister. The STRB reports to the prime minister on 'such matters as may from time to time be referred to the Review Body by the Secretary of State'. It usually reports annually and, following consideration and consultation on that report, a statutory instrument is passed containing the annual pay changes, the latest at the time of writing being the Education (School Teachers' Pay and Conditions) Order 1997 (SI 1997/755).

The Education Act 1994

This Act established the Teacher Training Agency and made provisions for training programmes based in schools.

The Disability Discrimination Act 1995

This Act introduced measures aimed at ending discrimination against the disabled. It deals with the rights of the disabled in employment, access to goods, facilities and services. Schools are required by the Act to provide certain information for pupils and parents.

The Nursery Education and Grant-maintained Schools Act 1996

This Act provided for the making of grants for nursery education (the 'voucher' scheme) and allows for borrowing by grant-maintained schools. The voucher scheme has now been scrapped. The School Standards and Framework Act 1998 contains new requirements for the provision of nursery education by LEAs in cooperation with voluntary groups and private nurseries.

The Education Act 1996

This is now the main Act regulating the provision of education in schools in England and Wales. Major changes were introduced by the Education Act 1993, which are largely repeated in the 1996 Act where they are consolidated with provisions from earlier legislation.

Many common terms are defined in the Act, such as pupil, school, primary school. 'Education' itself has no statutory definition. The Act also sets out the main powers of the Secretary of State for Education, the powers and duties of LEAs and the funding authorities (although the latter may shortly expire). There are separate sections dealing with different types of school – such as county, voluntary, grant-maintained, independent – setting out arrangements for their establishment and closure, financing arrangements, structure of governing bodies and so on. The other major provisions govern arrangements for children with special educational needs, the National Curriculum, religious education and worship, admissions, attendance, charging for education services, governing body functions and a number of miscellaneous matters. In addition, there are already vast numbers of regulations made pursuant to the Act. The 1996 Act has been amended in parts by the 1997 Act described below.

The School Inspections Act 1996

This is also a consolidating Act, bringing together provisions from earlier legislation governing the inspection of schools.

The Education Act 1997

This Act was produced with almost indecent haste in the dying days of the last Conservative Government, in part to set up the assisted places scheme, which has already been abolished by the first Education Act of the new Labour Government (see below).

Part II contains provisions relating to school discipline, including detention, restraint and exclusion. Part III deals with other disciplinary matters, such as double exclusions and home–school partnerships. Part IV deals with school performance targets and information about individual pupils, Part V with the new Qualifications and Curriculum Authorities and Part VI has further provisions relating to school inspections and LEA inspections. Part VII contains important provisions about careers education. Part VII has a number of miscellaneous clauses. The Act has a helpful index to the main expressions used and where to find the definitions.

The Education (Schools) Act 1997

The main provisions of this Act came into force on 1 September 1997, and it repealed the duty on the Secretary of State to operate the assisted places scheme and the other statutory provisions relating to that scheme. Those pupils already in the scheme were enabled to keep their places until the end of their primary or secondary education at their current school.

The School Standards and Framework Act 1998

This Act makes a number of changes to the education system, including limiting class sizes, setting up education zones, requiring local authorities to draw up education development plans, enabling the Secretary of State to take over failing LEAs and shut failing schools, creating new categories of school, providing for more parents on governing bodies and education committees, setting up adjudicators for admissions, setting up procedures for ballots to abolish grammar schools, restricting the extension of selection, enabling the Secretary of State to regulate on nutritional standards for school lunches, and abolishing the Funding Agency for Schools

The Teaching and Higher Education Act 1998

This Act establishes the General Teaching Council (GTC) to oversee the registration, qualification and training of teachers, and makes provision for the inspection of that training and for a code of practice. The GTC will also be a disciplinary body with powers to de-register a teacher if they are guilty of unacceptable professional conduct or serious professional incompetence or have a relevant conviction or to impose a reprimand, conditional registration order (for example, to undergo training before resuming teaching), suspension order (to prevent someone from teaching for a period of up to two years) or prohibition order (an indefinite ban, with the possibility of re-registration on application). A right of appeal to the High Court exists. It also contains provisions allowing the inspection of the training and careers service and amends the law on student grants and loans for higher education. Only the student loan and grant provisions came into force on the date the Act was passed (July 1998) – the remaining provisions will be phased in gradually.

Appendix II

Abbreviations

AC	Appeal Cases (part of main Law Report series)
All ER	*All England Law Reports*
CA	Court of Appeal
CLY	Current Law Year
CRE	Commission for Racial Equality
CTC	city technology college
DfEE	Department for Education and Employment
DC	Divisional Court
Ed. Law Monitor	*Education Law Monitor*
ELR	*Education Law Reports*
FCR	*Family Court Reporter*
FLR	*Family Law Reports*
GM	grant-maintained
HL	House of Lords
HMSO	Her Majesty's Stationery Office
HSE	Health and Safety Executive
ILR	*Independent Law Reports*
IRLR	*Industrial Relations Law Reports*
JP	Justice of the Peace
KB	King's Bench
LEA	local education authority
LGR	*Law Gazette Reports*
LT	*Law Times Reports*
OFSTED	Office for Standards in Education
PRU	pupil referral unit
QB	Queen's Bench
QCA	Qualifications and Curriculum Authority

QJP	*Queensland Justice of the Peace and Local Authorities' Journal (Australia)*
RPC	*Reports of Patent, Design and Trademark Cases*
SACRE	Standing Advisory Council for Religious Education
SENCO	special educational needs coordinator
SENT	special educational needs tribunal
Sol. J or SJ	*Solicitors' Journal*
TES	*Times Educational Supplement*
WLR	*Weekly Law Reports*
WWR	*Western Weekly Law Reports* (Canada) 1911–50, 1955–99

Useful addresses

Accident Line
(Law Society)
Freefone: 0500 192939

Advisory Centre for Education
Unit 1B
Aberdeen Studios
22–24 Highbury Grove
London N5 2DQ
Tel: 0171 354 8318

Andrea Adams Trust
Shalamar House
24 Derek Avenue
Hove
Sussex BN3 4PF
Tel: 01273 704900
Fax: 01273 417850
Call regarding workplace bullying.

Anti-bullying Campaign
10 Borough Hill Street
London SE1 9QQ
Tel: 0171 378 1446
Fax: 0171 378 8374

Arson Prevention Bureau
Melrose Avenue
Borehamwood
Hertfordshire WD6 2BJ
Tel: 0181 236 9700

Asbestos Information Centre
Limited (AIC)
PO Box 69
Widnes
Cheshire WA8 9GW
Tel: 0151 420 5866
Fax: 0151 420 5853

Association of County Councils
Eaton House
661A Eaton Square
London SW1W 9BH
Tel: 0171 235 1200

Association of Teachers and
Lecturers (ATL)
7 Northumberland Street
London WC2N 5DA
Tel: 0171930 6441
Fax: 0171930 5913
Web site: http://www.atl.org.uk

Association for Science in
Education (ASE)
College Lane
Hatfield
Hertfordshire AL10 9AA
Web site: http://www.ase.org.uk

Association of Metropolitan
Authorities
35 Great Smith Street
London SW1P 3BJ
Tel: 0171 222 8100

Boarding Schools Association
Westmorland
43 Raglan Road
Reigate
Surrey RH2 0DU
Tel: 01737 226450

British Activity Holiday
Association (BAHA)
22 Green Lane
Hersham
Walton-on-Thames
Surrey KT12 5HD
Tel and fax: 01932 252994
Web site: http://www.baha.org.uk

British Educational
Communications and Technology
Agency (formerly NCET)
Milburn Hill Road
Science Park
Coventry CV4 7JJ
Tel: 01203 416994
Fax: 01203 411418
Web site: see CCTA's web site

British Safety Council
70 Chancellor's Road
London W6 9RS
Tel: 0181 741 1231
Fax: 0181 741 4555
Web site: http://www.
britishsafetycouncil.co.uk/
e-mail: bscl@mail.
britishsafetycouncil.co.uk

British Broadcasting Corporation
(BBC)
Web site:
http://www.bbc.co.uk/education

Campaign Against Bullying At
Work (CABAW)
Chris Ball
MSF Centre
33–37 Moreland Street
London EC1V 8BB

Campaign for the Advancement of
State Education
158 Durham Road
London SW20 0DG
Tel and fax: 0181 944 8206

Careers Service National
Association (CSNA)
Shelagh Woolliscrogt
General Secretary
CSNA
2 Leabrook Road
Dronfield Woodhouse
Sheffield S18 8YS
Tel and fax: 01246 291541
Web site:
http://www.careers-uk.com

Carfax Publishing Company
PO Box 25
Abingdon
Oxfordshire OX14 3UE

Central Computer and
Telecommunications Agency
CCTA Government Information
Service
Web site:
http://www.open.gov.co.uk
Main link page for all government
departments, local authorities and
national government
organizations.

Central Bureau for Education
Visits and Exchanges
10 Spring Gardens
London SW1A 2BN
Tel: 0171 389 4004
Fax: 0171 389 4426

Centre for the Employment of
People with Disabilities
Employment Service
Disability Services Division
Level 3
Rockingham House
123 West Street
Sheffield S1 4ER
Tel: 0114 259 6437
Fax: 0114 259 6262

Centre for Education and Industry
University of Warwick
Coventry CV4 7AL
Tel for publications: 01203 523948
Fax: 01203 523617

Childline
Freepost 1111
London N1 OBR
Tel – 24-hour freefone number:
0800 1111
Web site:
http://www.childline.org.uk

Children's Legal Centre
University of Essex
Wivenhoe Park
Colchester
Essex CO4 3SQ
Tel for advice line: 01206 873820
Tel for publications: 01206 872466
Fax: 01206 874026
Web site:
http://www2.essex.ac.uk/clc
e-mail: clc@essex.ac.uk

City Technology Colleges Trust
(CTC Trust)
15 Young Street
London W8 5EH
Tel: 0171 376 2511

Commission for Local
Administration in England
(Ombudsman)
21 Queen Anne's Gate
London SW1H 9BU
Tel: 0171 915 3210

Commission for Racial Equality
Elliot House
10–12 Allington Street
London SW1E 5EH
Tel: 0171 828 7022
Fax: 0171 630 7605
Web site: see CCTA's web site,
special School's Zone page under
construction

Committee for the Employment of
People with Disabilities
Employment Service
Disability Services Division
Level 3
Rockingham House
123 West Street
Sheffield S1 4ER
Tel: 0114 259 6437
Fax: 0114 259 6262

Concerned Spouses of
Suffering/Stressed Teachers
(COSST)
Peter Lewis
22 Marlborough Rise
Aston
Sheffield S26 2ET
(SAE please)
Tel: 0114 2873087

Council for Licensed Conveyancers
16 Glebe Road
Chelmsford
Essex CM1 1QG
Tel: 01245 349599

Data Protection Registrar
Wycliffe House
Water Lane
Wilmslow
Cheshire SK9 5AF
Tel: 01625 545700
Web site: http://www.open.gov.uk/dpr/
e-mail: data@wycliffe.demon.co.uk

Disability Discrimination Act
(DDA) Information
FREEPOST MID02164
Stratford-upon-Avon CV37 9BR
Tel: 0345 622633

Department of Education for
Northern Ireland
Rathgael House
Balloo Road
Bangor
County Down BT19 7PR
Tel: 01247 279279
Web site: see CCTA's web site

Department for Education
Publications Centre
PO Box 6927
London E3 3NZ

Department for Education and
Employment (DfEE)
Sanctuary Buildings
Great Smith Street
London SW1P 3BT
Tel: 0171 925 5000; public
enquiries: 0171 925 5555
Fax: 0171 925 6000
Web site: see CCTA's web site
e-mail: info@dfee.gov.uk

Department of Health
Richmond House
79 Whitehall
London SW1A 2NS
Web site:
http://www.open.gov.uk/doh/

Eduweb
Web site:
http://www.eduweb.co.uk/

Equal Opportunities Commission
Overseas House
Quay Street
Manchester M3 3HN
Tel: 0161 833 9244
Fax: 0161 835 1657
Web site: http://www.eoc.org.uk
e-mail: info@eoc.org.uk

Fire Protection Association
Melrose Avenue
Borehamwood
Hertfordshire WD6 2BJ
Tel: 0181 236 9700

Freedom to Care
PO Box 125
West Molesey
Surrey KT8 1YE
Tel and fax: 0181-224 1022
Web site:http://www.members.
aol/FreeCare/Info.htm
e-mail: FreeCare@aol.com
Support for whistleblowers.

Funding Agency for Schools
Albion Wharf
25 Skeldergate
York YOP1 2XL
Tel: 01904 661661

General Council of the Bar
3 Bedford Row
London WC1R 4DB
Tel: 0171 242 0934

Grant Maintained Schools Centre
Red Lion House
9–10 High Street
High Wycombe
Buckinghamshire HP11 2AZ
Tel: 01497 474470

Health Education Authority
Trevelyan House
30 Great Peter Street
London SW1P 2HW
Tel: 0171 222 5300

Health and Safety Executive
(HSE)
HSE Information Centre
Broad Lane
Sheffield S3 7HQ
Tel: 0541 545500
Fax: 0114 289 2333
Web site: http://www.open.gov.
uk/hsehome.htm

HMSO
See under Stationery Office
Limited to purchase publications
Web site: http://www.hmso.gov.uk

Home and School Council
40 Sunningdale Mount
Eccleshall
Sheffield S11 9HA
Tel: 01742 364181

Home Office Police Research
Group
Publications
Room 456
50 Queen Anne's Gate
London SW1H 9AT

Incorporated Association of
Preparatory Schools
11 Waterloo Place
Leamington Spa
Warwickshire CV32 5LA
Tel: 01926 887833

Independent Schools Information
Service (ISIS)
56 Buckingham Gate
London SW1E 6AG
Tel: 0171630 8793/4
Fax: 0171 630 5013
Web site: http://www.isis.org.uk/
e-mail: national@isis.org.uk

Institute of Legal Executives
Kempston Manor
Kempston
Bedford MK42 7AB
Tel: 01234 841000

Kidscape
152 Buckingham Palace Road
London SW1W 9TR
Tel helpline for parents: 0171730
3300
Web site: http://www.dialspace.
dial.pipex.com/town/square/gaj28

Law Society
113 Chancery Lane
London WC2A 1PL
Tel: 0171 242 1222
Web site: http://www.lawsociety.
org.uk/home.html

Legal Services Ombudsman
22 Oxford Court
Oxford Street
Manchester M2 3WQ
Tel: 0161 236 9532

Local Government Association
26 Chapter Street
London SW1P 4ND
Tel: 0171-834 2222; enquiry line:
0171-664 3131
Fax: 0171-664 3030
Web site:
http://www.lga.gov.uk/lga

Local Government Ombudsman
(East Midlands, North)
Beverley House
17 Shipton Road
York YO3 6FZ

Local Government Ombudsman
(East Anglia, the South, South
West, West and Central England)
The Oaks
Westwood Way
Westwood Business Park
Coventry CV4 8JB
Tel: 01203 695999

Local Government Ombudsman
(London, Kent, Surrey, East
Sussex, West Sussex)
21 Queen Anne's Gate
London SW1H 9BU
Tel: 0171 915 3210

Lord Chancellor's Department
Selborne House
54–60 Victoria Street
London SW1E 6QW
Judicial Appointments Group
6th Floor
Southside
105 Victoria Street
London SW1E 6QT
Tel: 0171-210 8500
Web site: see CCTA's web site
e-mail: enquiries.lc@dhq.gov.uk
and, for court service,
cust.serv.cs@gtnet.gov.uk

National Accident Helpline
2 Castilian Street
Northampton NN1 1JX
Tel: 0800 444240
UK network of accident solicitors.

National Advisory Council for
Education and Training Targets
(NACETT)
7th Floor
222 Gray's Inn Road
London WC1X 8HL
Tel: 0171 211 5012
Fax: 0171 211 4540

National Association of Advisers
and Inspectors in Design and
Technology (NAAIDT)
16 Kingsway Gardens
Chandlers Ford
Hampshire SO5 1FE

National Confederation of
Parent–Teacher Associations
2 Ebbsfleet Industrial Estate
Gravesend
Kent DA11 9D2
Tel: 01474 560618

National Association of Governors
and Managers (NAGM)
Suite 36–8
21 Bennets Hill
Birmingham B2 5QP
Tel: 0121 643 5787; governors'
helpline: 0800 241242
Fax: 01444 472473
Web site:
http://www.rmplc.co.uk/orgs/nagm
e-mail: nagm@rmplc.co.uk

National Association for Primary
Education
National Office
Queen's Building
University of Leicester
Barrack Road
Northampton NN2 6AF
Tel: 01604 636326
Fax: 01604 636328
Web site: http://www.nape.org.uk

National Governors' Council
(NGC)
Glebe House
Church Street
Crediton
Devon EX17 2AF
Tel: 01363 774377
Fax: 01363 776007
Web site: http://www.ngc.org.uk
e-mail: ngc@ngc.org.uk

National Association of
Headteachers (NAHT)
1 Heath Square
Boltro Road
Haywards Heath
East Sussex RH16 1BL
Tel: 01444 472472
Web site: http://www.naht.org.uk/
e-mail: info@naht.org.uk

National Association of
Schoolmasters/Union of Women
Teachers (NASUWT)
Hillscourt Education Centre
Rose Hill
Rednal
Birmingham B45 8RS
Tel: 0121 453 6150
Web site:
http://www.teachersunion.org.uk
e-mail: visit web site for local
e-mail addresses

National Association for Special
Educational Needs (NASEN)
NASEN House
4–5 Amber Business Village
Amber Close
Armington
Tamworth B774RP
Tel: 01827 311500
Fax: 01827 315005
Web site: http://www.nasen.org.uk
e-mail: welcome@nasen.org.uk

National Children's Bureau
8 Wakley Street
London EC1V 7QE
Tel: 0171-843 6000
Web site: http://www.ncb.org.uk/

National Union of Teachers (NUT)
Hamilton House
Mabledon Place
London WC1H 9BD
Tel: 0171 388 6191
Web site:
http://www.teachers.org.uk

National Workplace Bullying
Advice Line
Dept C5
PO Box 67
Didcot
Oxfordshire OX11 0YH
Tel advice line: 01235 834548
Fax: 01235 861721
Web site: http://www.
successunlimited.co.uk/
Excellent web site.

NCET – see under British
Educational Communications and
Technology Agency

NCVQ – see under Qualification
and Curriculum Authority

Office for the Supervision of
Solicitors
Victoria Court
8 Dormer Place
Leamington Spa
Wawickshire CV32 5AE
Tel: 01926 820082/3; helpline:
01926 822007/8/9
Fax; 01926 431435
Web site: see the Law Society's
web site

OFSTED
Alexandra House
29–33 Kingsway
London WC2B 6SE
Tel: 0171 421 6800
Fax: 0171 421 6707
Web site: see CCTA's web site

Parliamentary Commissioner for
Administration (Ombudsman)
Millbank Tower
Millbank
London SW1P 4PU
Tel helpline: 0171217 4163
Fax: 0171 217 4160
e-mail:
opca-enq@ombudsman.org.uk

Professional Association of
Teachers
2 St James's Court
Friar Gate
Derby DE1 1BT
Tel: 01332 372337
Fax: 01332 290310
Web site: http://ourworld.
compuserve.com/homepages/fraser
_PAT/

Public Concern At Work
Lincoln's Inn House
42 Kingsway
London WC2B 6EN
Tel: 0171 404 6609

Qualification and Curriculum
Authority (QCA) (formerly NCVQ
and SCAA)
Newcombe House
45 Notting Hill Gate
London W11 3JB
Tel: 0171 229 1234
Fax: 0171 229 8526
Web site: http://www.qca.org.uk

Race Relations Employment and
Education Forum
DfEE
Level 4
Caxton House
Tothill Street
London SW1H 9NF
Tel: 0171 273 4857
Fax: 0171 273 5219

Redress: The Bullied Teachers'
Support Network
Jenni Watson
Secretary
Bramble House
Mason Drive
Hook
Goole
Humberside DN14 5NE
Tel: 01405 764432
Fax: 01405 769868
Web site:
http://www.successunlimited.co.uk

Royal Society for the Prevention of
Accidents (RoSPA)
Edgbaston Park
353 Bristol Road
Birmingham B5 7ST
Tel: 0121 248 2000
Fax: 0121 2438 2001
Web site: http://www.rospa.org.uk/
e-mail: help@rospa.co.uk

RoSPA in Wales
7 Cleeve House
Lambourne Crescent
Cardiff CF4 5GJ
Tel: 01222 250600
Fax: 01222 25061

Safety Association for Education
(SAFE)
University of Greenwich School of
Education
Mansion Site
Bexley Road
Eltham
London SE9 2PQ
Web site: http://www.gre.ac.uk/
directory/safe/index.htm

SCAA – see under Qualification
and Curriculum Authority

Schoolzone
Web site:
http://www.schoolzone.co.uk

Secondary Heads Association
(SHA)
130 Regent Road
Leicester LE1 7PG
Tel: 0116-299 1122
Fax: 0116-299 1123
Web site: http://www.sha.org.uk/
e-mail: info@sha.org.uk

SIMS Educational Services
Limited
The SIMS Centre
Stannard Way
Priory Business Park
Cardington
Bedford MK44 3SG
Tel: 01234 838080
Fax: 01234 838091
Web site: http://www.sims.co.uk/

Social Exclusion Unit
Cabinet Office
First Floor
Government Offices
Great George Street
London SW1P 3AL
Tel: 0171 270 5253
Fax: 0171 270 1971
e-mail: seu@gtnet.gove.uk

Society of Archivists
Information House
20–24 Old Street
London EC1V 9AB

Special Educational Needs
Tribunal
7th Floor
Windsor House
50 Victoria Street
London SW1H OHW
Tel: 0171 925 6925
Fax: 0171 925 6926

Stationery Office Limited
PO Box 276
London SW8 5DT
Tel: 0171 873 9090/0011
Web site: see HMSO's and CCTA's
web sites

Stress At Work
40 York Road
Northampton NN1 5QJ
Tel: 01604 259770

Suzy Lamplugh Trust
14 East Sheen Avenue
London SW14 8AS
Tel: 0181 392 1839
Fax: 0181 392 1830

Teacher Training Agency (TTA)
13th Floor
Portland House
Stag Place
London SW1E 5BH
Tel: 0171 925 3700
Fax: 0171 925 3790
Web site: see CCTA's web site

Teachers' Pensions (TPA)
Mowden Hall
Staindrop Road
Darlington DL3 9EE
Tel: 01325 745746
Fax: 01325 392552

Times Educational Supplement
Admiral House
66–8 East Smithfield
London E1 9XY
Tel: 0171 782 3000
Web site: http://www.tes.co.uk

UK School Resources
Web site:
http://www.liv.acuk/~evansjon

Welsh Office Education
Department
Government Buildings
New Crown Buildings
Cathays Park
Cardiff CF1 3NQ
Tel: 01222 825111
Fax: 01222 862111

Further reading

Bullying

Adams, A (1992) *Bullying at Work: How to confront and overcome it*, Virago, London

BBC *Bullying: A survival guide*, BBC Books, London

Children's Legal Centre (1996) *Bullying: A guide to the law*, Children's Legal Centre, Colchester
A legal information sheet available from the Children's Legal Centre (see Useful addresses section for address details).

Department for Education and Employment (1994) *Don't Suffer in Silence*, DfEE, London

Home Office (1995) *Preventing School Bullying: Things you can do*, HO, London

Careers

Department for Education and Employment (1997) *Careers Education and Guidance in Schools: Effective partnerships with careers services*, DfEE Circular 5/97, London

Department for Education and Employment (1998) *Careers Education in Schools: Provision for years 9–11*, DfEE Circular 5/98, London

Child protection

Bedingfield, D (1998) *The Child in Need: Children, the State and the law*, Family Law, Jordan Publishing, Bristol
Excellent on all aspects of the law relating to children and very good on historical background. Good section on children and education. Aimed at lawyers, but very readable and interesting human rights angle.

Children's Legal Centre (1998, 4th Edition) *Working with Young People: Legal responsibility and liability*, Children's Legal Centre, Colchester

Children's Legal Centre (1996) *Offering Children Confidentiality: Law and guidance*, Children's Legal Centre, Colchester

Council of Europe (1996) *The Rights of the Child: A European perspective*, Council of Europe Publishing, Strasbourg
Manual of source materials – of limited interest to the general reader.

Department for Education and Employment (1994) *Education of Children Being Looked after by Local Authorities*, DfEE Circular 13/94, London

Department for Education and Employment (1994) *Education of Sick Children*, DfEE Circular 12/94, London

Department for Education and Employment (1995) *Misconduct of Teachers and Workers with Children and Young Persons*, DfEE Circular 11/95, London

Department for Education and Employment (1995) *Protecting Children from Abuse: The role of the education service*, DfEE Circular 10/95, London

Department of Health (1995) *Child Protection: Messages from research*, HMSO, London
A summary of recent research findings on the child protection system post-Children Act. In itself probably of limited interest to teachers.

Hallett, C (1995) *Inter-agency Coordination in Child Protection*, HMSO, London

Home Office/Department of Health/DfEE (1991) *Working Together Under the Children Act 1989: A guide to arrangements for inter-agency cooperation for the protection of children from abuse*, HMSO, London

(1988) *Report of the Inquiry into Child Abuse in Cleveland 1987*, Command Paper 412, HMSO, London

Whitney, B (1996) *Child Protection for Teachers and Schools*, Kogan Page, London
Excellent, practical advice on child protection issues.

Disability

Department for Education and Employment (1997) *What the Disability Discrimination Act (DDA) 1995 Means for Schools and LEAs*, DfEE Circular 3/97, London

Discipline

Department for Education and Employment (1998) *Section 550A of the Education Act 1996: The use of force to control or restrain pupils*, DfEE Circular 10/98, London

Hamilton, C (July 1997) 'Physical Restraint for Children: A new sanction for schools', *Childright*, Children's Legal Centre, Colchester

Drugs

Department for Education and Employment (1995) *Drug Prevention and Schools*, DfEE Circular 4/95, London

Drug Education: Curriculum guidance for schools, SCAA, Qualifications and Curriculum Authority, London

Education law

Bennett, G and Meredith, P (eds) *Education and the Law*, Carfax, Abingdon

An academic journal, but with a wide audience in mind. Lots of useful articles on topical subjects by contributors from different professional backgrounds.

Education Law Reports, Jordan Publishing, Bristol

Reports of cases since 1994.

Gold, R, and Szemerenyi, S (annual publication) *Running a School 1997–98: Legal duties and responsibilities*, Jordan Publishing, Bristol

Written by a lawyer and a teacher, this is up –to date and jargon-free – very handy reference.

Harris, N, with Pearce, P, and Johnstone, S (1992) *The Legal Context of Teaching*, Longman, Harlow

Harris, N (1994) *The Education Act 1993: Text and commentary*, Sweet & Maxwell, London

Harris, N (1995) *The Law Relating to Schools*, Tolley, Croydon

A bit out-of-date, but otherwise an excellent book – *the* book on education law, aimed at lawyers.

McEwan, V (1996) *Education Law*, CLT Professional Publishing, Birmingham

Poole, K, Coleman, J and Liell, P (1997) *Butterworth's Education Law*, Butterworth, London

Looseleaf encyclopaedia.

Rabinowicz, J, Widdrington, T and Nicholas, K (1996) *Education: Law and practice*, FT Law and Tax, London
Written for lawyers, comprehensive and easy to find your way around.

Governors

Sallis, J (1995) *School Governors: A question and answer guide*, Butterworth-Heinemann, Oxford
Excellent, practical advice in question-and-answer format based on the TES column.
Wragg, E C, and Partington, J A (eds), (1995) *The School Governors' Handbook*, 3rd edn, Routledge, London
Good introduction to educational issues for governors.

Health and safety

Association for Science in Education (2nd edition, 1990) *Be Safe!*, ASE, Hatfield
Association for Science in Education (10th edition, 1996) *Safeguards in the School Laboratory*, ASE, Hatfield
Association for Science in Education (1996) *Safety Reprints 1996*, ASE, Hatfield
Association for Science in Education (2nd edition, 1998) *Topics in Safety*, ASE, Hatfield
Association for Science in Education *Safety in the Lab*, ASE, Hatfield
Brierley, D (1991) *Health and Safety in Schools*, Paul Chapman Publishing, London
Unfortunately out of date on some areas, but comprehensive.
Department for Education and Employment (1990) *Animals and Plants: Legal aspects*, DfEE Circular AM 3/90, London
Department for Education and Employment (1992) *The Use of Ionising Radiations in Education Establishments in England and Wales*, DfEE Circular AM 1/92, London
Department for Education and Employment (1996) *Improving Security in Schools*, HMSO, London
Department for Education and Employment (1996) *The 1996 School Premises Regulations*, DfEE Circular 10/96, London
Department for Education and Employment (1996) *Safety in Science Education*, HMSO, London
Department for Education and Employment (1996) *Supporting Pupils with Medical Needs*, DfEE Circular 14/96, London

Department for Education and Employment (1998) *The Health and Safety of Pupils on Off-site Visits: A good practice guide*, DfEE, London

Education Service Advisory Committee (1995) *Managing Health and Safety in Schools*, HSE, Sheffield

Health and Safety Executive (1992) *Managing Health and Safety in Schools*, HSE, Sheffield

Health and Safety Executive (1992) *The Responsibilities of School Governors for Health and Safety*, HSE, Sheffield

Health and Safety Executive (1994) *Safety Policies in the Education Sector*, HSE, Sheffield

Health and Safety Executive (1996) *Violence to Staff: A guide for employers*, HSE, Sheffield

Health and Safety Executive (1997) *Reporting School Accidents*, HSE 2/97 EDIS 1 C120, Sheffield

Health and Safety Executive (1997) *Workplace (Health, Safety and Welfare) Regulations 1992: Guidance for the education sector*, HSE (IAC)(L)97, Sheffield

Health and Safety Executive (1998) *Contractors in Schools*, HSE (IAC(L)98, Sheffield

Health and Safety Executive (1998) *Managing Work-related Stress: A guide for managers and teachers in schools*, HSE, Sheffield

Jewell, T (September 1997) Statutory nuisance and the educational environment, *Education and the Law*, **9**, 3

Lamplugh, D, and Pagan, B (1996) *Personal Safety for Schools*, Suzy Lamplugh Trust, London

National Association of Advisers and Inspectors in Design and Technology (1998) *Make It Safe*, NAAIDT, Chandlers Ford, Hampshire

NASUWT (1996) *No Place to Hide: Confronting workplace bullies*, NASUWT, Birmingham

NASUWT (1997) *Stop Personal Harassment*, NASUWT, Birmingham

Information

Department for Education and Employment (1990) *Records of Achievement*, DfEE Circular 8/90, London

Department for Education and Employment (1991) *The Education (Pupils' Attendance Records) Regulations 1991*, DfEE Circular 11/91, London

Department for Education and Employment (1996) *School Prospectuses and Governors' Annual Reports in Primary Schools*, DfEE Circular 11/96, London

Department for Education and Employment (1996) *School Prospectuses and Governors' Annual Reports in Secondary Schools,* DfEE Circular 12/96, London

Department for Education and Employment (1997) *Local Publication of 1997 Key Stage 2 National Curriculum Assessment Results in Primary School Performance Tables,* DfEE Circular 14/97, London

Department for Education and Employment (1997) *Reports on Pupils' Achievements in Primary Schools in 1996/7,* DfEE Circular 1/97, London

Department for Education and Employment (1997) *Reports on Pupils' Achievements in Secondary Schools in 1996/7,* DfEE Circular 2/97, London

Department for Education and Employment(1997) *School Leaving Date for 16-year-olds,* DfEE Circular 11/97, London

Department for Education and Employment (1998) *Reducing the Bureaucratic Burden on Teachers,* DfEE Circular 2/98, London

Department for Education and Employment (1998) *School Prospectuses in Primary Schools 1998/9 Onwards,* DfEE Circular 7/98, London
Replaces 11/96, but only regarding prospectuses.

Department for Education and Employment (1998) *School Prospectuses in Secondary Schools,* DfEE Circular 8/98, London
Replaces 12/96, but only regarding prospectuses.

Inspections

Department for Education and Employment (1993) *Inspecting Schools: A guide to the inspection provisions of the Education (Schools) Act 1992 in England,* DfEE Circular 7/93, London

Local government

Byrne, Tony (1994) *Local Government in Britain,* 6th edn, Penguin, London

Sharland, J (1997) *A Practical Approach to Local Government Law,* Blackstone Press, London

Management

Anderson, G, Boud, D and Sampson, J (1996) *Learning Contracts: A practical guide,* Kogan Page, London

Archimedes (1996) *TES Management Guide for Heads and Senior Staff,* Butterworth Heinemann, Oxford
Excellent and practical while accurate on law – based on the TES column.

Department for Education and Employment (1990) *Management of the School Day,* DfEE Circular 7/90, London

Department for Education and Employment (1992) *Induction of Newly Qualified Teachers,* DfEE Circular AM 2/92, London

Department for Education and Employment (1993) *Physical and Mental Fitness to Teach of Teachers and Entrants to Initial Teacher Training,* DfEE Circular 13/93, London

Department for Education and Employment (1993) *Protection of Children: Disclosure of criminal background of those with access to children,* DfEE/HO Circular 9/93, London

Department for Education and Employment (1993) *Schools Requiring Special Measures,* DfEE Circular 17/93, London

Department for Education and Employment (1993) T*he Use of School Premises and the Incorporation of Governing Bodies of LEA-maintained Schools,* DfEE Circular 15/93, London

Department for Education and Employment (1994) *Local Management of Schools,* DfEE Circular 2/94, London

Department for Education and Employment (1996) *Use of Supply Teachers,* DfEE Circular 7/96, London

Donnelly, J (1991) *A Handbook for Deputy Heads in Schools,* Kogan Page, London

Horne, H (ed) (1998) *The School Management Handbook,* 5th edn, Kogan Page, London

Nathan, M (1995) *The New Teacher's Survival Guide,* Kogan Page, London

NUT and SIMS (1998) *Law Management,* NUT and SIMS Educational Services Limited
Law management software especially designed for schools.

Miscellaneous

Blake, D, and Hanley, V (1995) *The Dictionary of Educational Terms,* Arena, Aldershot, Hants

Negligence

Robinson, J (1997) Damages for academic under-performance: pupils as plaintiffs, *Education and the Law,* **9**, 2

Pay and conditions

Department for Education and Employment (1997) *Early Retirement Arrangements for Teachers*, DfEE Circular 15/97, London

Department for Education and Employment (1998) *School Teachers' Pay and Conditions of Employment 1998*, DfEE Circular 9/98, London

Pupil behaviour

Department for Education and Employment (1991) *The Education (Pupils' Attendance Records) Regulations 1991*, DfEE Circular 11/91, WO 4/91, London

Department for Education and Employment (1994) *Education by LEAs of Children Otherwise Than at School*, DfEE Circular 11/94, London

Department for Education and Employment (1994) *Education of Children with Emotional and Behavioural Difficulties*, DfEE Circular 9/94, London

Department for Education and Employment (1994) *Exclusions from Schools*, DfEE Circular 10/94, London

Department for Education and Employment (1994) *Pupil Behaviour and Discipline*, DfEE Circular 8/94, London

Department for Education and Employment (1994) *School Attendance: Policy and practice on categorisation of absence*, DfEE May 1994, London

Department for Education and Employment (1998) *LEA Behaviour Support Plans*, DfEE Circular 1/98, London

Khan, AN (1997) Attendance requirements at schools, *Education and the Law*, **9**, 1

Whitney, B (1994) *The Truth About Truancy*, Kogan Page, London

Religion

Bradney, A (June 1996) Christian worship?, *Education and the Law*, **8**, 2

Department for Education and Employment (1994) *Religious Education and Collective Worship*, DfEE Circular 1/94, London

Hamilton, C (1995) *Family, Law and Religion*, Sweet & Maxwell, London

Sex education

Department for Education and Employment (1994) *Education Act 1993: Sex Education in Schools*, DfEE Circular 5/94, London

Harris, N (ed) (1996) *Children, Sex Education and the Law*, National Children's Bureau, London

Special educational needs

Department for Education and Employment (1994) *The Organisation of Special Educational Provision*, DfEE Circular 6/94, London

Department for Education and Employment (1994) *Code of Practice on the Identification and Assessment of Special Educational Needs*, HMSO, London

Friel, J (1997) *Children with Special Needs: Assessment, law and practice*, 4th edn, Jessica Kingsley, London
Good, practical book and relatively easy to follow. Aimed at parents and educators in particular.

Harris, N (1997) *Special Educational Needs and Access to Justice*, Jordan Publishing, Bristol
Summary of research on special education needs tribunals and so on.

Hinds, W (September 1996) Special educational needs and the local government ombudsman, *Education and the Law*, **8**, 3

Oliver, S and Austen, L (1996) *Special Educational Needs and the Law*, Jordan Publishing, Bristol
Comprehensive and thorough, but, because it is aimed at lawyers, it is not so easy for the lay person to follow.

Robinson, J (1996) Special educational needs, the code and the new tribunal, *Education and the Law*, **8**, 1

Teacher training

Department for Education and Employment (1990) *Treatment and Assessment of Probationary Teachers*, DfEE Circular AM 1/90, London

Department for Education and Employment (1991) *School Teacher Appraisal*, DfEE Circular 12/91, London

Department for Education and Employment (1992) *Induction of Newly Qualified Teachers*, DfEE Circular AM 2/92, London

Department for Education and Employment (1998) *Requirements for Courses of Initial Teacher Training*, DfEE Circular 4/98, London

Work experience

Department for Education and Employment (1996): *Work Experience: A guide for employers*, DfEE, London

Department for Education and Employment (1996) *Work Experience: A guide for schools*, DfEE, London

Department for Education and Employment (1997) *School Leaving Date for 16-year-olds*, DfEE Circular 11/97, London

Johns, A (1997) *Work Experience and the Law*, Centre for Education and Industry, Warwick University
A comprehensive summary, produced with DfEE backing.

Qualifications and Curriculum Authority (1998) *Learning from Work Experience: A guide to successful practice*, QCA, London

Equal Opportunities Commission (1985) *The Code of Practice for the Elimination of Discrimination on the Grounds of Sex and Marriage and the Promotion of Equality of Opportunity in Employment*, Equal Opportunities Commission, Manchester

Index